A Veterinary Life

Adrian Arnold

To my grandchildren, Harrison, Noah, Jemima and Jude,
one of whom who is considering a veterinary career, and with my heartfelt thanks to my soulmate, Jen.

Confessional

Memoirs and autobiographies tend to fall into one of two categories. In the first category we find those impressive works by soldiers and politicians supported and documented by diaries kept assiduously year after year. The second group includes those which rely upon the frailty of human memory. This book is firmly rooted in the second camp. It is based on facts, many of which happened many years ago, that have acquired a certain amount of garnishing, mild inaccuracy and occasional exaggeration for dramatic effect. In spite of these provisos all the accounts related in these pages are based on the truth as I remember it - and to those friends and family whose memories differ to varying degrees I can only apologise. Several of the names in these recollections have been altered to avoid any embarrassment.

If you are looking for a misery memoir, please put this book back on the shelf I don't want to disappoint you. In spite of tragedy I have enjoyed a wonderful life that I would like to share with those of you who are looking for sunlight to brighten these dark days.

Index

Chapter 1

The decision to become a vet

It was on our return from a theatre trip to London late one night at the age of fifteen in 1954 when I told my father I wanted to become a surgeon.

He replied "Adrian, to become a surgeon you need brains which you haven't got and luck which you might not get. Why not become a vet?"

It was not really the response I was looking for but then my father was often quite blunt in his opinions and it made me think further about my future career.

What makes someone want to become a vet? A love of animals? I have pointed out in the many career fairs I have attended, that this affection can be a disadvantage. We vets are often called upon to perform several unpleasant and even painful tasks on our patients. I have a love for our own family pets and I like animals in general but I cannot afford to love my patients.

A wealthy lifestyle? Forget it - despite what the pet-owning public thinks of the exorbitance of veterinary fees. But the challenge of diagnosing a patient who tells the truth, nothing but the truth but, not always, the whole truth and the sense of achievement in taking an animal, deformed or damaged, and restoring it to a healthy life make a veterinary career very rewarding.

It is the challenge of the unexpected. The doctors in their consulting rooms can be almost certain that their next patient will look rather like you or me. The vet, when she calls "Next, please", does not know whether the patient will have two, four, six, eight or a hundred legs, covered in fur, feathers, skin or scales and be more likely to bite, scratch, kick or maul her. This unpredictability was a great attraction to me.

Other reasons will become clear as the story develops but you ought to know that there is nothing particularly special about me except that I have been lucky.

Lucky to have survived the first waves of V-1 rockets. In 1944 the

Germans escalated the war on London by launching V-1 And V-2 rockets, known as buzzbombs or doodle bugs. In the hall at Pebworth Road in Harrow we had a Morrison shelter. It had a thick steel top and bottom with wire mesh at the sides and ends. Mum, Pete and I slept in it every night. One night Mum heard a 'buzzbomb' engine cut out as it started its descent. If you heard the engine cut out you knew it would not hit you as the glide would take it further into the city. She dragged me out of the front door and pointed to the black shape as it raced across the moonlit sky.

"That's a buzzbomb," she said. "Now get back into bed."

I can still see that shape in my mind's eye to this day. It was at this point that it was decided that my mother, brother and I should move away from London to our Liverpool grandparents to avoid the last throes of the Blitz.

I was lucky to have recovered from diphtheria in an isolation hospital in Liverpool which was suffering its own Blitz. Lucky to have survived further evacuation to Derbyshire when my mother tied a label to the lapel of my coat and put me on the train to Derby where I was met by the other set of grandparents.

Yes, I have been lucky, and I have had the nerve to take up opportunities before they showed their true potential. Who else would propose to a girl twenty-two days after our first meeting and find that union still stronger fifty-seven years later?

So where did I come from? My great-grandparents came from the Cambridge area which is where many of my wife, Jen's, family originated. My paternal ancestors were grooms whose children graduated to boot making and then to teaching. The maternal side followed a similar path from cattle dealing to publican and finally teaching. All four grandparents were teachers.

My parents, especially my father, vowed to improve their standard of life and became both an accountant and property developer. There had never been any history of medical or veterinary careers in my ancestry.

On his way to making the money he had dreamed about, my father became one of the nouveau riche. A class of the community he often denigrated although he was one of them himself.

His favourite poem was Rudyard Kipling's "If" and he felt that he could "walk with Kings - and not lose the common touch" but beneath the outward confidence he never felt completely comfortable in the company of either.

That is quite enough about my ancestry but the question of why I became a vet has only been partially answered. There are many events in one's life that accumulate to form a decision. I have always been interested in the "workings" of living bodies even from the earliest biology lessons in which we had to dissect a worm and I found its heart. I dissected a frog for "O" level when the arrangement and function of the various organs fascinated me. I even researched the pond life of sticklebacks as my "O" level project. Hence my surprise when I learnt that I had failed Biology "O" level. This was one of many life lessons that I took to heart which only made me more determined to pass the exam a few months later as a re-sit. I have never had any fear of blood but heights were a different matter. If I ever got to the fifth rung of a ladder, I demanded the DFC and Bar!

My reasoning for this career choice was that my father had been a very successful businessman both as a consultant chartered accountant and a property developer. I knew I could never achieve his level of business acumen and I did not fancy the idea of being compared to him for the rest of my life. I wanted to join a profession as far removed from his own as possible. Besides this, he had an overwhelming respect, bordering on worship, for any member of the medical professions. I had no desire for the acclaim but I felt I could be my own man and earn his respect in a field about which he knew nothing. Veterinary surgeons were considered to be a few rungs down the professional ladder from doctors who had their own class structure. When the family doctor visited the house of a patient, he was admitted by the front door while the vet was directed to the rear entrance in those early days.

Following the conversation with Dad, I had a chat with our local vet and a great friend, Roger Massey. When he came over for drinks one evening, we took a stroll around the garden, just the two of us. We were beside the chicken run - I can picture it to this day. We were discussing the prospects of a newly qualified vet when he said "Adrian, you will never make a fortune being a vet. You can either live a frugal life and retire on a small pension or you can live a reasonably comfortable life and work til you drop. I have adopted the second choice and never regretted it."

His decision later proved to be the right one as he died at the early age of 58 from kidney failure. Roger had style, as later anecdotes will prove, but just one will suffice at this point. On his death bed, he had his wife on one side of the bed with his mistress on the other chatting happily to each other across his failing body while he had a faint grin on his lips.

My earliest memories are of our life in North London during and after the war.

Chapter 2

Early schooldays

My first school, after kindergarten or nursery school, was Byron Court School in Wembley, North London where I wore high lace-up boots later known as "bovver boots". We recited the Lord's Prayer every morning and the lessons concentrated on the three "R"s – Reading, Writing and 'Rithmetic'.

Taking the entrance exam for Felsted Junior School in Essex at the age of eight was a new experience for me. At the time I did not understand how important the exam so I did not worry too much about the result. I was more fascinated by a fellow examinee, John Reynolds, who was completely bald having lost his hair because of the repetitive shock of Blitz bombing during the war. He later grew a very fine head of hair.

After passing the entrance exam - rather better than anyone else had expected, Mum and Dad drove me to the school for my first term. After a short conversation with the Headmaster, Bryan Morris, they handed my trunk and tuck box to Matron, Mum kissed me on the cheek and Dad shook me by the hand and they left.

I felt completely alone.

I stood in the long entrance corridor to the school which was lined with school notices - all of which I read at least a dozen times while older pupils swept past me in waves of chattering sparrows. There was a further long dark corridor leading to other parts of the school but I only managed to venture about ten steps towards this unfamiliar world before returning to the safety of the noticeboards. After a couple of hours, a swarm of young boys moved past the entrance corridor and, feeling a sense of safety in numbers, I joined the crowd which congregated at the entrance to the dining room. Even here there was a ritual which involved showing both sides of our hands to Matron before being allowed into the dining room. Any dirty hands were directed to the nearest wash basin.

I was initially placed in Class 2 alongside another new boy, Willy Spouse. The first lesson I remember was held in the Old Schoolroom in the High Street of Felsted. It is the only remaining building of the original school dating back to its foundation in 1564 by Richard, Lord Riche, who had been Lord Chancellor to King Edward VI. (History does not paint a complimentary picture of the man.)

At the back of the classroom was a storeroom with shelves lined with the dust of several centuries and a murky window looking over the street. I was dispatched to this lookout point by one of the senior boys to keep "Cave!" I hadn't a clue what the word meant never mind knowing what the master looked like so it was only when the roll call was made that I was found to be 'missing'.

This first lesson was Latin. At Byron Court School I was under the impression that the whole world spoke English so any other language was completely foreign to me and 'dead' languages were beyond my comprehension. The master, Mr Walker, pointed towards me and asked me to parse the verb "amo". "Parse", "verb", "amo" - what on earth what was he talking about?

"Spouse? Can you tell Arnold how to do it?"

"Amo, Amas, Amat, Amamus, Amatus, Amant," came the confident reply.

"Well done! Now decline the noun 'puella'."

"Puella, puella, puellam ..."

I felt I had entered a different galaxy. This was unadulterated gobbledegook. What was a "pure lamb" any way? I was completely out of my depth so it was with relief that I found myself demoted to Class 1 where, at least, they spoke the same language as me.

If this all sounds rather psychologically traumatic, forget it. There were, and still are, young children going through the same anxieties. Some last a lifetime which is unbelievably sad, while others, like me, have a difficult few days before beginning to enjoy life in a new environment. I began to explore this new exciting world of French, Algebra, Mathematics (rather than Sums) and sports like hockey, rugby, cricket and swimming.

Some of the masters were inspiring like Hugh Waters, the Maths teacher, who also coached the rugby team and athletics. He was a bachelor who kept a cottage on the Norfolk Broads for use during the holidays. He was an inspirational teacher - both in the academic and sporting fields. One of his responsibilities was the boy's postage accounts at the end of term. He would come into the classroom with a load of files and call out sums of money which we had to add up very quickly. They were the postal accounts and it was his way of speeding up our mathematical thinking while, at the same time, getting us to add up the accounts. He was also a very gifted amateur photographer,

11

developing his own films in a cubby hole in his rooms that he had converted to a darkroom. He used these photos as records of rugby matches, training methods and athletic skills. He would take us on 'away' rugby matches on an ancient school bus. Instead of the senior boys grabbing the prized seats at the back every boy wanted to be as close to 'Drip' Waters, sitting beside the driver, to hear his experiences of having been a Lancaster bomber navigator during the War. He had been shot down three times but survived.

Within a couple of hours of the end of a rugby match he would post his report of the game together with wonderful black and white photos of the action on the school noticeboard. It only came to light after his death that he had been the anonymous provider of the annual strawberry tea at the end of the Summer term for both parents and boys.

Autograph books were a common hobby amongst us boys and there was a long waiting list for Mr Walker's autograph which consisted of a pen-and-ink sketch of the famous Johnny Walker Whisky gentleman that featured in the advertisements of the day. Another master who lives in the memory was Mr Mason, who taught French, and had been a prisoner of war and tortured by the Gestapo during the War when they had pulled out all his finger nails.

The second headmaster, Derek Ross, later became a family friend. He was an ordained vicar who won Blues at Oxford for both hockey and cricket and, in spite of a marked stammer, preached the best sermons in the senior school's chapel. He always took his text from one of the Sunday papers of the day he was preaching. Following his retirement in his mid-sixties, he became the parish priest at Black Notley, a small village outside Chelmsford.

After four years at the Junior school where I had become 'top dog', I moved across the road to the Senior School where I was, once again, a small minnow in a much larger pond.

Senior school

I had learnt a lot about coping with new environments at the junior school so by keeping my head down, while not exactly adhering to all the school rules, I managed to develop my own character. It was at this stage that I began to appreciate the value of asking "Why?" which has stood me in good stead throughout my life. I do not readily accept the first answer to a problem or question. "Why?" has a twin brother, "Why not?", who can often offer unconsidered solutions to life's problems.

I was not particularly gifted academically – about halfway down the upper set of two in most subjects – although my English was good both in the written and spoken forms. Biology fascinated me while Physics I found almost completely inexplicable, how I passed it at "A" level I will never know. Our chemistry master, John Lee, had his own unit of measurement and law of chemistry. His smallest unit of measurement of volume was 'half a drop' - think about it! - while Lee's law of chemistry stated that if an experiment did not turn out as expected, the answer given to the question "Why, sir?", was "Just does!"

So it was to my surprise that I passed "A" level exams in Biology, Chemistry and Physics. The next challenge was to find a college that might accept me with my limited academic achievements. At the time there were eight universities which offered a veterinary degree - London, Bristol, Cambridge, Liverpool, Glasgow, Edinburgh, Trinity College, Dublin and University College in the same city. My exam results were OK but hardly Oxbridge material and I had set my heart on the Cambridge vet school.

In those days one either passed or failed an exam. There was no grading by letters or numbers. If the student was extremely gifted they might get a pass with distinction. Cambridge was the closest and, since "one doesn't get if one doesn't ask", I applied. I had little anticipation of success. However I had not accounted for the support I would receive from both my head- and house-masters and the luck of being injured on the hockey field.

Clare interview

These were the two main reasons which may explain how and why I got into Clare College. Both my headmaster and housemaster were old Clare men and both went up to Cambridge to plead my case with the Master of the college, Sir Henry Thirkill. He listened to them and offered me an interview when the second piece of luck came into play. The day before my interview I had been playing in a hockey match and, in the heat of the game, I collided heavily with the opposing goalkeeper. Somehow his stick caught my collar bone and dislocated it inwards. This closed off my oesophagus (foodpipe) and diverted my trachea (windpipe) so swallowing was not possible and breathing was a bit difficult. Someone took me to the Broomfield hospital in Chelmsford where I found myself under the care of the resident orthopaedic surgeon, Mr Harris, known to many of his patients as 'The Butcher'. Collar bones normally dislocate outwards so Mr Harris was rather unfamiliar with the inward dislocation. I remember him placing a textbook on my chest while he read the instructions which involved grabbing the bone through the skin and pulling it out while pressing my chest down. I had a figure-of-eight bandage strapped across my shoulders, neck and back to hold the collar bone in place, given painkillers and sent back to school.

The next morning my father collected me from school for the interview at Clare. With the strapping, lack of sleep and being doped up to the eyeballs with Veganin, a compound mixture of paracetamol, caffeine and codeine, I was not in the most sparkling frame of mind for the most important interview of my life. One of the college staff admitted us to the hall of the Master's lodge in the corner of Old Court where we waited for some time. Me, in a haze of painkillers, and Dad in uncharacteristic silence. Eventually the Master invited us into his study.

The dark room was lined with heavy mahogany bookshelves, the books stacked like guardsmen on parade, an Oriental carpet, its long-forgotten pattern indecipherable under years of accumulated academic tobacco smoke and vintage wine stains. The Master sat behind the massive desk, a dark silhouette against the lead-lined window panes of the one bay window. While Dad remained at the back of the room I sat in a small chair facing the desk which resembled a catafalque with all its dire connotations. To this day, I cannot remember a single question asked by Sir Henry. I simply stared through my analgesic haze at the carpet beneath my feet. My only memory was one of extreme embarrassment at my exaggerated laughter at what I thought was a joke he made which turned out to be a deep and meaningful observation. At the end of what felt like an eternity, we stumbled out into Old Court. I stopped and took what I thought would be my last look at Clare College, Cambridge.

In complete contrast, Dad was uncharacteristically excited by the whole atmosphere of the college and town. He insisted on taking me on a tour of the town explaining that the main bookshop of the town, Heffers, had been founded by some very distant relative. It was the first time I realised how much he regretted turning down the university offer in his younger days despite his denial of such feelings for many years.

I am certain that Sir Henry took pity on me because he offered me a place if I passed an exam called Part 4 of the First MB which was a medical exam in biochemistry, a subject Felsted rarely taught at the time. I failed at the first attempt during my last term at school and went to a 'crammer' in

Holland Park for three months where I learnt no more biochemistry but they did teach me examination technique. As a result I passed at the second attempt.

My feelings have always been that I got into Cambridge by the side door and often wondered whether I was something of an academic fraud. Some thirty years later, at a reunion of Clare Vets and Medics, I learnt from a medical colleague, who went on to a highly successful academic career in psychiatry at a world-renowned university, that he had experienced identical thoughts of low self-worth.

I had five months to fill before taking up my place at Cambridge. Having been pre-occupied by exams for so long I decided that I needed a complete change of life style and stretch my brain in a different direction so I took myself off to Paris. Where else?

France

I have always enjoyed stretching my mind in different directions (the family call them 'Dad's Enthusiasms') so I took the opportunity to stay with a French family, the Massus, in Saint Germain-en-Laye, a commune, or suburb, about 19 kilometres from the centre of Paris. Madame Massu spoke excellent English but only used it on the day of my arrival. She insisted on French being spoken at all other times. She and her husband had three children ranging in age from 10 to 19 and I lived en famille.

French family life was an eye-opener for me. Not only did they drink wine liberally, but they insisted on watering it down. They introduced young children to the fruits of the vine as early as three or four years old. Arguments between members of the family were frequent and often quite dangerous with kitchen knives being the preferred weapon of both attack and defence. Mosquitoes were a constant irritation so much so that every night each room would smoulder with fire papers that released an insecticidal vapour.

To improve my "O" level French I enrolled in the Sorbonne in the Latin quarter of Paris to study French for foreign students. I took the train to central Paris in the mornings when we had a series of lessons after which I found a cheap brasserie for lunch and then spent the afternoon exploring the city. One morning an impressive uniformed officer came into the classroom and asked if there were any native English speakers in the class. An American girl, who always sat at the front of the class and asked the intelligent questions, raised her hand at the same time as I did. The gentleman explained that he needed someone to teach Air France stewardesses how to speak conversational English. I pointed out that the girl in the front row did not speak English - she spoke American!

I got the job.

It was only for a couple of days a week and was a lot of fun but it was brought to an abrupt end when I was diagnosed with suspected appendicitis and repatriated to the UK where the "appendicitis" mysteriously disappeared and I made a full recovery - until the first year of our marriage five years later when it struck again - but that is a story for later.

Paris is a good place for a 19yo Philistine schoolboy intent on a scientific degree to appreciate some finer points of the Arts. I saw operatic performances from a box at L'Opéra; watched one of the great Shakespearian actors of the day, John Neville, give his performance of Hamlet at the Théatre Sarah Bernhardt and understood most of the dialogue in the long-running French farce, "J'y suis; J'y Reste" ("I'm here and I'm staying"). The Hamlet performance was interesting in two ways. The first was that the large majority of the audience never looked at the stage at all but had their heads buried in copies of the play as they followed the narrative and second, because of the length of the play, I had to leave halfway through Act Four to catch the last train home to St Germain. Happily, Peter Ustinov's play, The Love of Four Colonels, was shorter and I was able to stay to the end and still catch my train.

Those three months opened my mind from the narrow confines of veterinary science to a much broader view of life which was an invaluable preparation for the next stage of my education - university.

Farm experience

Before going up to Cambridge one had to have completed 6 months of farming experience. In my case this involved getting up at 4.30am driving a few miles to a large dairy farm where milking started at 5.30 and was very primitive compared to the modern machinery of today. There was a vacuum line that ran the length of the milking shed to which you connected a portable canister with four suction caps which had to be attached to the cows' teats. This looked simple in hands of an experienced cowman but it took me several days to learn the technique before the caps stopped falling off the teats. There were still half a dozen cows that would not take to the machines and had to be hand-milked. The milking parlour was frequently a couple of inches deep in slurry despite a daily hosing and brushing down of the central aisle.

There was little evidence of record keeping and the farmer relied on the cowman's opinion of the productivity of each cow. In fact "productivity" was not a word used in those days. It was only in the later years of the 20th century that the word entered the national vocabulary.

After milking we had to clean everything up and then go about other farm business. This included collecting pea haulms (harvested pea plants to you and me), lifting sacks of animal feed and general cultivation of the fields. The other farm workers played a trick on me when we had to carry sacks of wheat, barley and beans up a ladder to the upper storage level of the barn. The other two suggested that I took the bean sacks while they moved the wheat and barley sacks. I saw little difference in the bags until I went to lift the first bean sack. What I didn't know was that the cereal sacks weighed one hundredweight or 112 pounds (50kg) while the bean sack were larger and held 1½ hundredweight - half as much again - and I had to carry them up a ladder! Fortunately I was nineteen, I was fit and I could take a joke - but I slept well that night.

I used to have a sandwich lunch before afternoon milking which finished at 4.30 after which I drove home again. This was a 7 days a week job, so I had little social life during the school holidays.

On another occasion my fellow workers had even more fun with me. I had just impressed myself by reversing a tractor and trailer into the cart shed and I had a very smug look on my face. The men applauded my skill then suggested that, since I had done the first one so well, I might as well reverse 'that trailer over there' into the shed.

No problem.

What I hadn't realised was that the first cart had two wheels while the second one was a four-wheeled trailer. I made a complete mess of it. The men stood around and laughed at my embarrassment for a good 20 minutes before one of them took pity on me and backed it perfectly into the cart shed bay within thirty seconds. My arrogance evaporated like the morning dew but I had learnt a precious lesson. Later on, in Dunstable, there would be a particular cat that brought my supposed superiority down several notches teaching me a similar lesson.

This farming experience is an important introduction to veterinary medicine. To be accepted by the farming community, we had to learn the farming terminology. Unfamiliar terms such as tup, keds, hoggetts, hogs, gimmers, wethers, dagging, mule, raddle, shearling, teg, scrapie and scab had to become familiar - and these are all just sheep farming terms!

Dad had bought a 500-acre farm, Ulting Hall, about a mile away from our home in Hatfield Peverel in 1963. It had always been his ambition to own a farm. Not just any farm but one at the cutting edge of agricultural practice. As a result he installed several innovations such as Cropstore grain silos, a barley beef unit and automated feeding in both the calf and pig units. For several years he was at the forefront of farming technology and the farm's visitor's book held the signatures of at least nine agriculture ministers including those from USA, France and Russia. He asked Dr David Sainsbury, who taught pig medicine at the Cambridge vet school, to oversee the design and implementation of the new pig unit. The farm featured in many of the leading agricultural publications of the time including Farmers Weekly and Country Life.

The previous owners, the Frenches, a brother and sister, had run the farm for the previous fifty years and it was stuck in something of a time warp. When they moved out of the Queen Anne farmhouse, we could not wait to explore the rambling building. My brother and sister rushed upstairs, but I had seen a rather plain door in the corner of the kitchen. The haze of cobwebs surrounding the lintel suggested that it had not been used it for some time. The door creaked as I pulled it open to reveal an old wooden staircase leading down to a vaulted cellar. I swung my torch around the large rectangular room which seemed to be empty until I caught sight of an alcove in a far corner. Looking closer I saw wine racks holding about 40 bottles of wine.

The Frenches had been teetotal all their lives so they could be interesting. There were about a dozen bottles of home-made wine dating back to the 1920s, six bottles of 1923 champagne and 18 bottles of port. The home-made wine was poured down the drain while the champagne corks were in a dangerous state of decomposition and I handled these like Molotov cocktails before disposal. However, the port was a real find. Many of the bottles still had the wax protection on the corks with imprints which showed that the wine had been shipped to the old port of Maldon, five miles away, in 1894. It had not been a notable year for port but, after eighty years, it was liquid velvet and only brought out on very special occasions. The last bottle was drunk in the Isle of Man, where my parents retired, in about 1980.

Chapter 3

Tripos years at University

To the undergraduate of today, college life at Cambridge in the 1960s would have bordered on the medieval. My room in Clare Old Court resembled something out of an Elizabethan drama. There was no running water. A college servant called a 'gyp' delivered two large jugs of hot and cold water first thing in the morning so that I could wash and shave in the basins provided. The bathrooms were in the crypt of the chapel which had disbelieving American tourists reaching for their cameras as sleepy-eyed students shuffled across Old Court in their dressing gowns on their way to have a bath. I only ever stayed that one night in Old Court when I went up to the university to sit the Organic Chemistry exam demanded by the Master.

I spent my in-college years over the river on P staircase in Memorial Court, known to Clare graduates as 'Mem' Court, which was built in 1926 to commemorate the Clare men who gave their lives in the First World War. Those living in 'Mem' Court enjoyed the luxury of running water and gyps to clean our rooms but no bathrooms. While Old Court echoed the age of the Restoration, 'Mem' Court reflected the Edwardian era - more Brideshead than Samuel Pepys.

A gyp was a male valet to the students while "bedders" were their female counterparts. The smooth running of the college was the responsibility of the portering staff overseen by the Head Porter, Charlie. Charlie collected your post, relayed messages from friends and teaching staff, arranged transport within the city and further afield. In the late evening he patrolled the grounds and reported any student caught trying to climb in after the staff had locked the gates. The Porters work three rotating shifts (7am to 3pm, 3pm to 11pm and 11pm to 7am).

One of the favoured accesses to the college after hours was up the east wall, across the roof and through the fellow's bathroom on the top floor. This nightly practice led an eminent Professor of Theology, Charlie Moule, to post a note on the main noticeboard which stated that "Professor Moule would like to draw to the attention of those students climbing in through the Fellow's bathroom, that he takes his baths between 1pm and 2pm on Tuesdays and Fridays. He would appreciate being left in peace during those times."

Charlie, the Head Porter, was one of those talented people who had the gift of remembering names. It was at least fifteen years after I left Clare that Jen and I took the family up to Cambridge to hear her brother, John, preach at his old college, St. Johns. As we wandered back to the car, I took them though my old college. It was during Finals Week when a large notice informed visitors that entry was restricted to college members. The children grabbed me by the arm. "Look, Dad," said Kim pointing at the notice. "You can't go in. It says the College is closed to all but members."

"But I am a member," I replied and continued through the gate much to the embarrassment of the family. I poked my head round the door to the porter's lodge where Charlie was distributing the post into the pigeon holes.

"Good evening, Charlie," I said.

He looked up with a quizzical expression on his face. "Good evening, sir. Don't tell me. Just give me a minute." He only had to think for a minute or two before his eyes lit up. "Mr Arnold! Vet! Nice to see you again, sir."

College members were expected to dine in Hall, wearing their undergraduate gowns, at least five times a week. Below the High Table where the Master and Fellows dined, were three long tables with bench seating. Dinners, which were always preceded by a lengthy Latin grace from one of the classical scholars, were served by the kitchen staff rather than the cafeteria systems of today. Although the food was good it never tried to emulate the excesses of Porterhouse Blue and, never having dined at the High Table, I cannot vouch for the quality of the college's cellar. I am a nostalgic by nature and consider myself very lucky to have enjoyed the atmosphere of a Cambridge education which had an undercurrent of style. My granddaughter has made her modern views quite clear in that she would never consider applying to Oxbridge. "They are all ineffectual snobs" is her eighteen-year-old opinion and I applaud her for expressing it - I just feel that she may modify her criticism in the years to come.

The centre of Cambridge today is a nightmare for anyone travelling by car because of the traffic restrictions in the heart of the town. It was quite different in our student days when traffic consisted largely of murmurations of starling undergraduates, black gowns flapping in the breeze, cycling their various ways to lectures, laboratories and tutorials throughout the town.

Extra-curricular activities

To me, Cambridge was simply an extension of my school education while the more mature students, those who had done National Service, had seen much more of life. I was an innocent schoolboy while the military experiences had knocked a few juvenile chips from their shoulders. They were prepared to miss the occasional lecture or practical to enjoy the other activities afforded by the university. If I missed an academic appointment because I had a sporting engagement or some other call on my time, I felt ridiculously guilty.

Despite this virtuous mentality, I still played hockey for the college when we won the Inter-College championship - called Cuppers. I acted in three dramatic productions including the lead in George Bernard Shaw's "The Doctor's Dilemma" which we played for four nights at the Arts Theatre in Cambridge. Enjoying sport, I played a lot of squash in the college courts behind Mem Court, took fencing lessons which were exhausting, punted up to Grantchester on the river Cam and drank in the Blue Boar in Trinity Street. I got drunk on about six occasions - which only taught me that I didn't like it! In retrospect I could have made more friends from other disciplines and colleges but hindsight is only useful if it is preceded by foresight.

As vet students we followed the same lecture curriculum as the medical students while dissecting animals rather than the human body. There would usually be two hour-long lectures every morning and a practical class two or three times a week. I am guessing now but I think that the main medical lecture theatre held nearly 200 students. The very clever students sat in the front few rows and persistently raised their hands to ask erudite questions. The majority of us sat next to friends in the higher rows of seats and tried to pay attention to the wisdom of learned academics and research fellows as it was passed on to comparative ignoramuses - or is it ignorami?

Two medical lecturers stand out in my memory. Professor John Boyd, lecturing on embryology, would arrive an hour before the start of his lecture to fill the four sliding blackboards with chalk diagrams in full colour which were works of art in themselves. The other was the pharmacology lecturer who fascinated us with a lecture on the most painful ways to commit suicide! (Swallowing drain cleaner if you need to know!) He also had the ability to drink any undergraduate under the table.

We would devote the rest of the day to practical sessions of dissection, pathology, histology and other ancillary subjects. As veterinary students we had our own additional lectures on the variations of other animal's anatomy, physiology and embryology.

During one of these laboratory afternoons a research team tested us all - medics and vets - for various forms of colour blindness. Positive results came as quite a shock to more than a dozen of our fellow students who had no previous knowledge of their condition.

I spent many of my evenings writing up my lecture notes while other students were out drinking and socialising. With this schoolboy mind-set, I did not take the fullest advantage of the opportunities that Cambridge offered me. I went as a schoolboy and there was still a lot of the innocent left in me when I qualified 6 years later.

The first weeks at Cambridge were a strange experience. Getting to know the geography of the town and college, beginning to recognise members of the college, learning the routines of college life, meeting my fellow vet students and exploring the endless opportunities offered by a university education were all part of the excitement of a new environment.

We travelled everywhere on our bikes which had our designated college number painted on the back mudguard – mine was CL57. Everywhere we went during the working day we wore our short and rather tatty black undergraduate gowns which flapped like ragged witches wings behind us as we rode through the town.

Not that I can take much credit but I take great pride in the fact that I am 'semi-unique' in the history of Clare College founded in 1326 which is second only to Peterhouse in the antiquity of the Cambridge colleges.

How can one possibly be semi-unique? It would seem to be an oxymoron.

The reason is that I was one of the first two veterinary students that Clare had ever accepted since its foundation. The other was Richard Dyball who took the academic route as a career, first lecturing at Bristol University before moving back to Cambridge where he is now a Fellow of Clare. Our tutor was Dr Gordon Wright who lectured in medical neurology and tutored the Clare medical students. He was a very kind man but slightly out of his depth when presented with the college's first two vets. Over the years Gordon became a fixture at Clare and I had the honour to attend the celebration of his 100th birthday in 2015 together with more than a hundred of his tutoring charges over the years. Even at that age he was still actively engaged in the research of the neurology of the human hand - having married his second wife five years previously. He died in 2019 at the age of 104.

My first year's accommodation was room eight on P staircase in Memorial Court otherwise known as P8. We were an eclectic bunch on P staircase which included two theologians, two engineers, a medic, a historian, a geographer and me, a vet. Our backgrounds varied as much as our academic choices. We were the offspring of shopkeepers, a knighted admiral, a captain of industry, average businessmen, a farmer and a Wolverhampton taxi driver. I may have gone to Cambridge to train as a veterinary surgeon but my true education came from our conversations sitting at the bottom of the staircase at two o'clock in the morning, discussing cars, religion and women - in that order - with such a diverse mixture of experiences and opinions.

Various memories still linger on, such as the first time I met our year of vet students in the veterinary anatomy building on Tennis Court Road.

Compared to the antiquity of many of the university "schools", the veterinary school was remarkably basic. Having left the huge medical lecture hall after our first lecture with the medics, we made our way round the corner to a rather neglected building which we entered through a dilapidated set of double doors down into a concrete basement. There was an acrid smell to the place explained later by the discovery of three large galvanised iron tanks filled with a strong formaldehyde solution holding the bodies of the greyhounds that we would spent the next year dissecting.

This was the first time we had met together as a group and everyone felt a little awkward. As I looked round the bunch of prospective vets, I caught sight of a familiar face. It was a student against whom I had played both hockey and rugby at school when we played his alma mater, Mill Hill. (I didn't play cricket against him as he was a much better cricketer than me.) This was Paul Scammell. We were both happy to see a familiar face. Over the next six years we were to become very good friends and, several years later, Paul and I would set up our own practice in Crawley - but that is another story.

There were 18 vet students in my year at Cambridge. A motley collection of 3 ladies and 15 men (and boys). At the end of the six years of training all but three eventually qualified. There was no excuse for not qualifying bearing in mind that the teaching staff probably outnumbered the students by a factor of two to one. Our first casualty came before the end of our first year. The lady in question was the wife of an Addenbrooke's consultant surgeon in her early fifties who may have thought that being a vet would while away the idle hours between bridge parties. How she gained admission to the course was a matter for serious conjecture but she lost interest early in the first year never to be seen again.

The second casualty was a gentle giant of a man, Brian Hogben, who was never cut out for the academic life, failed the second year exams and took up a post with the Initial Towel Company.

Our third 'loss' was more of a manoeuvre than a lack of academic ability. This was Harry Sunkwa Mills, a student from Ghana, who had a driving ambition to become a doctor but found that the Ghanaian authorities had already allocated the two government sponsored places to the Cambridge medical course. Undeterred, he searched through reams of Ghanaian bureaucratic paperwork to find that there was an obscure government sponsorship for a veterinary student at the university. Veterinary students had to attend all the medical lectures and their own specific subjects so, by the end of the first year, Harry had attended all the necessary medical lectures. He wrote back to the Ghanaian authorities saying he now realised that his true vocation was to human medicine and not veterinary practice. They could either fly him home and let another student take his veterinary place or he could walk across Tennis Court Road in Cambridge to the department of medical anatomy. The Ghanaian government saw the practical sense of his suggestion and agreed to his transfer. Clever man, Harry.

They divided the eighteen of us into nine pairs. They allocated each pair a part of one of the greyhound bodies such as the abdomen, foreleg or head so that several students could work on the same body. They replaced the bodies at the beginning of each term to give everyone a chance to dissect the whole carcase. We wore long white lab coats but the smell of formaldehyde seeped into our daily clothes. We eventually got so used to the burning sensation in our nostrils that we hardly noticed it after a time but our friends left us in no doubt that we needed a bath.

As I have said, during the first three years, we had to attend all the medical lectures as well as having our own veterinary anatomy lectures and dissected animals – a dog, a goat and a horse – instead of humans. So we learnt human embryology, human pathology, human physiology and anatomy, human neurology, toxicology, pharmacology, parasitology and some basic medical law. All this meant that our Finals exams at the end of the third year were a long ordeal. The exams themselves usually lasted for three hours in one of the Examination Halls situated in various locations throughout the city.

We wrote our exam papers using fountain pens and most examinees carried two or three fully loaded pens just in case the first one ran out of ink.

These pens are largely collector's items nowadays and names like Waterman, Platignum, Conway Stewart, Parker and Sheaffer are fading into history. They regarded Lazlo Biro's invention of the ballpoint pen as rather too common to use in the major exams of one's life. At the end of four weeks of endless calligraphy we all had a deep dent in the side of the writing finger from pressure of the pen which only recovered after a few weeks.

There is a lot of news coverage about the stress university life puts upon students as if it was a new phenomenon. It was less newsworthy in those days but there were still students who succumbed to the rigours of concentrated study. One poor guy spent the three hours of one Final exam paper simply signing his name on fourteen sheets of exam paper. If we had a problem, we discussed it with our tutors who treated our anxieties with the confidentiality of the confessional. The good ones - and there were many of them - would have been called counsellors today.

Over the years the university has collected mountains of regulations, rules, statutes and ordinances of which many have never been amended or repealed. This can result in some rather quaint anachronisms.

One of these, which may be apocryphal, states that it entitles an undergraduate sitting a Finals examination to a pint of ale on his desk. One enterprising student wrote to the examination board pointing out this edict and, much to his surprise and delight, found a pint of bitter on his allotted desk. As he took a long draught in front of his envious colleagues, he felt a tap on his shoulder and turned to see the invigilator standing beside him.

"Excuse me, sir, but where is your sword?"

Spluttering a little, the candidate said "Sword? I have no sword."

"Exactly, sir. You should have consulted the university ordinance of - it was some year of the 17th century, I believe - which states that all Finals examinees should wear their sword during the exam period. Failure to do so incurs a fine of £5 or, in these days, about £50. I will expect your cheque by the end of the day."

It proved to be a costly pint

At Cambridge we took a degree in Natural Sciences, which included veterinary medicine, and sat our Finals exams after three years to get our B.A. degree. After that, the medical students went on to the teaching hospitals while we vets went up to the vet school on the Madingley Road, a couple of miles outside the city. This was where we learnt the practical side of becoming a vet.

In our third year we had to move out of college to "digs", or lodgings, in the town. I found a room with Mrs Bass in Hillside at the top of Castle Hill where she looked after five students one of whom became a close friend, a medic by the name of Julian Habershon. His father had been a missionary in India and somehow received a letter from England addressed to The Rev. Habershon, India. Those were the days when the Post Office took their responsibilities seriously.

Somehow or other Julian had persuaded Gordon Wright, our tutor, to allow him to bring his MG 'A' to the university which he parked on the steep drive up to the house. We ordinary mortals had to leave ten minutes before Julian to get to dinner in Hall each evening so I decided to take a little, rather childish, revenge. I begged two large potatoes from Mrs Bass and stuck them on the twin exhausts of the car as I left for college. In Hall, Julian came and sat beside me at one of the long tables. He mentioned nothing about the car and our conversation carried on as normal so I thought the potatoes must have fallen off or he had not noticed them. It was only when I got back to my room and went into the small washroom and found two half potatoes stuck on the ends of the taps that I found that my game had been discovered. He told me the next morning they had fired off with a loud bang when he started the car and the potatoes narrowly missed a pedestrian walking along the pavement at the bottom of the drive.

Julian proved himself a determined man. There was a ferocious physiology professor who was admissions tutor for Christ's College by the name of Dr Pratt. Somehow he even made us all feel nervous when lecturing us on the finer points of the Krebs Cycle but he had a very attractive daughter, Liz, towards whom he was frighteningly protective but Julian was not to be deterred in his courtship of the lady. I am happy to say they have now been married for fifty years despite his father-in-law's initially violent objections. Faint heart never won fair lady.

One Sunday, another great friend of mine, Mike Kirk, and I were bored. To exercise both our minds and bodies, we spent the day playing alternate games of chess and squash. I seem to remember that we ended up that evening, very tired, having played six games of each. Mike later joined the family business, didn't like it, and took up teaching. He taught first at Stowe then became the headmaster at the Gordon Boys School in Surrey before taking up the headship of the RHS Holbrook, a major boarding school for service families in Suffolk. He had been with the Gurkhas during his National Service so was familiar with the service life.

We were as irresponsible as most students are from time to time. I was walking back to college at about 11 o'clock along Trinity Street when I noticed a fellow vet student, Ken Whimster, a good friend, leading a cow out of Jesus Lane. A few more cattle followed him and ambled their way towards the Market Square. At that moment a police car came round the corner just as the rest of the herd came galloping round the corner and surrounded the trapped vehicle. Ken fled on guilty heels.

It turned out that he and a group of friends had released a herd of bullocks which had been grazing on Jesus Green. Ken had led the way; a few more fellow students had guided the main body of the herd while a couple at the back brought up the stragglers. It was these last two who had urged the animals into a gallop. This caused the charge down Jesus Lane into Sydney Street swamping the police car. In those days we carried out these "pranks" in style wearing our short undergraduate gowns - not the scruffy T-shirts and torn jeans of today. Ken was chased through the streets of Cambridge by one of the frustrated policemen for about 20 minutes. Apparently they both ran out of breath about 50 yards apart and sat on convenient doorsteps. The policeman made one last effort to catch him when Ken dragged himself to his feet and staggered off.

"Oh, bugger off home, you little tow-rag," came the exhausted comment from the officer as he made his way back to the Market Square.

Rag Day in Cambridge was a pre-cursor to Live Aid or the Save the Children fund-raising events. The colleges competed with each other to raise as much money as they could for various charities. RAG standing for Raising and Giving, is still raising money today but on a much more professional basis. My contribution was to dress in a dinner jacket, a black cape with a red silk lining and a top hat. In this outfit I did conjuring tricks for the passing pedestrians. They even allowed me onto the town's buses - free of charge- to amuse the passengers. But not everything was plain sailing.

I was walking through the Backs from Old Court to Memorial Court when I met the college dean, Dr John Robinson, who had been a major prosecution witness in the Lady Chatterley's Lover trial a few months earlier. I performed three card tricks for him and his family and held out the collecting tin, which was on a loop round my wrist, with my palm facing upwards. It must have been mid-November because he took a Remembrance Day poppy from his lapel, stabbed my hand with the metal stem, laughed (in a Victorian age the word would have been "guffawed") and walked on without a contribution. The college Chaplain, Dr Bill Skelton, was a far more Christian man - and preached a far better sermon. It was only when researching this book that I found out that Bill, the gentlest of men, had experienced an eventful wartime career in the RAF. I quote from his obituary - "Known as "the night hawk partners", Skelton (as navigator) and Branse Burbridge (as pilot) were officially credited with destroying 21 enemy aircraft, one more than Group Captain "Cat's Eyes" Cunningham. Skelton's brilliance with airborne radar over Britain and Germany was recognised with the awards of a DFC and Bar in 1944 and a DSO and Bar in 1945." I wonder how many of his Clare contemporaries knew anything of these wartime exploits.

Speaking of my conjuring skills, my main interest was with card magic, but I could supplement my grant by giving more general magic shows to College professor's children's parties. It was always the same show while the price varied dependent on the last trick when I brought a small animal from the top hat. It was either a white mouse, white guinea pig or white rabbit that I gave the animal to the birthday child at the end of the show. They all came free from the laboratories animal technician with whom I had struck up a friendship. If the parents wanted the snob value of a white rabbit, my fee was £5 while the guinea pig was £3 and the mouse a pound.

Another friend from P staircase, Jim Russell, found another outlet for my conjuring skills. Jim was one of the kindest men I knew but had an unjustifiably low opinion of himself. He was the oldest child of Admiral Sir John Russell and his younger brother had been page to the Queen so he had lived in the shadows of an illustrious family for too long. He was a medic who later qualified at Guys Hospital. While at Cambridge, he realised that there were a lot of families coping with Downs children - we called them 'mongols' in those days which was cruel. Jim set up a "respite" club every Thursday evening in a church hall to give the parents some welcome time to themselves. He asked me to give a show one evening to which I agreed but asked about the age range of the group.

"They vary from about twelve to nearly forty," he replied.

"What are their mental ages?" I asked.

"Between two and ten."

This would be a challenge. I devised three routines based on the likely understanding of three age groups and started with one trick from each routine. I had asked Jim whether any of the audience would be afraid of "bangs" to which he instantly said "Betty! She is terrified of loud noises."

I told him that if I had to go into the easiest routine, there would be trick involving the bursting of a balloon and, that if that was the routine I would use, I could give him a signal and they would move Betty out for a couple of minutes. It was obvious, from the reaction to the trick from the second set of illusions, it would have to be the easiest routine. I gave him the signal, they moved Betty away for a few minutes and the evening was a great success.

Jim later started similar clubs in London and Bristol but remained embarrassed by any public acknowledgement of his work. I met him in the lift of Crawley hospital many years later. A successful GP, married with a young family but still slightly uncomfortable in his own skin. He died a couple of years ago and I was proud to have known him.

Teddy Boys

As we get older, we begin to feel that everything was so much better "in the old days" which is rarely true. Things were different but not necessarily better. Recorded violent crime figures are remarkably similar between the the 1970s and today. We have street gangs today rather like we had Teddy Boys, Mods and Rockers in the 60s and 70s although they were sprats compared with the County Line sharks of today. I nearly became the victim of one of these gangs in Cambridge late one evening.

Walking back to college past the Round Church at the top of Magdalen Street, a group of about half a dozen Teddy Boys confronted me with their slicked hair, drainpipe trousers and thick crepe-soled shoes. Each one was carrying a bicycle chain hanging from their wrist. It was lucky that I had taken Annabel out with me that evening.

Annabel was an 18th birthday gift from my parents. She is an innocent-looking walking stick with a silver band just below the handle. There was no point in running as one or more of them would be faster than me so I waved Annabel feebly in their general direction. While I held my breath, the leader of the group made a grab for the stick which was what I was hoping for. Once he had taken a firm hold, I pulled back on the handle to reveal two-and-a-half feet of sharp Wilkinson steel - Annabel was a swordstick. My luck held in that the gang leader dropped the wooden end and fled with the others as I flashed the blade in their direction. Annabel still lives with us today.

Learning

One or two episodes during my Cambridge years taught me the value of questioning almost everything. Not necessarily accepting current or even learned academic thinking. Experts seem to have an ingrained habit of getting many things wrong.

I remember one physiology essay I had written on the function of the human kidney. During one tutorial held in one of the ancient rooms of Clare Old Court, the tutor, Dr Willmer, questioned my use of a particular fact I found in a respected textbook on the subject.

"You are quoting a drawing - not a proven fact," he said.

"Well, if you can't trust such a highly respected academic work, who can you trust?"

"Exactly," he replied. "Is the illustration a diagram?, an anatomical drawing?, a photograph or copied from someone else's inaccurate work?"

It quite put me out at the time and it took a few months for me to appreciate his words. Words confirmed a few months later when I attended a lecture by Roger Akester, the avian anatomy lecturer. He recommended a particular book for us to read regarding the anatomy of a chicken but the recommendation came with a warning.

"Just ignore the respiratory system illustrated on page 127," he said. "At the time of its original publication, dissection techniques were not accurate enough to define the delicate airways of the bird. The air travels through the lungs, down to air sacs in the abdomen and even into the bones.

"We knew about the sacs but the delicate passage ways were left blank because nobody had been able to dissect them accurately. The author sent his drawing of the incomplete respiratory system to the illustrator who may have been offended by the lack of continuity between the lungs and the air sacs used his imagination to draw in his approximation of where he thought they ought to be. This illustration appeared in several subsequent textbooks until someone eventually solved the puzzle and corrected the illustration some 20 years later."

I always felt that almost all of my fellow vet students were cleverer than me except for Brian Hogben who had failed the exams at the end of the second year which, in my mind, left me next for the chop. So in the final exams I was surprised to learn that, while I had passed, three others had to re-sit their exams which only proved that you can be quite wrong about your own capabilities. (I had had to re-take my Biology "O" level and failed Anatomy at the end of my third year which meant I had to re-sit the exam in the Autumn so my confidence was always rather low.)

Chapter 4

Seeing practice

During the vacations we were expected to "see practice" with a variety of veterinary establishments to gain practical experience and, while doing so, we had to keep records of the more interesting challenges and experiences we encountered, while shadowing our mentors, in the form of a case histories. These would form part of our final year examination when one the senior examiners interviewed us during an hour of conversation. This was known as a "viva". I don't know whether many teaching schools still use the term to describe such an examination. It may form part of today's "course work".

I wish I still had that case book but it formed part of the final exam and had to be submitted to the examining authorities. It would have fascinating to compare the notes of veterinary practice in the 60s to today's scientific powerhouses.

Despite the lack of facilities and knowledge, amazing feats of medical and surgical expertise went on behind the doors of ordinary detached houses in suburban streets which were the veterinary practices of those days. The most common intravenous anaesthetic was sodium pentothal, often referred to in old war films as the "truth serum", or either chloroform or ether would be administered by mask to the struggling patient. Most surgery was fairly basic such as the castration or spaying of household pets, suturing the odd skin wounds, castration of farm livestock and Caesarean sections of farm livestock carried out under paravertebral local anaesthesia in a cow barn or pig sty. Small animal surgery provided more stimulating surgical challenges such as the pinning and plating of broken bones, retrieval of a variety of foreign objects from the intestines and the removal of a wide range of tumours.

An inventory of surgical equipment would include scalpel handles; Swann Morton disposable scalpel blades; Gillies, McPhail and Mayo needle holders; Mayo and curved-on-flat scissors. We used Spencer Wells and Halstead's mosquito forceps to stem bleeding and larger forceps, both curved and flat, for gynaecological and intestinal surgery. So many surgical instruments carried the name of their designer that they almost had individual characters that one got to know over the years. The American Mayo Clinic in Rochester, Minnesota was a centre of surgical excellence and developed their own specific forceps, needle-holders and scissors. Spanish doctors, known for their ophthalmic surgical skills, designed the Castroviejo scissors for detailed surgery of the eyes. Suture materials included various sizes of catgut, monofilament and braided nylon and even silk tapes.

Massey and Mitchell

My first choice for seeing practice was with our wonderfully mad vet in Chelmsford, Roger Massey, who had encouraged me to enter the veterinary profession. He was in partnership with a Mr Mitchell but the two of them never spoke to each other following a long-forgotten argument. If they wanted to pass any information to the other they would ask the receptionist, or me if I was there, to convey the comment to the opposite partner even when they were in the same room! It was all rather bizarre.

"Adrian, would you tell Mr Mitchell that I shall be visiting Small's Farm in Bannister Green this morning? Does he have any medications he would like me to take for their horse?"

"Tell Mr Massey that I delivered the drugs to Charlie Small yesterday afternoon."

It went on like this for over 12 years.

Roger was one of the Radio Vets who spoke regularly on BBC radio farming programs for many years. These broadcasts involved a visit up to Broadcasting House in Portland Place at the upper end of Regent Street. One day Roger had been investigating the sudden death of a pig which he suspected might have had anthrax - a highly infectious disease in both humans and animals. He had put the dead pig in the boot of his car intending to take it to the local Ministry of Agriculture, Fisheries and Food (MAFF) laboratory on his way back home after the broadcast. He was running late so left his car outside Broadcasting House and rushed in to do the recording. Returning to where he thought he had left the car, it was gone. He contacted the police who said they had no record of it being towed away so Roger explained that they had better find it soon as it may have an anthrax pig in the boot. He took the train back to Chelmsford. It was two days later that the police rang to tell him they had found the car - in the police pound! Whether it was the smell of the rotting pig that led them to the car, or not, I cannot say but the car boot needed a deep clean on its return.

I soon learnt not to be surprised by the unexpected. One client presented Roger with a cat that had a history of limping on a front leg occasionally as well as retching and a lack of appetite. There was no obvious discomfort in either front leg, chest or stomach area so Roger decided to X-ray the animal to see what showed up. Luckily, Roger accidentally placed the cat on the X-ray plate too far forward to show the lower end of the abdomen but this turned out to be rather fortuitous. There was nothing wrong in the chest or abdomen but just in front of the left shoulder was the thin white shadow of a needle that the cat had swallowed. This got stuck in the oesophagus, or foodpipe, and when the left fore leg stretched forward the needle pricked the shoulder joint caused the cat to wince. Roger's treatment was unscientific but effective. Under an anaesthetic he manipulated the needle through the oesophagus and out through the skin at the base of the neck and after a course of antibiotics it made a full recovery.

There were no qualified veterinary nurses at this time. The first Animal Nursing Auxiliary qualified in 1961 and they were only allowed to call themselves veterinary nurses in 1984. The receptionist would step in to hold an instrument during a complicated operation, give post-operative injections, renew dressings and comfort distraught owners. Some of these ladies built up a great deal of experience during their years with the practice. They were also the bookkeepers, the peacemakers and became the beating heart of the practice.

Owners rarely paid for treatment at the time. Accounts were rendered monthly in guineas which were the currency of the professions in those days. There was no itemisation of the work done. The account page would simply state the words "To Veterinary Fees" with the amount in guineas. (A guinea was £1 1s and the unit for professional fees and horse-racing circles - hence the One Thousand and Two Thousand Guineas classic horse races.) For the first few years of my veterinary career the average consultation fee was five shillings which, in today's decimal currency, is 25p.

Speeding E-type Jaguar

While I was seeing practice with him, Roger found himself the beneficiary of a legacy and chose to spend the money on a bit of luxury - in the form of a brand new Jaguar "E" type sports car. Unfortunately as a result of that decision, Roger lost a very valued farming client. There were two Jaguar dealerships in Chelmsford the owners of which both owned large farms in the area that were clients of the practice. Both garages offered him enticing deals over the car and he had to choose one over the other. Once he made the choice, the owner of the losing dealership informed him he would no long require his services as vet to his farms. Roger took the news in his usual good spirits saying that "it was all water under the bridge" but we all knew that the petty vindictiveness of the farmer hurt him deeply.

Losing the client did not prevent him from enjoying his new toy to the limit. He enjoyed stretching the capabilities of the car on his way home after surgery on summer evenings. As he rounded a tight corner on such an evening he was confronted by a policeman pointing a speed-gun at him. As will become familiar throughout this book, the police, doctors and vets had a close working relationship which often became friendships with individual officers.

"Evening, Mr Massey," said the constable.

"Good evening, Billy. How is life treating you this lovely evening?"

Billy ignored the niceties and asked "And what speed do you think you were doing just now?"

Roger thought for a moment and realised that the police normally <u>told</u> you what speed you were doing rather than <u>asking</u> you.

"I don't know, Billy. What does your gun say?" Innocence radiating from his face like a medieval saint.

"You bugger!" replied the policeman. "You know damn well you were speeding, but the battery has just given up on the speed gun so I can't tell you."

He threw the speed gun into the back of his car and muttered "Get off home.... Slowly!"

In those days there was still a local policeman in most of the larger villages and the vets and doctors got to recognise and respect members of their local force.

Strychnine

As I think a reader will have realised by now, veterinary medicine was rather primitive in the 1960s. James Herriot had painted a remarkably accurate picture of rural veterinary life but, understandably, he omitted some of the more unpleasant aspects of that life. An example of which, I was about to experience in the Chelmsford practice.

One afternoon Roger had to deal with a particularly wild, and very strong, feral cat that the RSPCA inspector had trapped and asked him to put down. There was no safe way to get the animal out of the metal cage so Roger went to the small locked cupboard which contained various dangerous drugs. This was the DDA cabinet of the practice. DDA stood for Dangerous Drugs Act which stipulated that certain drugs had to be held under lock and key and hold a DDA Register into which every drug movement in and out of the cabinet had to be recorded. He removed a small bottle of clear fluid into which he pushed a small tuft of cotton wool held by a pair of long forceps.

"I don't like doing this, Adrian, but sometimes it is the only solution."

He pushed the forceps through the bars of the cage when the cat savagely bit at the cotton wool end. Within a few seconds it developed a series of seizures before dying horribly within minutes. The fluid was strychnine.

With today's arsenal of sedatives, heavy tranquillizers and anaesthetics, the animal would have suffered far less, but it was still a primitive age of veterinary medicine. We had to use what was available and I still remember that cat.

Winter of 1963

The winter of 1963 was one of the coldest on record with an average temperature throughout January of -2.1°C or 28.2°F. The first snow fell in mid-December and drifted, in places, to over 20 feet. Snow lay 6 feet deep in Manchester city centre while the last of the frost ended on 6th March. Country roads were often impassable with cars completely buried as wind drift filled the local lanes to the height of the roadside hedges. It was a bad time for the whole country and farmers suffered worse than most but they still called out the vets.

One of my jobs while seeing practice with Roger Massey was to start his car engine when morning surgery was ending to defrost the vehicle ready for the day's visits. After surgery Roger would check the calls that had come in from the farming clients. They all insisted that their own farms were accessible despite the weather but Roger had an arrangement with the milk tanker drivers. They would call in to the surgery letting us know which farms were accessible, and those that were still snowed in. The local councils did their best to keep most of the main roads open but there was a time when we came to a T-junction at which Roger stopped and appeared a little confused.

"You may be wondering why I am hesitating here, Adrian. My problem is that this is not actually a T-junction but a crossroads. We need to go straight across," he said, pointing at a ten foot high wall of snow in front of us. At least he stopped which was not the case the next day.

We were driving along a well-cleared road, chatting to each other, when Roger suddenly flung the car into a hard right turn onto a side road. We had been so pre-occupied that he had forgotten about the turn until the last moment. Because of this manoeuvre we were sailing sideways down the minor road straight into the path of an oncoming car whose elderly owners had been driven out into the snow to get vital food supplies. It must have been a frightening sight to see a huge Ford Zephyr careering sideways towards them. Roger threw the wheel across to the left and we nosedived into the ditch just as the other car passed us on the road.

"Rather a brilliant bit of driving, I thought," said Roger as he looked down on me in the passenger seat - the car was canted at a 45-degree angle.

"Brilliant?! That was bloody mad."

"Well, if I'd turned the wheel the other way we would have hit them. Now just walk across that field and ask John Titmus if he could bring his tractor over and pull us out."

He was a wonderfully exasperating man but I still wonder whether those pensioners got back home safely.

A few weeks later I was back at Cambridge and I braved the weather to spend the weekend with Jen at Stock, a small village outside Chelmsford, where she was working as a nanny. During the night it snowed heavily again and we were unable to get my MG 'A', Susie, out of the drift so I had to get back to Cambridge by train. The following Friday the roads had cleared a bit and, unknown to me, Jen decided to drive Susie back to Cambridge where I was living at the George and Dragon pub on Jesus Green. It was about 4.30 in the afternoon when Harry, the landlord, called up to say there was a phone call for me. It was Addenbrookes hospital.

"Was I the fiancé of Jenifer Tarrant?" they asked.

"Yes," I said nervously.

"She has been in a road accident and we have got her here in Casualty," (They called it Casualty then instead of A&E.)

"How is she?" I asked.

"I'm afraid I cannot tell you that over the phone. You will have to come and see for yourself."

Mike Vaughan, a fellow vet and another lodger at the George and Dragon, had an Austin Westminster and he offered to drive me to the hospital. I have never been driven so fast through the streets of a major city in my life.

Fortunately Jen was only bruised and shaken despite turning the car over into a ditch. She had tried to overtake a slow-moving bus and hit the hard ridge of compacted snow in the middle of the road and lost control. Many sports cars had wooden floors in those days and there was a round hole in the passenger foot well. Gazing through the hole, Jen could just make out the line of feet of the passengers of the bus which had stopped to help. They turned the car sufficiently to allow Jen to crawl out but not before trying to push it the other way - on to her - at which she yelled at them to stop and roll the car the other way. It was all very frightening at the time but we got her back to the spare room in the pub to sleep off the shock. We went back home to Stock on the Sunday by train. It was so cold that the shoulder of Jen's sheepskin coat had frozen to the window of the train by the time we got to Liverpool Street station.

One farmer took advantage of our generation of vets to whom dedication to their clients was more important than bottom line profit. It happened to Peter Grant who was later to become my senior partner in Woking. In 1947 he worked that winter in the Lake District when he got a call late one snowy afternoon to an emergency case of milk fever. Having struggled through the snow, he arrived at the farm to find the farmer at the front door with a suitcase in his hand.

"I'll pay you for the milk fever if you get me to the station. None of the taxis would come out."

I have no record of Peter's response to this wilful deception and abuse of his good nature. He was a Scot, so it was probably colourful.

Early general practice surgery

Operating surgery in Chelmsford was still pretty primitive. There would only be one or two small animal operations a day as the practice treated mainly farm animals. Roger attended the farms and Mr Mitchell treated the equine clients. There were no kennels so any operative patients were tied up in the office, having had a sedative injection, where they would wait until their time came for the operation. This took place after morning surgery with the examination table doubling as an operating table.

Anaesthesia was by sodium pentothal given intravenously. The margin of error in this anaesthetic's dosage was quite narrow and quite deep levels of anaesthesia were needed to achieve adequate pain relief. The syringe was taped to the patient's leg, and the anaesthetic topped up as and when necessary during the operation. There were no intubation or anaesthetic machine facilities and recovery could take as long as two hours depending on the length of the operation. Barbiturates act by being taken up selectively by fatty tissue and since the brain is the fattiest tissue in the body, this is where the immediate effects are seen. Initial recovery takes place as the redistribution of the drug to the other fat depots in the body reduces the amount in the brain before being metabolised (broken down) and excreted. This has significant implications in breeds such as the greyhound which have small amounts of body fat and therefore experience prolonged recovery times.

We used catgut to suture the internal muscle layers and blue monofilament nylon to close the skin. Cat spays would take no longer than 10 minutes while a bitch spay might last as long as 45 minutes resulting in an in-coordinate patient being sent home that evening. There were no hospital facilities on the premises although Roger would occasionally take a severely ill patient back home with him after evening surgery.

Major surgery such as orthopaedic work, enterectomies, pyometras and caesarean sections often carried poor prognoses because of the lack of facilities for controlled anaesthesia and intravenous fluid therapy. There was little dentistry performed, apart from the occasional removal of a loose tooth. In fact I cannot remember any teaching of dental techniques given by the vet school.

Apart from neutering operations, the most common surgery was the removal of foreign bodies from the intestinal tract. Pets will swallow almost anything and we removed baby's teats, wooden toy crocodiles, woollen nappies and rubber balls from the intestines of cats and dogs. These all paled into insignificance compared to the experience of one of my vet school colleagues, Neil Cotton, who had a practice in Torquay.

Someone presented him with a young border collie of about 16 weeks which was persistently trying to swallow something. Apart from this strange behaviour and a lack of appetite it was perfectly happy. Neil examined the pup and noticed something strange at the back of its throat.

"Are you missing a poker?" he asked the anxious owners.

"A poker? What on earth are you talking about? We came here to find out what was wrong with our pup not to discuss the contents of our house."

At this point the wife of the owner tapped her husband on the arm, saying "Actually, we have lost the small poker by the fireplace. I told you about it yesterday."

"Why do you ask?" came a suspicious question from the husband.

"Because I think your dog has swallowed it."

X-rays later confirmed his diagnosis and, during a short anaesthetic, he gradually withdrew it from the throat. The retrieved poker was twelve inches long while the puppy was seventeen inches from tip of nose to tip of long collie tail. A sword-swallowing pup.

It was the same Neil Cotton who was asked to examine a 'rattling' dog. Every time it moved, it rattled. Even when lifted onto the examination table, it rattled. This time X-rays discovered sixteen pebbles from the town's beach in its stomach which were later removed successfully.

Christian Scientists

One incident that found its way into my casebook was a call from a particular farm saying they had a sick pig. "That'll be erysipelas," said Roger. I had had it drummed into me by all the professors at the vet school not to make diagnoses before examining the case so I challenged his assumption.

"Their father is a Christian Scientist and will not allow any vaccination of his livestock. Any pig of his that is sick is invariably erysipelas - but, you are right, one should not diagnose before examination."

On our arrival at the farm a very large round man of about 70 who I assumed to be the Christian Scientist met us. Roger later informed me it wasn't him that held the religious beliefs but his 90-year-old father who ruled the farm and his two sons with a rod of iron. Sure enough, it was a case of erysipelas which responded well to the penicillin treatment. This case proved to be a lifeline during my final viva examination as it distracted the examiner from asking me any more probing questions but that is another story for later.

The wrong cat

Another practice I spent time with was in Thaxted, a small Essex market town. The single-handed vet was a Mr Bennet who had a veterinary degree from Glasgow and a doctorate from some American university. His consulting premises were in a shop front on the high street with a large barn in the back garden which was where the operations were carried out as well as housing several cages for boarding cats.

He used me as unpaid labour to mind the practice while he was away on visits or on the golf course. One of my first calls nearly proved to be a disaster.

"Is that the vets?" asked a frantic voice.

"Yes," I replied.

"Come quick. It's Steel's Farm. We've got a cow with milk fever. She's down and not looking good."

They rang off.

I had no idea where Mr Bennett had got to so I just had to wait. When he eventually arrived back at the surgery an hour later, I gave him the message.

"That's fine, Adrian. Unfortunately I don't have a Steel's farm on my books. What did they sound like?"

"It was a man and he sounded as though he was panicking - apart from that I haven't a clue."

Luckily, the farmer rang back later, identifying his farm as Wheels farm, and the cow was saved.

On another afternoon a client rang to say she had returned from her holidays and could we deliver her cat home? The labelling of the boarding animals was rather haphazard so again I waited until Mr Bennett returned. He identified the animal and asked me to run it back to the owner. By the time I arrived at the house she was nowhere to be seen. Presuming she had gone shopping for essential supplies, I left the cat in the basket on the front doorstep and returned to the surgery.

By the time I got back the owner had returned, only to find it was not her cat! I was then dispatched to retrieve the "wrong" cat. The owner was understandably not best pleased. "Mine is a black and white cat, not a ginger, and Mr Bennett spayed (neutered) her!" I muttered grovelling apologies and went back to the surgery.

"We were supposed to have spayed the cat while the owner was on holiday," I said.

"Oh God, quick!" he said. "Let's do it now. It will only take about 20 minutes and we can get her back home before evening surgery. We can tell her we have been very busy and only just had time to operate on the cat this afternoon."

The animal was quickly anaesthetised, and he found the uterus but it looked abnormal. Instead of the ovaries lying at the ends of the uterine horns, there was just a curious cluster of blood vessels. Anyway we paid no notice and completed the surgery.

When he had said "we" would return the cat, it meant me. So I packed the drowsy animal into the basket and set off yet again. This time the owner was in and relieved to have her beloved pet returned. That was until she opened the basket and I explained the reason for the cat's drowsy appearance.

"Why has she been operated on?" she shrieked. "Mr Bennett spayed her two years ago!"

Apparently she thought we could identify a spayed cat several years after surgery. This is easy with tom cats but with queens any scar is very fine and hidden deep in the fur.

By this time I was totally speechless and fled. I recounted the sorry tale to Mr Bennett who slapped his hand to his forehead. He then remembered that, two years ago, he did ovariectomies (removal of the ovaries) instead of the full operation. At that point I told him he could explain the mistakes to the owner. It was experiences such as this that made me begin a list of "Things I will Never Do To My Staff" in the back of an old diary. I found that diary in the loft many years later.

Dunstable

The final practice I spent time with as a student was the practice of Martin Senior and Clive Halnan in West Street, Dunstable. Jen and I were married by this time, my final year at Cambridge, so she joined me while I was seeing practice. This did not always turn out well as Judith Halnan, Clive's wife, looked upon her as an unpaid nanny to her two children. Jen spent large parts of the day entertaining the children while Judith enjoyed her social activities around their home village of Studham. So when the second opportunity to see practice with them we decided that Jen would stay at home in our rented flat in Great Shelford and I would return home for the weekends.

Then, as now, practices often take advantage of students using them as cheap labour. This is fine so long as the student is gaining practical knowledge but, too often, they are making tea and answering the telephone. I learnt most from Roger Massey who took great pains to explain what he was doing and why. He encouraged me to perform my first injections, monitor my first anaesthetics and examine cattle by rectal palpation. He was always happy to answer my juvenile questions and treated them with a seriousness that few of my other mentors ever achieved.

The Dunstable practice had the advantage of the experience of Martin Senior with the modern scientific approach of Clive Halnan, who had qualified from Cambridge some 5 years previously. Although they were as different as chalk and cheese, I learned a lot from both men both in the

42

veterinary and social fields. So when they offered me a post as an assistant, subject to passing my final exams, we accepted. The starting salary of £1050 per annum was the second highest offer of a post in our year of students.

Norwich VI Centre

While spending most of my vacations seeing practice in Chelmsford and Dunstable, I spent one month with the veterinary investigation centre in Norwich. My lasting memory of this posting was of endless post mortems of escaped coypus, or nutria. Large rodents imported as a cheap alternative to the more expensive furs of the fashion trade. It was either that or endlessly plating up bacterial samples onto agar gel in petri dishes. This was to identify the infection and its susceptibility to the antibiotics of the time. The permanent staff seemed to spend a lot of their time jostling for political advantage to further their career in the service rather than investigating diseases.

The time spent at the veterinary investigation centre in Norwich was valuable in that it confirmed my opinion that I wanted to work with people in general practice and not in the sterile atmosphere of a laboratory run by governmental bureaucrats.

Chapter 5

The Era of the 50s and 60s

At this point it might be helpful to describe the way of life in the early days of my veterinary career. The grumpy dinosaurs of today are often reminding us that things were so much better in their day. I know this because I frequently behave like one of those dinosaurs. We complain about today's trains arriving late and overcrowded forgetting the ever-present soot, grime and filthy carriages in the days of steam railways. I love those nostalgic newsreels of steam trains racing through the tunnels and over the bridges but forget about the smuts of congealed smoke that invaded the carriages, the delays caused by fallen trees, livestock on the line or a broken-down train blocking the line. But there was far less overcrowding even on the fewer train services since most people lived and worked locally.

We forget that private telephones were a luxury and to get a line at all, householders often had to accept a shared line with a neighbour. Local exchange operators were the primary source of gossip in the community which usually turned out to be as accurate as the information we get on social media today. Telephones were a luxury, not an essential fashion item for the under-fives at primary school. They also had the advantage of working most of the time instead of being unable to find a mobile signal. Telephone numbers involved exchanges and the number. Everyone on the country knew the telephone number of the Metropolitan Police at Scotland Yard was Whitehall 1212 while our telephone number at home was Hatfield Peverel 12. There was even one London exchange named Arnold! Transatlantic calls were rare and only used by ordinary members of the public on birthdays and Christmas. Even then the call had to be booked for a particular time and duration several weeks ahead. On the other hand, we spoke to our neighbours and raised our hats at passers-by instead of keeping our eyes glued to the screen of our mobiles.

Electricity cuts were part of daily life with emergency candles and matches placed at strategic points throughout the home. Central heating was the stuff of dreams. Most people simply put on an extra cardigan and added an extra blanket to the bed clothes. We considered duvets rather foreign until the arrival of skiing holidays in the late 70s when returning winter holidaymakers asked for these unfamiliar, but effective, methods of keeping warm in bed.

Household pets often lived outside in kennels or outhouses. There were many more mongrels in the community because either the owners could not afford the cost of neutering or the local veterinary practice did not have the skill to perform hysterectomies. We fed dogs on scraps left over from the owner's table or horse meat and condemned cattle carcases from the slaughterhouse. Mum used to have a delivery of meat from the slaughter man once a week. They painted it with a deep green dye to prevent it entering the human food chain. She would cut the meat into cubes and boil it on the range for about three hours. The sickly smell pervaded the whole house for the day.

Cats ate cheap fish scraps from the fishmonger to supplement their 'pest control' diets. It was a few years before commercial pet food arrived in the form of Pedigree Chum, Chappie and Spillers Winalot biscuits for dogs. Family cats might get Whiskas tinned food and they were often given saucers of milk before tuberculin testing eliminated the risk of tuberculosis. This led, years later, to one lecturer teaching us that while dogs were prone to human TB from the coughing owners while cats were more likely to contract bovine TB from the untreated milk.

Dairy cattle were still being hand-milked with most dairy farms breeding Ayrshire or Dairy Shorthorn cattle. Guernsey and Jersey breeds provided the small demand for luxury milk. The ubiquitous black and white Friesian of today was only beginning its dominance of the country's dairy herd.

We had three postal deliveries a day to compensate for the lack of e-mails and text messages. We expected next day delivery by first class postage long before Amazon Prime and other online retailers promoted "next day delivery" as if it was a technological leap into the future.

Cars were serviced at least every six months or a few thousand miles. Windscreen wipers often had to be operated from inside the car but, because windscreen washers were still a thing of the future, they simply spread the mud across the glass. Headlamps on most cars were weak while the best guide when driving in fog was the pile of leaves in the gutter.

News came on the radio, and later television, about three times a day. We got information about events that affected our daily lives instead of the 24/7 undigested news-fest they subject us to today. No sooner has someone taken a mobile video of a big wave in the Marshall Islands than it is the third item on News at Ten.

Medical practice was also very different. Doctors either wore long white coats or a three-piece suit if they were a consultant. Nurses all wore uniforms denoting their rank in the hospital hierarchy. These uniforms easily identified matrons, staff nurses, sisters, nurses and orderlies. Doctors and vets listened and examined before making a diagnosis and prescribing treatment. Today they stay glued to their computer screens, order up a multitude of tests and then order medications whose side effects cause more problems than the original condition. But it is time I put this grumpy old man back in his kennel and got back to the story.

Villages

The effects of the war were still evident in daily life. Petrol rationing ended in 1950 but sweets were still rationed up to 1953 and, while sugar rationing ended later the same year, meat and other food products remained rationed until July 1954. Economically, the country teetered on the edge of bankruptcy and our playgrounds around North London were often bomb sites.

We moved to Hatfield Peverel in about 1950 when my parents bought a large mock Tudor house, surrounded by a large garden together with a gardener's cottage where Mr Gray lived with his wife and son. There was a large paddock at the back of the house. The property cost £8500 which stretched their financial resources to the limit.

Hatfield Peverel was a small village six miles east of Chelmsford housing about 1200 people most of whom worked on the surrounding farms or the nearby towns of Witham, Braintree and Chelmsford. These were also the early years of the commuter age. Dad would join about 15 people on the platform of Hatfield Peverel station to catch one of about 3 trains to Liverpool Street in the City in the mornings.

In these villages and small towns, the days of the squire, doctor and vicar of Treasure Island were fading but there was still an unspoken hierarchy within these small communities. The large land owner and the doctor sat at the top of the tree while the policeman, butcher, greengrocer and other tradesmen occupied the lower branches. The blacksmith was still repairing farm implements and carts but was also servicing the occasional car.

Hatfield Peverel had three pubs, the White Horse and Duke of Wellington on the main A12 with The Sportsman's Arms lying to the south of the village towards Ulting. The Sportsman's had a large chestnut tree on the green outside and a hitching rail for the occasional farm horse that might

46

have been ridden to the pub after a day's work. My brother Pete and I would saddle up the two old nags on the farm and amble down to the Sportsman's for a few pints. We hitched the horses to the post under the chestnut tree and then let them take us home at closing time. It was a very peaceful life.

Village people wore hats. Men doffed them or tipped them to passers-by. Ladies wore them everywhere and kept them on in church while the men removed theirs. Church services on Sundays were well-attended social gatherings especially in the villages where the congregation exchanged the current gossip. Most churches would hold both Morning Service and Evensong on Sundays rather than the Communion services of today.

There was a petrol filling station and small garage in the High Street. The butcher's shop stood on the green with the grocer, Ken Lawrence, at the other end of the A12 as it ran through the village. Mum would phone in her weekly order of groceries every Thursday which Ken would deliver the next afternoon in his small, dark green Morris van. We were largely self-sufficient in vegetables with Mr Gray, the gardener, dropping in to the kitchen in the morning to ask Mum what she needed for the day.

The doctor's house, which doubled as the surgery, stood across the road from the grocers. There were no appointments. You turned up at morning or evening surgery, sat in the hall and waited your turn to go through to the front room for the consultation. Sydney Emerick may have been just our village doctor, but he was a man of many parts. There was something of the polymath about Syd.

Working with Marconi of Chelmsford in the 1950s, he invented a medical radio-transmitting device. This recorded the foetal heartbeats of pregnant women sending information to the maternity hospital in Chelmsford. He could explain Einstein's theory of relativity in simple terms; navigate sailing vessels across the Channel while taking time out to captain the village's second cricket team. They also elected him a Governor of the London Hospital in Whitechapel despite practising in the outer reaches of Essex. A great deal of any clinical expertise I developed as a vet was down to Syd.

We had our own policeman in the village whose house acted as the local police station. There was little going on in the village he didn't know about and levels of petty crime were so low that people never locked their homes when they went out shopping.

The village cricket team included a postman, a wheelwright, an insurance agent and a couple of farm hands. Our best batsman, who regularly scored 50 or more in a match, ran a slightly dubious trade in what he used to call "necessities". The population of the village may have been a little over a thousand but it fielded two cricket teams and a football side.

Village life was still very insular. I remember, when playing cricket for the village side, sitting on the boundary next to Frank Selby, the village postman, I said "It's great coming to a village like this from North London with so many of the team being native to the village."

"Native!" he exploded. "Oo do yer think's a native in this side?"

"Well. There's you, Frank."

"That's right. Oi'm a native but 'oo else do you think is a native?"

"Snowy Bright's a native."

Snowy was the other opening bowler for the team alongside Frank. He wore the thickest glasses I have ever seen and was invariably dispatched to the outfield when not bowling. If the ball came in his direction, the shouts of the other members of the team had to guide him towards it.

"Snowy's not a native."

"He was born over the wheelwright's shop on the High Street."

"'Ee may have been but his mother came from Tarlin."

Terling, pronounced Tarlin, was an even smaller village two miles away. I gave up at this point and walked around the boundary. Every match day an elderly lady dressed in widow's black brought out her kitchen chair to watch the game. As I approached her, she asked if I was going on holiday that summer.

"Yes. We are all going to Spain for ten days," I replied.

"Oooh, Spain! That'll be abroad, won't it? I haven't been abroad. The furthest I've been was on my honeymoon to Braintree." Braintree was just under ten miles away.

Roy Claydon ran the garage on the High Street. He wore a new white coat every day. There was no self-service at the pump - only the one, as we had no unleaded, super or otherwise, and diesel was only available in the larger towns. Roy or his mechanic would fill the tank for you after you had told him how many gallons and "shots" you wanted. "Shots" were squirts of an upper cylinder lubricant called Redex put into the tank before filling up. The cost of a gallon of petrol in 1971 was 6/6d or 33p. For those who never knew Imperial measures, there are 4.5 litres to a gallon so a litre, in 1971, would have cost a fraction over 7p.

New cars were "run in" to bed the engine down. Speed was limited to about 35mph for the first thousand miles although the oil was changed after the first five hundred. Servicing cars involved an oil change, sandblasting the spark plugs and greasing of between 20 and 40 grease nipples at the various joints of the cars suspension and transmission. After a while the engines had to be de-coked which meant stripping down the cylinder head and grinding out the accumulated debris in the cylinders and valves which was reducing the engine's efficiency. Without MoT tests in those days or the improved petrol technology of today, vehicles pouring dense black smoke from the exhaust were a common sight.

In the 50s and 60s there were many car manufacturers dominated by Morris, Austin and Ford, most of whose models were available only in black. The Austin 7 was one of the earliest affordable cars followed by the Morris 8, Austin 12, Ford Popular and Ford Anglia. The latter cost £310 in 1950. Only the pensioners of today remember cars like Singer, Hillman, Armstrong Siddeley, Wolseley, Humber, Talbot, Standard, Lagonda, Allard, AC, Riley, and Alvis. There were limited numbers of foreign cars such as Mercedes, Alfa Romeo, Lancia, Toyota, Nissan, Renault, Citroen, Simca and Peugeot. Most of these have gone now, swallowed up by the uniform efficiency of the industry today.

These cars were not the most efficient, most economical or safest, but they had a character which is sadly lacking in most of the vehicles of the 21st century. I'm getting nostalgic again - until I remember the journeys to Cornwall for the annual fortnight holiday taking the best part twelve hours. There were no motorways and the dreaded bottleneck on the West Coast route was the Exeter bypass which itself could take hours to negotiate. There were no speed limits outside the towns but then few cars could exceed 65mph.

The Towns

The larger towns of Chelmsford and Colchester housed a much wider community and offered more facilities than the small market towns and villages. Every town would have several branches of banks - many of which are now long gone in the quest for efficiency. Banks like Martins, District and National Provincial and more provincial companies such as Williams and Glyns, William Deacons and the Yorkshire bank have all disappeared. The latter even produced its own bank notes that were accepted throughout the country. There was usually a professional part of the town which housed the lawyers and accountants in musty Victorian offices.

Unemployment in 1974 was 3.8% - exactly the same as in 2019 – but inflation was running at 16% instead of today's 2%. The average salary in 1974 was £2168, the average house price was £8915 and a pint of beer cost 14p.

Shops offered a broad range of goods from national chains of fishmongers like Mac Fisheries or the nationwide butchers, Dewhursts, to department stores which sold most items except food. There were no supermarkets, so one had to queue at the greengrocers for vegetables then on to the fishmonger or butcher before queuing again at the fruiterers to buy all the ingredients for a special meal. The nearest we had to a supermarket was Sainsbury's who dealt in perishable foods at the various counters in the shop each of which had its own queue. Housewives only bought food for special occasions in the towns relying on their local village providers for meat and vegetables.

Boots was the largest national chain of chemists, having just absorbed Timothy Whites and Taylors, which not only filled prescriptions, dispensed medical sundries but also offered an extensive library service. We would borrow two or three books a week from the Boots library in Chelmsford.

Department stores often had a cashier seated in a glazed cubicle at the back of the store. Wires ran along the ceiling to this central hub from each counter where the salesperson would place the sales slip and cash in a metal tube they hooked onto the wire. A handle pulled sharply down sent it on its way to the cashier who returned the receipt and change to the counter a few minutes later. As youngsters we were fascinated by the aerial traffic whizzing above our heads. Some innovative stores later replaced this antiquated system with a network of vacuum tubes to carry the transaction documents up to Accounts on the top floor.

As in the villages, there was a strata of society in the larger towns. Knights and other lords of the realm at the top, and there weren't many of them, with the professionals such as surgeons and barristers on the next rung. These were followed by other doctors, solicitors, bank managers, city businessmen, managing directors and factory owners most of whom would be members of the golf club. Vets were lower on this scale. Doctors would enter by the front door of a patient's home while they sent vets round the back.

Chelmsford had two larger hospitals, the Broomfield and the Chelmsford and Essex while Colchester boasted three mental asylums and a general hospital. The local doctor, district nurses and midwives formed teams to cover their local area. Without hesitation, they would visit the old, weak and those just too ill to get to the surgery. There were no appointments at the surgery but, if you turned up within surgery hours, they would see you that day. If you had to stay in hospital, your local GP would often visit you in hospital, check that all was as well as could be. They also answered any questions you were too afraid to ask the important consultant. Most hospitals still relied on matrons to keep the organisation in order. All of them were strict, some were battle-axes, but most had a kindness below the surface.

From the matron, authority passed down to the ward sisters, staff nurses and juniors. The nursing staff wore the distinctive uniform of their rank while all the doctors wore long white coats except perhaps the senior consultants who carried their authority without the need of uniform. You could always tell the difference between the staff, patients and visitors which can be difficult today. Hospitals were run on rigid lines with visiting hours often reduced to an hour in the afternoon and another in the early evening. Mornings were too busy to have visitors cluttering up the wards.

Banks were also very different in those days. The bank manager was an important person in most people's lives. He gave advice on financial matters, authorised overdrafts, loans and mortgages and was a person of some standing in the local community. There were no cash machines and the interiors were more like railway station waiting rooms (but we don't have them anymore) with one side of the large room occupied by bank clerks, known as "tellers", who would receive and dispense cash and cheques. Some of them became friends after a while and they all greeted you with a smile. In towns the size of Chelmsford banks would have at least ten or twelve branch offices often next door to each other.

Daily lives were much more structured in those days. People normally worked a five and a half day week with Saturday afternoons and Sundays off. Few shops were open on Sundays and annual holidays were usually limited to one or two weeks. Many families had predictable meals on every day of the week. Roast meat on Sunday, cold meat on Monday and Tuesday, shepherd's pie on Thursday and fish on Friday. Eating out at a restaurant was a rare treat and restricted to celebratory occasions. Pubs only provided snacks such as pickled eggs, pork scratchings and packets of Smith's Crisps.

Cities

There were probably two or three commuter trains from Hatfield Peverel station each weekday morning. Each businessman would have his own favoured train which he would board to sit in the same seat in the same compartment and the same carriage every day. The passengers would read the morning's papers or try to complete The Times crossword before reaching Brentwood further down the line. Others might glance at a few business papers but, as far as I can gather, apart from conventional greetings, there was little actual conversation during the journey which took about an hour to get to Liverpool Street. These businessmen were uniform in their dress which would have included a bowler hat, an umbrella, brief case and a heavy dark coat over a three piece suit. They would have noted anything "flashy" with disapproval.

We lived life at a far more leisurely pace in the 60s. A friend of my father's who commuted to the City from Colchester would park his car on the grass green outside Colchester station to catch a train around 8.00am in the morning and return on the 4.45pm from Liverpool Street. He always travelled first class and, in the evening, as he settled into his compartment. a white-jacketed steward would greet him.

"Good evening, Mr Kay. How was your day?"

"It was a good day, thank you, George. How was yours?"

"Mustn't grumble, sir. Can I get you your usual?"

"That would be kind. Thank you."

The steward would move off to the bar carriage before returning with a pink gin on a silver-plated tray. It was an era that must seem alien to the generation of today but there was a courtesy that came naturally to most people in those days.

Dad first had an office in Africa House in High Holborn before moving to a larger office with an attached flat on the third floor of 19a, Cavendish Square just behind the John Lewis store on Oxford Street. The area has completely changed today. In the 50s they railed the central garden off with several access gates to which the residents of the square had keys. There was no underground car park, in fact there were no parking meters or yellow lines. Drivers would happily double park around the square and even, on occasions, triple-park.

Many of the houses had doormen dressed in top hats, green frock coats and toecaps polished to a mirror-finish on their boots. Our doorman was Mr Taylor, a tall man with a natural military bearing and, invariably, a smile. He lived with his wife and family in the East End. When I arrived in my old banger at the flat on a Friday night, he would come over to the car as I got out.

"Evening, Mr Adrian. How's life with you?"

"Pretty good, thanks, Mr Taylor and how's the family?"

We would catch up with each other's news as I handed him the car keys. Everyone gave My Taylor their car keys so he could manoeuvre the vehicles about trying to make sure that any car was ready to move off when the owner returned.

"When do you need the car next?"

"Not 'til Sunday afternoon."

"Right you are then. Charlie will have the keys when you need them."

He was one of the kindest men I can remember of that time but it never paid to cross him. Lew Grade, one of the great show business entrepreneurs of the day, owned the office on the first floor of 19a Cavendish Square. One afternoon a young film star client of his parked his Rolls Royce alongside the kerb outside the building. Mr Taylor approached him and asked for the keys,

"I don't give the keys to my Roller to every Tom, Dick and Harry. Anyway I will only be here for an hour at the most," he replied as he dashed up the steps to the front door.

That was not the way you treated Mr Taylor. Two hours later the arrogant young man came out of the building to find cars parked in front, behind and beside the Rolls Royce. He saw Mr Taylor a few yards down the pavement and he snapped his fingers at him.

"My man, would you mind moving these cars? They are blocking my car in."

"Sorry, sir, they didn't leave me the keys."

The Rolls remained penned in until ten that evening and nothing further was said.

While Mr Taylor stood sentry at 19a, just across the square on the corner of the John Lewis store was the "pitch" of the local news vendor with his cry of "Noos, Star and Sta-a-ndard", these being the three evening newspapers of the City. At about six o'clock he would leave the pile of papers on his stand and slope off to the Phoenix pub just round the corner for a leisurely pint of mild and bitter, a drink you never hear of these days. Businessmen would collect their paper and leave the change on top of the pile of papers. No-one would ever think of taking the money - or short-changing the vendor - while he was away from his post. It was a measure of the trust that was a mark of the times.

Enough of these nostalgic memories we need to get back to veterinary life.

Chapter 6

Vet school years

Life at the vet school on the Madingley Road was a much more intense period of learning. There would be one or two hour-long lectures each morning with sometimes another in the afternoon. Practical sessions might replace lectures. The vet school divided us into pairs alphabetically so my partner was Dave Bachelor. By this time there were only 16 of us left in our year so, in effect, we had the benefits of personal tuition. Even then some of us managed to fail part of our final exams.

They allocated each pair to a rota which designated which professor or lecturer we would shadow for two weeks. Thus, after a fortnight studying large animal surgery under Colonel Hickman, we night find ourselves under the tuition of Peter Bridge who taught farm animal management. Other specialities included small animal surgery, anaesthetics, public health, veterinary law, parasitology, radiology and pathology in all its forms. At least once a week we attended the RSPCA clinic in the town supervised by the small animal medicine lecturer, Dr Douglas. Dr Leslie Hall and Professor Robert Walker formed the teaching hub of small animal surgery.

Leslie Hall was an inspiring anaesthetist whose devoted white Boxer followed him throughout the school buildings like a shadow. White Boxers were rare in those days because the colour was not a recognised breed standard by the Boxer community and white puppies were normally destroyed at birth. In several breeds such as the Dalmatian, various terriers and collies there is a congenital association with a white coat and deafness. One theory about the breeder's dislike of the white pigmentation is that Boxers were used as "war dogs" in the First World War and white was too easily seen by the enemy. How much truth there is in the story I don't know but it always seemed sad that, for aesthetic reasons, healthy puppies were destroyed for reasons of colour. It might have been described as canine apartheid.

After each lecture they would recommend us to various learned articles found in the textbooks and journals lining the walls of the library. The recommended veterinary journals were not always UK based. Two other favoured sources being the Ondestepoort Journal from South Africa and JAVMA, the Journal of the American Veterinary Medical Association. If we were not in the lecture hall, operating theatre, the small animal clinic or the farm, we studied in the library.

I cannot remember too much about individual lectures or practical sessions but two demonstrations have stuck in my memory throughout my life. They are examples of how the simplest of lessons can have lasting effects. Before we assisted the teaching surgeons in the theatre, they taught us a few basic techniques. These included scrubbing up, wearing the sterilised clothing, maintaining sterility while operating and keeping a cool head when procedures go wrong. Scrubbing-up sounds simple. We applied an antiseptic soap solution to our hands and lower arms before scrubbing every surface with a stiff nailbrush. The important words here are "every surface". It sounded easy and after a few practice sessions we felt we had grasped the technique.

The tutor had a novel way of demonstrating our failing such a simple task. He provided a bag of soot and told us to bury our arms up to the elbows in the clinging black powder. Then he blindfolded us, led us to the sink and told us to remove all evidence of soot from our hands and lower arms. We could take as long as we liked but our hands had to be clean when we took the blindfolds off. Every one of us failed miserably. We all had tell-tale streaks of black down the sides of our hands, the corners of nail beds and between the fingers despite our concentrated scrubbing. A lesson like that lasts for life.

The other demonstration cured most of us of the new surgeon's fear of blood loss. There was a particular wall at the back of the vet school which they whitewashed once every year. The tutor collected a sealed container of blood from the local abattoir. He put this on the ground before handing out syringes of varying capacities - 2ml, 5ml, 10ml, 20 and 50ml. He told us to fill the syringes with the blood and squirt them onto the wall. It is amazing how far 10ml of blood could spread over a pure white wall. Even 2ml makes a significant mess. So when we learnt that while an average Labrador carries over 2.3 litres (5 pints) of blood and even a cat has 250ml, our fear of haemorrhages dropped to more reasonable levels. Blood loss should be respected but not feared.

I often felt that the teaching staff felt that general practice was slightly beneath them and they were more interested in producing research graduates rather than practising veterinary surgeons. At the end of the course, only three of our year of 16 made a career of academic research, one of whom was my Clare colleague, Richard Dyball, who enjoyed a distinguished career in veterinary research.

I recently looked up the veterinary curricula of both Cambridge and Bristol veterinary schools. They frightened me stiff. There is no way I could qualify as a vet today. It is largely science-based. Everything has to be measured, accounted for, tested by laboratory analysis, risk assessed and recorded. There seems to be little room left for the "art" of medicine. I can remember waiting for clients in the consulting room of my first practice in Dunstable and reading the framed copperplate certificate of the senior partner. This illuminated document stated that he "had satisfied the examiners in the Art and Science of veterinary medicine." Looking back it occurs to me that, at the time of my qualification in 1964, veterinary medicine comprised 85% art and 15% science. Today the figures would approach 95% science and 5% art. I find this sad. I'm afraid you may find this disapproval of my past profession something of a recurring theme in this memoir.

Extracurricular activities

One of the great advantages of being a Cambridge undergraduate was the wide range of extracurricular activities on offer. Of the many clubs and societies that vied for one's attention was the Canada Club which chartered an aircraft to fly members across the Atlantic during the Long Vac. in the summer. There were about 170 of us aboard the Boeing 707 as it left Heathrow. We all had arranged varied employment for the three months we would be in North America. Three students had jobs delivering school busses from the East coast to San Francisco while others, like me, would work as builders' labourers, farm workers or office boys. The aircraft was one of the early versions of the 707 and, being a charter flight, the seating was configured as a single class - first-class seats and business class did not exist then - so there was just one long aisle down the centre of the plane with a bar at each end. Students being students most of us collected at the rear bar which, after a few hours, ran out of supplies so we all moved up to the forward bar. We were about two-thirds of the way down the central aisle when the captain came over the speaker system telling everyone to stay completely still. The transfer of weight of about eighty students from the back to the front had put the aircraft into a dive and he was busy trying to correct it. He gave us the all clear a few minutes later.

Our flight landed at Idlewild airport in New York - now known as JFK. A bus took me downtown to the Greyhound bus station where I got my first experience of the variety of food available in America compared to the rationing which still prevailed in the UK. There was a street stall which offered over fifty kinds of sandwich on about twenty different varieties of bread. Choosing the most bizarre option I opted for a fried egg sandwich on rye which proved a novel experience but one I would not care to repeat.

I caught the Greyhound bus to Toronto, a distance of nearly 500 miles, which took over 10 hours to complete. For the next month I worked as a general dogsbody on a building site between King and Queen Streets in downtown Toronto while staying with friends of my parents in the suburbs. The building became the Physics faculty of Toronto University.

I spent the next month on a polled Hereford stud farm on the banks of Lake Ontario. We drove a huge truck called a "rig" or "semi" (pronounced 'sem-eye') from one county fair to another carrying two huge bulls, twelve cows and six calves. We slept in the straw with our charges before getting up at 5.30 to prepare them for the day's show - shampooing, brushing, combing and braiding until they looked their best for the parade ring.

For the final month, four of us bought a Canadian Ford Meteor car which we drove from Toronto to Vancouver, down to San Francisco and back to New York via the Grand Canyon, Death Valley and New Orleans. During our drive through the ice fields of Jasper National Park we rounded a corner where we were confronted by a large bull moose. The other three decided that, since I was the veterinary student, it was my job to persuade it to move out of our way. I don't know who was more apprehensive - me or the moose - but it eventually ambled off into the roadside brush.

Among several strange coincidences I have experienced in my life nothing matched the one on the edge of the Grand Canyon. Jane Reekie, the daughter of my old headmaster, had been working in a department store in Toronto but she had not been on duty on the couple of times I had visited the store during my time in the city. As we parked the car in the main car park of the visitor area to the canyon, I looked out at a group of students gathered at the edge of the canyon only to see Jane at the far side of the crowd. I got out and tried to make my way round the large crowd to have a word with her when I accidentally bumped into another girl in the group.

"Adrian? What are you doing here?" she asked in a very surprised voice. Surprised, because we had been on the same skiing trip two winters previously. She was with a group of Exeter university students which had just met up with Jane's group from London University which had just become a triumvirate with our Cambridge quartet. It is a very small world.

After visiting New Orleans, Atlanta and Washington we finally arrived at New York where I found the biggest veterinary hospital I had ever seen. It occupied fourteen floors on the East River Drive. The staff welcomed this very inexperienced vet student from England and even invited me to run an intravenous line into a dog injured in a traffic accident. I messed up the right front leg vein followed by the veins in the other three legs without success when a young nurse offered to do the job for me. Without a moment's hesitation, she found her way through the mess I had created and hit the vein first time. It was another of those times when I felt very small and incompetent.

We had covered just over 8000 miles on the trip and the whole three months cost me about £80 which included the full costs of the trip less the wages earned in the first two months.

The giraffe

Back at the vet school, morning studies paused for half an hour around 11.00am when students and staff retired to their respective Common Rooms to have a cup of coffee, smoke a cigarette and play an obscure card game named Skat. It involved no money, and the rules were both flexible and never understood by visitors. It was during one of these mid-morning breaks that a great friend of mine, Ken Whimster, announced that he was feeling sorry for one patient out in the hospital block - a circus giraffe. They had admitted the animal to treat a cough. One could say that a giraffe with a cough has something of a problem. There was no suitable accommodation for the beast so they housed it in its travelling truck parked behind the main car park. The truck had a hydraulic mechanism that could raise or lower the roof whenever it encountered a low bridge. In this situation the giraffe was led out, ducked its head under the bridge while the truck driver lowered the roof to negotiate the bridge then raised it again to allow the giraffe to return to the vehicle.

Ken felt it should enjoy a taste of fresh air and be allowed to stretch its legs for a while. We suggested that he went to the clinician in charge of the case, Colonel Hickman, and ask if we could take the giraffe for a walk. He agreed rather reluctantly, and we tied a few reins together so we could attach a bridle to the animal's head. Ken climbed a ladder inside the truck and attached the head collar. Four of us, two on each long rein, gently encouraged the huge animal out of its confinement.

Then it all went wrong.

The giraffe, seeing the opportunity of freedom charged out of the box, dragged four helpless veterinary students through the school's car park as it careered into and through various vehicles. On arrival at the entrance to the car park it took a sharp left turn towards the main frontage of the school. An immaculate lawn, guarded by warning notices to "Keep Off The Grass", surrounded the entrance.

Giraffes can't read.

On arrival in the middle of the sacred turf, the poor animal stopped, panted a few times and dropped dead. Watching an adult giraffe collapse is an awesome sight. Even more worrying was our responsibility for its demise. After some debate, we agreed that Ken should inform the Colonel of the fate of his patient.

Within ten minutes stunned members of the teaching staff and a host of laboratory technicians surrounded the inert carcase. To their great credit they arrived at a diagnosis within 24 hours.

The animal had been suffering from tuberculosis. This raised another problem. Just across the approach road to the school was a large paddock where the university's prize flock of Clun Forest sheep were happily grazing. Tuberculosis is a highly infectious disease so not only did the sheep have to be moved to new pasture but the "sacred turf" had to be disinfected with a flamethrower following the removal of the body. As a result, throughout the summer of that year, the hallowed lawn displayed a scorched outline of a giraffe.

Interestingly, the story does not quite end there. Tuberculosis comes in various forms, human, bovine and avian among them, and the particular strain from the giraffe was human TB. This prompted the question how the animal came to be infected. The school contacted the circus and who told them that the previous keeper of the giraffe had left the circus. He was now working as a mechanic in a Birmingham garage. Two health inspectors visited the handler at home and asked him if he was suffering from a cough. "Funny you should ask that," he replied, "I have had this cough for several months now." He was later treated successfully for his TB infection.

Training for surgery

One of our year, John Race, had a traumatic experience on his surgical rota. John was a great guy - son of a Cambridge fireman who had been killed on duty and the fire brigade sponsored his education. He was not a large man but athletic and got a soccer "Blue" from the university. He and Mike Vaughan were the two members of our year who were members of the Hawks Club, the elite sports club of Cambridge, only open to students who had represented the university in their chosen sport.

One afternoon John was due to perform a cat spay under the watchful eye of Professor Walker, the senior small animal surgeon. The patient in question was rather fatter than usual but he anaesthetised the animal, scrubbed up, sterilised the operating site on the left flank and prepared to make his incision. Several layers must be transected before the contents of the abdomen are reached. They are the skin, the underlying fat layer and the three muscle layers - the external oblique, the internal oblique and the transversalis.(Sorry about the technical language.) John made it through the first two muscle layers when he came across a thick layer of fat which he thought was in the abdominal cavity. He started to explore the fatty mass to find the uterus not realising that this was an additional fatty layer above the transversalis muscle and he had not entered the abdominal cavity.

He spent nearly 40 minutes in increasingly desperate attempts to find the uterus while Professor Walker looked on without a word. Eventually the professor suggested that he looked a little deeper where he found the final muscle layer, entered the abdomen and completed the hysterectomy. It was a cruel lesson. Did he learn from it? I don't know but I remember seeing John and the Prof exchanging surreptitious winks when they passed each other in the corridor a few weeks later so I doubt it did any permanent psychological damage.

John later took one of the bravest decisions of all of us when, immediately on qualifying, he married his Danish fiancée, moved to Denmark, learnt the language and set up a very successful practice.

There was a small university veterinary society which used to arrange talks by outside speakers once or twice a term. One of these speakers was Eddie Straiton, a well-known radio and television vet who was the studio advisor to the BBC series of All Creatures Great and Small based on the novels of James Herriot. He spoke on the subject of life as a practising large animal vet. He had many funny anecdotes and some useful practical advice.

At the end of this light-hearted evening Eddie brought us up short with the last story. It concerned a difficult calving of an over-sized calf. Eddie had attached the calving ropes around the head and forefeet of the calf and the farmer and cowman pulled as Eddie tried to guide the calf out. It was hard work, and they needed more muscle power to get the job done. The only available help came in the form of a mentally disabled lad of about 20 named Billy who did menial jobs around the farm. They called him in to lend a hand and eventually the calf arrived with such a rush that the farmers fell over backwards including Billy who unfortunately fell backwards into the slurry pit. This resulted in a lot of good-tempered laughter and they all repaired to the farmhouse for a clean-up and a cup of tea. After 10 minutes the cowman left to tend to the cow and her calf but he rushed back into the kitchen within 2 minutes. "Come quick," he shouted. "Billy's hung himself in the barn." Despite cutting him down and trying all forms of resuscitation, Billy was dead. The laughter had shamed and embarrassed him to take his own life.

You could hear a feather drop to the floor of the room in the silence that followed, and we all had a lot of food for thought at the end of that evening.

Final exams

One would have thought that the experiences of my final exams would have been seared into my memory but the recollection of some events can be as clear as age-altering memory will allow, while others form a complete blank in the mind. So it was with my Finals. I have little recollection of the written papers but very distinct memories of wading through the many ring-binder files of lecture notes. I studied in silence in the spare bedroom of our flat every evening while Jen patiently wrote letters, created baby clothes or watched black and white television programs broadcast by one of only two channels available at the time - BBC and ITV.

What does live in my memory is the final viva exam. This was conducted by Prof Robert Walker who walked me past various organs, both healthy and diseased, laid out on tables for identification. I identified a pig's kidney, a dog's tibia and the reticulum of a cow. Then placed the captive bolt pistol at the correct angle to dispatch a fatally injured horse. I was still very nervous when we walked out to the large animal housing where he floored me with his next question. We were standing outside a loose box that housed a boar that was under investigation by the school.

"What would be your first question to the owner?" he asked.

"How long has it been ill?" The Prof shook his head.

"What symptoms he has noticed?" More head-shaking.

"Is it off its food?"

"Has it recently arrived at the farm?"

"How old is it?"

Every question got a shake of the head and I was getting more and more desperate so much so that my brain just froze. I ran out of alternatives and stood with my head gazing down at the concrete as if it held the answer. In desperation I looked up at the Prof and saw that there was a kind smile on his face.

"Not all veterinary medicine is about science," he said. "A lot of it is common sense. The question I was waiting for was 'What is he like?' Male animals can be unpredictable and you must keep your wits about you. It is always best to get an initial opinion from the owner before you start your examination and, even then, be prepared to make up your own mind."

I later remembered the Prof's advice when Roger Massey told me of a vet friend of his who had been examining a docile boar in its sty before turning to the farmer to discuss his findings. After about three minutes the boar crept up behind him, thrust a tusk into the back of his leg and tore it upwards through his buttock rendering him lame for the rest of his life. It is not just the male of the species that can be dangerous, the female of the species can also be unpredictable.

Many years later in Crawley, Paul Scammell and I got an urgent call from the owner of a nursing German Shepherd bitch saying that it had bitten our assistant, Judy Townsend, in the face. She was bleeding badly according to the owner. We rushed to the address and got Judy to the hospital where they did a great job in repairing the tear in her cheek. What had happened was that, knowing the bitch well from previous visits, she had bent down to stroke her while she was nursing her litter in the whelping box. Nursing mothers can be very protective of their young offspring and she leapt to protect her young. Always be on your guard but avoid any suggestion of fear - if you can.

The rest of the viva went much better since we spent most of the time discussing the philosophical implications of the case of the Christian Scientist pig farmer's objection to the erysipelas vaccine I had recorded in my case book until I was dismissed with a great feeling of relief.

It was then just a matter of waiting for the results which took about a week to come through. Rather to my surprise, I had passed while three of our classmates had to re-sit their finals. Two of whom I had felt were a shoe-in for a pass which only proves how wrong one can be of our own capabilities. The results came more of a relief than a celebration as it meant that our impending family - Jen was now nearly eight months pregnant - was financially secure for the near future.

Chapter 7

Marriage

During all this time studying I met my life's lover, best friend and soul mate so let me describe how this happened.

Jen and I met at a mutual friend's 21st birthday party in 1962. I had not been that keen to go, and I was making my way to the front door to slip away from the party at about 9.30 when another friend, Ian Peek, came in with this girl. My friend and I exchanged pleasantries before he moved on to the party leaving the girl standing in front of me.

"Aren't you with Ian?" I asked.

"No," she said.

So we started a rather stilted conversation during which we felt we had little in common until we found that we read the same kind of book. The Saint books by Leslie Charteris and Dennis Wheatley, both authors who were the Tom Clancys and James Pattersons of their day but now long forgotten. Matters progressed quite quickly after that and it was three hours later that the birthday boy found us in his father's study with Jen on my knee. He told her that he had invited her to the party to be his girlfriend for the evening.

I should point out that this kind of behaviour was totally out of character for both of us. Why? What were our characters at that time? I normally felt clumsy and awkward talking to girls - social ability was not my strong point. We both had slightly low opinions of ourselves. Spontaneity was not our strong point. She was working as a nanny to a family in Stock outside Chelmsford where Roger Massey lived. To cut a short story even shorter, I suddenly proposed to her while at another birthday party in Sussex twenty-two days later - a proposal which, to the surprise of both of us, she accepted.

Not unexpectedly both sets of parents were a little shocked. They made us to wait at least a year before getting married - especially as I still had two more years study before I qualified. My next problem was that I had already invited another girl to the Clare May Ball!

Reading this gives a completely false impression of my confidence with girls. I had had only one mildly serious girlfriend up to this point and that was only to please my parents who were friends with her parents. The May Ball girl was the daughter of another doctor and the sister of two school friends of mine. I had only invited her as a last resort just so I had someone to take to the Ball.

Looking back on this passionate whirlwind of romance both Jen and I still can't believe we behaved in such an abandoned manner which was completely alien to both our characters but it has worked out wonderfully.

We were married on 8th June 1963 and we returned to Cambridge for my final year as a married couple. We lived in a small flat, one of a block of eight, in Great Shelford. Jen worked in an unmarried mother's home on the Trumpington Road.

She checked her watch late one afternoon and announced that she had to rush home to cook her husband's supper.

"What? You mean you're married?" asked one of the girls.

"Of course, I am," said Jen "What do you think this is?" waving her wedding ring at them.

"Oh, we all wear those," she replied. "We thought you were just another one of us."

Our flat was one of a low block of eight close to the railway line. Many years later Jen and I took the family to listen to her brother, John, preach at his old college, St Johns. On our way home we decided to drive past the block of flats to show the children our first married home. On seeing the small building one of them asked "Which half did you live in?" and we had to explain that the building contained eight flats. I don't think they really believed us.

Living on a small grant and Jen's wages meant that we had to "make do and mend". Jen made the curtains, decorated the walls and made bedside tables out of old orange boxes on their sides decorated by some left-over fabric. Money was tight and with Jen pregnant with Kim, I just had to pass my Finals and get a paid job.

We were the only married couple in our year and we used to invite a number of my fellow students over for the evening when they would help us decorate the flat in exchange for a home-cooked meal by Jen. She also became pretty clever at bar billiards when we went out with the others to a pub in the evenings. She had this ability to leave a tempting red ball close to the black peg. Our cocky opponents invariably took up the challenge and knocked the black peg over losing all their previous points. There was a lot of hard work being done but it was a very happy time.

Wedding

We were married on June 8th the next year, 1963, on a blazing summer day. The local policeman held up the traffic while we and the wedding party crossed the road from the church to the Vicarage on the other side. My brother, Pete, acted as my best man and four of my vet student friends acted as ushers. Mum insisted on Jen having her hair "permed", the memory of which she has hated to this day. Nevertheless it was a wonderfully memorable day even if Roger Massey did present Jen with a pair of bloodless castrators as we left the wedding party.

Dad was very generous and lent us his beloved three litre Alvis to leave the reception. I had hidden our MG 'A', Susie, at the local dentist's home. Our boisterous friends painted "Just Married" in toothpaste on the boot lid of the Alvis and tied two lines of tin cans to the exhausts. As we stopped two miles down the road to remove the clanking tins we were caught by Chris Ward. It had been at his 21st birthday party we had met. He presented us with a bottle of champagne and three glasses and we drank another toast together before getting on our way to collect our Susie from the dentist's garage. Breathalysers were still to be invented.

Perhaps we should not have underestimated the guile of our young friends because they had found the MG 'A', despite the secret hiding place, and decorated it suitably. We drove with the hood down until we arrived at the Mayfair hotel where I closed the hood of the car only for a cloud of confetti to burst out. The uniformed commissionaire simply said "Congratulations, Sir and Madam," before carrying our luggage into the hotel. The next morning we left for our honeymoon in Majorca - the Bahia Palace hotel. It quite put Mum out that we spent so much money on a fancy London hotel when they had a perfectly serviceable flat in Cavendish Square we could have used.

It was only on the first day back at the vet school in the Autumn term we learnt of one wedding prank had failed rather miserably.

Paul Scammell greeted us with the words "How did you fancy the kippers?"

"What kippers?" we asked.

"The ones we tied to the engine block of the MG."

We had not smelt a thing and the only sign left of the fish were two charred skeletons still hanging onto a length of wire when we lifted Susie's bonnet in the vet school car park.

Jen was extremely anxious about her standard of cooking when we returned from our honeymoon saying she was only used to cooking for a hundred at the Barnardo's home she had worked in.

"I can only cook boiled eggs or peeled potatoes for fifty," she cried.

A few weeks later we had Mum and Dad over for Sunday lunch when she produced a magnificent Poulet Algerienne of onions, garlic, mustard, balsamic vinegar, and cayenne pepper decorated with halved grapes. This impressed them enormously and I was so proud of her.

Appendicitis

Towards the end of my final year when Jen was about seven months pregnant with Kim, I woke up one morning with a dreadful stomach ache. Jen told me to do some of her relaxation exercises to no avail so we called our doctor, Dr Bevan, to come out. I had tried pressing McBurney's Point which is a definitive sign of appendicitis but found no pain. Dr Bevan came in and pressed the point in the correct position and I leapt up with an "Ouch!" When he said I needed the operation, I mentioned that we had just joined an organisation called BUPA.

"Does it make a difference?" I asked.

"Certainly," he said, almost rubbing his hands with glee. "I will book you in to the Evelyn Nursing Home where I will do the anaesthetic."

This frightened me more than the operation. Most Clare undergraduates went to Dr Bevan who was a "rowing" doctor, whose mantra was that nothing should interfere with rowing. A friend of mine went to him after coughing up blood and wondered whether he should give up rowing.

"Give up rowing, boy? Never!"

So you can imagine that I was a little anxious to place the responsibility of my anaesthesia in his hands. The clutch on the ambulance was faulty, and we lurched our way to the Evelyn with me in considerable pain. The nun in charge of me during my stay was Sister Norbert, a lovely Irish lady with a wicked sense of fun. One morning I filled the bed bottle so full I had to hold it vertical while I pressed the call button. She burst in, stopped dead, clasped her hand to her heart and said "For a wonderful moment there I 'tort' that was a bottle of Irish whisky!"

On another afternoon I noticed that she seemed even busier than usual.

"Are you short staffed today, sister?" I asked.

"It's the younger ones. They're away on a retreat."

"So why aren't you on retreat?"

"My dear," she said. "When you get to my age you lose all hope of redemption."

Laughter is painful after an appendectomy.

All this drama happened just a few weeks before my final exams. This, together with the fact I passed my Tripos exams from a room above the public bar of a busy pub, implies that distractions are not necessarily a bad thing just before important examinations although as a general rule I would not recommend them as an examination technique.

Despite pregnancies, abdominal surgery and revision, Jen and I had our fanciful dreams of the future. Jen's sister lived in California and I had spent three months in North America so emigrating from an England that was suffering under a stale Labour government had a lot to commend it. Unfortunately simple practicalities soon put an end to this idea. We would have to live in the state of our choice, California, for six months during which time I could not work, before sitting the state veterinary exams in Sacramento. Veterinary surgeons in the States were only licensed to practice in their home state with two exceptions - Mississippi and Missouri and the two Dakotas which had reciprocal arrangements regarding certification. I had been taking important exams for nearly nine years and decided that even more study of American veterinary practice with exams at the end was a step too far and we abandoned the idea.

The second dream lingered for a few years longer. This was to set up a practice in the UK then move to Canada, which recognised the British qualification, and set up another practice there. Once we had established that practice we would move on to open practices in South Africa and Australia so we could spend our time travelling the world supervising our veterinary empire! The whole idea was totally mad but you must have dreams even if the wilder ones fail to materialise.

Before all this could happen I had to pass my final exams.

Chapter 8

Beyond the Vet School

I used to collect antique veterinary and animal husbandry books. I found one fascinating bound volume of the year's monthly publications of "Animal World"", the journal of the Society for the Prevention of Cruelty to Animals before receiving the royal warrant to become the RSPCA. The journals dated back to 1861. They contained articles as various as shooting captured wild birds at the Hurlingham Club to the case of a carter who had killed a rat by picking it up from the floor of a pub and biting it across its back. The dying rat turned and bit him on the cheek infecting him with rabies. The carter died in severe distress a few weeks later.

We forget that rabies used to be endemic in the UK. For instance in 1895, 672 cases of human rabies were reported and yet, by 1922, we had eradicated the disease from the British Isles. How? I have no idea. There was no treatment or vaccine available. It is one of life's mysteries.

Some engravings in the Journal were works of art and would sell well in an auction sale today. The most interesting section for me was the advertisements on the back pages. One of these notices stated that "A Mr Harrison, veterinary surgeon on the Harrow Road, London, was pleased to announce his fees for consultation as 5/0d (25p) and visits at 5/0d per mile." The consultation fee at the Dunstable practice in 1964 was still five shillings a hundred years later.

The Hurlingham club trapped wild birds of every kind. They kept thrushes, blackbirds, sparrows and starlings nettled from the hedgerows and seabirds from the coast in domed wicker baskets until the day of the shoot. The club members placed these inverted baskets at various points in the grounds of the club. When the 'guns' were ready, a staff member would pull on a rope to lift the basket releasing the birds into the paths of the 'sporting' party.

There was real cruelty in many aspects of Victorian life which we have forgotten. We have only replaced by them with more modern forms of cruelty such as the stalking and bullying of our own species. Yesterday's Victorian callousness has been replaced by today's activism of behalf of persecuted wild life which is often misplaced.

Animal welfare societies

I have always had the greatest respect for the national animal welfare charities such as the RSPCA and RSPB. But I have also suffered the well-meaning intent of local organisations who feel it is their responsibility, alone, to care for the needs of such wildlife as badgers, grey squirrels and urban foxes. In the 1980s, if news got around that our practice was treating a badger injured in a road traffic accident, we would soon receive urgent phone calls from about five different badger groups. Each one insisting they were the ones with the greatest knowledge about the release of injured animals. We should grant them the responsibility of releasing the badger on its recovery. The aggressive antagonism between these groups was unbelievably petty.

Urban foxes are another example of well-meaning interference having unintended results. The population of these foxes in London has quadrupled in the past twenty years so there are now around eighteen urban foxes per square kilometre in the capital. While they are a pleasure to watch playing in suburban back gardens, they ransack our waste put out on the roadside for recycling adding to the problem of litter in our streets. The press feed us with dramatic stories of foxes invading homes and threatening babies. So the public cry out for the authorities to act.

The public tend to "cry out" quite a lot today - about a lot of different issues. Well-meaning people feel sympathy for the persecuted, cunning-but-cute fox. The fact remains it is a wild animal. In the 1990s there were about 33,000 foxes living in towns and cities. That figure had risen to nearly 150,000 by 2014. Dustbins replaced rabbit warrens as the foxes' supermarket. What do the authorities do? They round up as many urban foxes as they can and then transport them to more rural areas such as those around Colchester. By this time these foxes are used to meals from dustbins and rubbish sacks not from rabbits grazing in the fields.

Myxomatosis had arrived in Britain in 1953 and, for the next decade, infected rabbits often blinded by the disease were a common sight on country roads. It wiped out 99% of the rabbit population until the few resistant animals began to breed and restore a smaller population.

This destruction of the fox's natural prey probably contributed to their migration to the towns. In these new urban territories they soon learnt the layout of the roads, rubbish tips and waste ground and could navigate the area quite safely. In an alien town, they soon became the victims of road accidents requiring attention by the overstretched RSPCA or the veterinary practices of the area. We must have attended over thirty dead and injured foxes in the practice before the authorities released them elsewhere after another public outcry.

Then there is the question of badgers and tuberculosis in cattle. How can the government sanction the slaughter such news-friendly creatures? Because they are a source of the tuberculosis (TB) that resulted in the slaughter of over 35,000 dairy cattle in the twelve months ending in June 2018. Brock from the Sam Pig stories and Badger from Wind in the Willows are the sanitised images we have of a creature that is more often covered in brown mud than elegant in clean-cut black and white stripes.

Yes, badgers do carry TB. It is present in their saliva and urine that leak onto the farmers' fields ready for the cattle to graze. But tuberculosis was only diagnosed in badgers in 1971 while it has been endemic in the cattle population for more than a century. What is not so well known is that foxes also carry TB and have done so for far longer than badgers so, while we shoot badgers, we legislate against foxhunting.

We do not know enough about the transmission of the disease which was rampant in Victorian England. It was almost eradicated at the end of the 1960s but is now widespread across the country. I don't pretend to have an answer to the problem but I am certain that neither the government nor the activists are close to solving it.

Addenbrookes experience

Back to the vet school, I was in my final year when I decided that I had seen several veterinary operations and it would be interesting to experience some human medical surgery. Through a complicated web of friends and relatives I managed to get an introduction to the senior general surgeon at Addenbrookes hospital, Mr Tunnicliffe. He was kind enough to allow me to shadow him for a week which proved to be a fascinating experience. He was a kind man, generous with his time and expertise. I was curious about the atmosphere in his theatre. There was a lot of light-hearted banter between the surgeons, anaesthetist and nurses often during the most taxing procedures but the team seemed to know when total concentration demanded silence. I asked him about this, saying I was a little surprised at the casual chat during surgery.

"Interesting that you should notice that, Adrian. Many surgeons maintain a rather strict atmosphere during surgery but I actively encourage the banter as you call it."

"Does it help you relax?"

"To a certain extent I suppose it does but my main reason is to prevent silly mistakes. I remember one eminent German surgeon who demanded complete silence during his surgery. One day he was performing an enterectomy (removing part of the gut) and closed off both ends of the resected intestine instead of suturing them together. His team was so in awe of the great man they were too afraid to point out his mistake and the patient died three days later. By encouraging a chatty atmosphere in the theatre I like to think my team would quickly point out any silly mistake I was about to make. We are all human after all."

There were many similarities between the theatres of Addenbrookes and the vet school - the tables, anaesthetic trolleys, drip stands, electrocautery machines even the instruments were largely the same although there was less use of retractors at the vet school and the team of supporting theatre staff was larger at Addenbrookes. One piece of equipment that caught my eye was a small television screen suspended from the ceiling on an adjustable arm. These were the days long before they had seriously considered CCTV for security reasons and only a minority of private homes owned a television set. I asked Mr Tunnicliffe what they used the device for.

"It connects to the radiography unit so that if I have a problem during a procedure, I can call up my friends in the X-ray department and they will display the relevant X-ray image on the screen."

I was impressed at this advanced piece of kit until I saw it in use. In fact, they only used once during my week with Mr Tunnicliffe and that was when he called up his radiographer colleague and suggested that they met at the University Arms for lunch once he finished the operation!

Another lesson I learnt at the hospital was not to take things or people at face value. We were scrubbing up before a complicated operation to remove a diseased section of intestine from a 6-month-old child. This would be the fourth procedure suffered by this poor mite in his short life but essential if his life was to be saved. As I looked over my shoulder, I saw a small elderly man walking with the aid of a stick looking like Father Time's older brother without the scythe.

"Who is that?" I asked.

"That's Dr Haskeard, the paediatric anaesthetist."

To say I was shocked would be a gross understatement. To put the life of a tiny child into the shaking hands of an old man who could barely walk seemed to border on negligence. With some difficulty I subdued my righteous indignation and said nothing. (Righteous indignation can become the default state of the young who are convinced that they already know it all.)

After greeting the surgical team the 'pensioner' returned to the pre-op room and, after five minutes, returned following the anaesthetised child on a stretcher bed. They transferred the tiny patient from the bed to the table where Dr Haskeard set up intravenous lines into the minute veins previous catheterisations had almost destroyed. It was then I noticed that he was no longer using his stick and his hand was steadier than mine. He was in complete charge of the situation. The operation lasted about an hour and a half before the patient was returned to the recovery room under the supervision of Dr Haskeard.

Half an hour later, while we were preparing for the next operation, Dr Haskeard re-appeared, leaning on his stick with a distinct tremor back in his hands, just to thank the team for their co-operation during the whole procedure. He may have been an old man but, in his element, he was a supreme artist.

Another specialist was the thoracic anaesthetist. A complete contrast to Dr Haskeard, he had his own customised anaesthetic trolley which he had fitted with small slots on the back of the machine to hold vials of every conceivable drug he might need during a long complicated operation. While Dr Haskeard was the artist, this man was the gifted technician. They both had their parts to play.

Association of Veterinary Students

During my penultimate year I was elected President of the Association of Veterinary Students (AVS), the body charged with the welfare of the vet students throughout the country. This involved visiting several of the other veterinary colleges for committee meetings as well as an annual conference. This gave me a fascinating insight into the lives of the other vet schools. One thing that struck me every time was how insular the other schools were compared to Cambridge. During our discussions over supper after the committee meetings, the conversations would be restricted to veterinary subjects. Absorbing accounts of cattle caesareans, treatment of scabies in dachshunds and the comparative benefits of different anaesthetic techniques were all very well for a time but after a while became mind-numbingly dull. These other students seemed to have no other life outside veterinary medicine and led very blinkered existences. It was then that I realised how lucky I was to be enjoying the broader experience of a Cambridge college staircase discussion at two in the morning. These informal debates with students studying engineering, medicine, theology, geography and music, covered a wide range of subjects but usually ended up discussing the subjects that fascinated young men of a certain age – cars, religion and women.

At the Bristol committee meeting we finished drinking at about one in the morning and were making our wandering way back to our boarding house when one of our group pointed out a car which stood some distance from the kerb. We improved the parking by bouncing the vehicle into a better position. We then saw another car that needing moving so began to bounce that one. By this time net curtains had begun to twitch. Soon enough, a police car came round the corner at considerable speed. Being students we knew what to do - scatter. There were eight of us and only two police officers so most of us would escape and make our way back to our lodgings. We came down to breakfast the next morning to find an exhausted and rather dishevelled Irish delegate sitting at the breakfast table.

"What happened to you, Sean?" we asked.

"De bastards," he muttered,

"What happened?"

"De bastards," he repeated. "Dey caught me, put me in the back of the car, took me seven moiles out into the countryside, pushed me out and told me to walk home. Oi've only just got here."

Perhaps a little cruel, but imaginative policing just the same. At least he did not get a police record.

As AVS President I was an official guest at the BVA conference held that year in Llandudno. One prestigious college professor, Joan Joshua from Liverpool, gave a lecture on some small animal subject the content of which I have forgotten during which she made some very scathing comments about the qualities of the current crop of students. As their representative, I felt it was my duty to defend my fellow students so, when the meeting opened to discussion, I took a deep breath and walked up to the microphone in the middle of the lecture hall. This was in front of about 200 of the 'great and good' of the profession so it was rather nerve-wracking. My reply acknowledged that some students may not come up to her high expectations but that a number of the profession's teaching staff fell somewhat short of our expectations and gave a few examples. Much to my surprise I got a standing ovation as I walked back to my seat at the back of the auditorium.

The conference lasted for five days during which poor old Jen had to put up with the company of the many geriatrics lodging in our hotel or watch the only two films being shown at the local cinema several times. There is only so much knitting a girl can do.

There were other times when we had fun together, like the invitation to the Royal Vet College's annual dinner. As official guests, we were to be seated at the top table but someone had forgotten us and had not allocated us our seats. We explained that we were happy to sit in the body of the hall until a member of the organising committee rushed up to say that two of the official guests had cried off so we could have their seats. As we took our honoured places at the High Table, we noticed the name cards in front of our seats - Lord and Lady Dalrymple-Champneys! We sat down after grace was said and whispered to each other that we could have some fun with this situation so for the next 20 minutes we assumed the roles of the absent guests talking about the finer points of managing a 300 acre deer park and the difficulties of keeping the visiting public away from our private apartments. We could not maintain straight faces for longer than twenty minutes before we confessed our deception which, fortunately, went down well with the other dignitaries. The Dalrymple-Champneys were established patrons of the college. There was even an award in their name for academic achievement at the college but they rarely attended college functions despite receiving respectful invitations so few people knew what they looked like hence the success of our impersonations.

The highlight of my year as AVS President was the annual International Veterinary Students Union (IVSU) conference which, that year, met in Hanover and West Berlin. This was the time when the Cold War was at its height. Many of our German vet student hosts had escaped over The Wall. One afternoon they had arranged a coach trip to visit East Berlin. We travelled in a convoy of four coaches which stopped two miles from the border post to allow the escapee students to get out. They did not want to go anywhere near the Wall. At Checkpoint Charlie the East German border guards searched each coach with a tooth comb. When one of our group took a photo of the search, his camera was confiscated and destroyed on the pavement outside.

My lasting impressions of East Berlin on that occasion was of the depressing poverty of the city contrasted by the magnificence of the Russian military cemetery dominated by a huge statue of Mother Russia. The trip was an education, but we were all glad to return through Checkpoint Charlie to West Berlin, comparatively, a City of Light.

On the last night of the conference we had a farewell party in a Berlin bierkeller or beer hall where, for some unaccountable reason, I behaved completely out of character. I climbed onto the top of a table in the middle of the large hall and led the assembled international company in a full rendering of the French folk song, Alouette - all 13 verses, five of which I made up as I went along!

Unknown to most of us during the evening a group of half-a-dozen delegates had decided to see how far they could travel on the Berlin underground - the U-bahn - towards East Germany. After a few stops they were surprised, and slightly anxious, when they read the name of the station, Friedrichstrasse, which was the main passenger train station in East Berlin. What to do? They decided to stay on the train to the far terminus where they crossed over to the other line and caught a train back again. By the time they got back to Friedrichstrasse their confidence had returned and they decided to get out and walk towards the main line platforms where every exit was patrolled by East German guards. Discretion soon became the better part of valour and they returned to the U-bahn station and caught the underground back to West Berlin. This all seemed very unlikely to us as they recounted their experience and we put it down to extreme luck. Recently while investigating this unlikely story, I found a possible explanation on a travel website which read -

"So when the East Germans built the wall that sealed off West Berlin, they made sure to add metal and glass barriers to divide the platforms of Friedrichstrasse as well. The station became an international oddity, in that it was located entirely in East Berlin, but some of its train platforms and all of its underground services were only for West Berliners. Passengers would often have to make a border crossing when moving from one story of the building to the other. For the next 28 years, it was, effectively, a three-dimensional border, one drawn not between north and south or east and west, but between up and down."

My lasting experience of my year as AVS President was how lucky I was to be at Cambridge. Talking with students from the other colleges - Edinburgh, Glasgow, Liverpool, Trinity College Dublin and London - the blinkered view of life shown by the vet students at these colleges depressed me. The major themes of any conversation in a social situation seemed to be veterinary - the fascinating case of a ruptured spinal disc in a Dachshund seen last week, the comparative benefits of Gillies and

McPhail's needle holders or the latest techniques involved in orthopaedic surgery. They seemed to have few outside interests or opinions which led to dull conversations. You must stretch your mind in different directions to keep it fresh.

Chapter 9

Dunstable Practice

When I joined the Dunstable practice, the premises formed part of Martin Senior, the senior partner's, home at 65, West Street in the middle of a row of three-storied Victorian terraced houses. Clients approached the house up a flight of stone steps from the pavement to the side door. Our receptionist, Elisabeth Shoemaker, sat at a desk at the head of the stairs with the waiting room in the neighbouring hall of the main house. Once the consultation was over they left by the front door down a further flight of steps. There was no parking or even a garage but then most clients arrived on foot.

I remember sitting in my car outside the surgery one evening waiting for Martin Senior to finish his surgery before I could discuss a case with him. A couple came out of the front door carrying their newly-vaccinated puppy.

"If he thinks I'm going to keep this pup isolated for the next two weeks, he's got another think coming," said the husband and he put the put the pup on the pavement and walked it home. You can only give advice, it may not be accepted.

Once morning surgery was over, the consulting room became the operating theatre. It also formed the pharmacy, office, a basic laboratory and whatever other storage space was needed. The premises were dark and claustrophobic, so it was a relief to get out into the car and start a round of visits.

For at least the first ten years of my career, I saw more patients on visits than I did in the consulting room. You must remember that at that time only a minority of the population owned a car. We would record the daily visits into large page-a-day diaries provided free to the practice by the pharmaceutical company, May and Baker.

Each of us would perform an average of 15 visits a day to both small animals and farm livestock. The practice also rented a small terraced house in Houghton Regis, a small village two miles away towards Luton where it was my job to conduct a half hour surgery on Tuesday and Thursday afternoons. Besides treating any patients brought to the door, I collected cats for neutering at the main surgery. I picked them up on Tuesday and brought them back for collection on Thursday.

One morning I had a longer list of visits than usual and I was late for lunch so I grabbed a sandwich and rushed off the Houghton Regis surgery to find a patient queue of four clients waiting on the pavement outside the front door. It was then I realised that in my hurry I had forgotten the key to get in. I went down the narrow alleyway to the back of the premises where there was an old-fashioned sash window. I used a large stone to smash a pane of glass which allowed me to release the lock, open the window and climb in. But even the best laid plans have a habit of going wrong. In this case I had not realised that the sash cord of the window was broken, so, when I released the lock, the upper window fell down impaling the back of my hand under the broken shards. It took me a few minutes to extricate my hand before climbing in and unlocking the front door from the inside - leaving a trail of blood behind me. I decided to become the first patient of the afternoon using gauze dressings, cotton wool and various bandages to stem the flow before I treated the remaining veterinary patients single-handed. At least it gave the clients something to talk about for the next week or two and I suffered no serious injury that a few stitches could not resolve.

The Powders

The very first professional task given to me by Mr Senior was to make up the red powders. A word of explanation is needed here. The red powders formed part of a trio of powders, the others being the green powders and the black powders. Each consisted of magnesium sulphate or Epsom Salts. This is a chemical compound which has a wide variety of uses both medical and cosmetic but "The Powders", as we used them, were a simple laxative. Adding small amounts of vegetable dyes coloured the white Epsom Salts.

If we found a cow, sheep or pig suffering from an unidentified illness, we would prescribe three days of the 'green' powders. If there was no improvement we would suggest three further days of the 'red' powders followed by a further three days on the 'black" powders. The general theory was that if the animal had completed the course of nine consecutive days of laxative Epsom Salts it was either cured or dead. As I have mentioned before, veterinary medicine was still pretty primitive both on the farm and in the surgery.

Covered in a red dust I was feeling quite proud of myself having filled a large two pound Winchester jar with the red powders when Martin Senior returned from his morning visits. He took one look at the jar and poured the contents down the Belfast sink. I stood in open-mouthed amazement as he launched into a furious tirade about the uselessness of modern students.

"It was the wrong colour of red, boy," he shouted. "Do it again and, this time, get the colour right."

"But... but... Sir, I..."

He would not be placated. He dismissed the fact that the dye had no effect on the action of the powders as irrelevant. I went home that night furious at the petty nature of my employer's behaviour.

Since that time I have been able to reflect on the episode. In a way, Martin Senior was right. His farming clients recognised the authentic colours of the practice powders and anything that varied from that normality was not to be trusted. A powder of a different shade of red may be a cheaper alternative for which they would charge him the same amount. Even worse, it might be a totally new treatment that meant that they were being experimented on without their knowledge.

We made many other remedies on the premises with the various mixtures, tinctures and solutions dispensed in glass bottles of varying sizes from 2 fl.oz. up to 16 fl.oz., each with a cork stopper. We may have left the old apothecary's measures of drachms, scruples and minims behind but the metric system of millilitres (ml) and milligrams (mg) was only just arriving. Tablets were issued in paper envelopes with the necessary instructions written on the outside.

Besides the medications prepared by the practice, we were using commercial drugs from various pharmaceutical companies, many of whom no longer exist. Companies such as Glaxo, May & Baker, Upjohn, Boehringer Ingelheim, Pfizer, Astra, Eli Lilly and Bayer were the market leaders of the day. A company by the name of Arnolds held a near monopoly over the supply of veterinary surgical equipment. Their A4 hardbound catalogue ran to something like 200 pages offering a wide range of implements from horse gags, calving winches and captive bolt pistols to the most delicate of ophthalmic surgical retractors.

Drug company reps used to visit practices once every one or two months providing information about new drugs and local gossip while taking the orders for the month. There were no veterinary wholesalers as there are today until Vestric, an offshoot of Glaxo appeared on the scene in the late 70s. Our limited arsenal of antibacterial drugs included procaine penicillin, Streptopen, chloramphenicol, Lincocin, Terramycin, Betsolan and Acriflavine most of which are never heard of today. The injectable drugs came in glass bottles of varying sizes - 30, 50 and 100ml - with a rubber top held in place by a metal cap.

Diagnostic facilities were non-existent apart from urine dipsticks which gave simple indications about blood proteins, glucose, ketones and blood in the urine by changing colour to indicate a value. Using our own microscopes we did our own blood counts, skin scrapings and parasite identification.

For more extensive investigation we would send samples to the nearest veterinary investigation laboratory. We had no X-ray facilities so abdominal problems would be investigated by palpation, auscultation (use of the stethoscope) and, as a last resort, laparotomy (opening the abdomen). We examined chests by percussion and stethoscope and diagnosed fractures by palpation. Over the years our hands, ears and eyes became our most reliable diagnostic aids. A newly-qualified graduate would often have difficulty in diagnosing simple pregnancy in a bitch while his experienced employer might be able to identify the number of pups in the uterus.

We treated all fractures with plaster casts–even comminuted fractures of the femur. If you don't know what that word means, you have not been paying enough attention to your orthopaedic lectures. It means broken into more than two pieces. Martin Senior was an artist in reducing these femoral fractures using simple traction under anaesthesia before applying the plaster cast. By the time he had finished plastering the limb it looked like a piece of sculpture.

The classification of fractures often confused the client. We classify a bone broken into two pieces as a "simple" fracture. This does not mean it is simple to repair. A compound fracture, which many people thought was a multiple fracture, simply means that the bone has penetrated the skin and is therefore more liable to infection. (A fracture in which the bone is broken into more than two pieces is classified as a comminuted fracture – not a compound break.) Many years later I was to spend a long hour in a witness box acting as an expert witness in a case of alleged malpractice trying to explain that "simple" in orthopaedic terms did not mean "simple" to repair.

During my time at Dunstable the practice moved from the cellar in West Street to a larger Edwardian house in Princes Street together with a small collection of old farm buildings in the yard outside. It may even have been a town dairy in the past. Unlike the West Street house, the premises are still there in Princes Street where it forms one of the premises of the Icknield Veterinary Group. These improved facilities allowed for consultations and the office work to be conducted in one building while another provided a dedicated operating room.

The waiting rooms of those days simply had a collection of loose chairs and a receptionist's desk. There were none of the advertising and advisory notices that decorate the veterinary waiting rooms of today. The only decoration in the Dunstable waiting room was a very large glazed and framed certificate in beautiful copperplate script which I would read during the long gaps between clients. (Clients much preferred to see one of the partners than the 'new boy'.) The certificate stated that "Martin Senior had satisfied the examiners in the Art and Science of Veterinary Medicine and Surgery and was therefore awarded the degree of Bachelor of Veterinary Medicine."

That certificate has always given me food for thought. I genuinely believe that when I qualified in 1964 veterinary medicine comprised about 85% Art and 15% Science. Today I believe the position is reversed with science forming at least 90% of a veterinary surgeons armoury.

Settling in

The practice provided us with accommodation in the form of a two-bedroom flat on the first floor of a new block of flats called Viceroy Court. It stood on the main A5 as it passed through the centre of the town. We had to provide our own transport. Knowing how much equipment the partners carried in the boots of their cars I suggested that I might get an estate car. These were the 5-door cars of the time also called station wagons. I got a stern letter back from Mr Senior saying that did not consider an estate car "to be in style and keeping with the practice". So we opted for a standard Ford Cortina at a cost of about £960 (or £12,300 in today's currency.)

The boot of a vet's car in those days would carry most of the drug inventory of the practice and a lot of equipment. We had to carry rubber overalls and boots, bandages, dressings, i/v drip equipment, scalpels, scissors, artery forceps - everything necessary for minor surgery in the field. Tuberculin syringes and callipers, Burdizzos, trocars and cannulas for bloated farm stock, horse gags, stomach tubes, casting ropes, disinfectants and a captive bolt pistol all formed the mobile arsenal of a visiting vet of the times. Our cars were travelling dispensaries. They carried not only the veterinary equipment but also cardboard boxes filled with the home-brewed medications in their glass bottles and the bulk containers of the commercially produced drugs. So the large boot of the Ford Cortina was full to the brim once the car was loaded for a round of visits. To this manifest of veterinary equipment must be added the smells and rubbish that accumulated after rubber boots, protective aprons and towels had been used while delivering calves on frosty mornings, treating mastitis in the slurry of a milking parlour, rescuing sheep that had nearly drowned in a flooded stream and transporting bleeding car accident victims that were so terrified that they could not help emptying their bowels and bladders over the upholstery. There is something unique about the aroma of a car belonging to a vet in mixed general practice. Once smelt, never forgotten.

I remember our first week at the practice as if it was yesterday. Jen and I had packed up our small flat in Great Shelford and drove to Dunstable followed by a small removal van. On our arrival, the manager of Viceroy Court met us. When asked for the keys of number 77 on the first floor, he told us he had specific instructions to withhold the key from us.

With the removal van about to arrive within the next half an hour, we drove round the corner to the veterinary surgery in West Street which was also Martin Senior's home. I was furious. He calmed me down explaining that there had been a mix-up in transferring funds between solicitors and the problem would be resolved within the hour. He instructed us to go down the High Street to the Sugarloaf Hotel and buy a nice lunch for the two of us. Everything would be in order on our return.

All this anxiety did not help Jen who was eight months pregnant with Kim. All I can remember of that meal was that Jen had Coquilles St Jacques as I tried to calm her worries while fuming with anger inside.

Sure enough, they eventually produced the key, and we moved our small load of possessions into the flat. Later that afternoon Martin Senior came round to make sure we had settled in. He also said he was expecting us to attend Holy Communion at the parish church the following morning when we would be joined by the other members of the practice. The other members being Clive Halnan, his wife, two daughters and the receptionist, Elisabeth Shoemaker. We all sat together in the front pew just below the pulpit. Sunday services were just as much social gatherings of the community as divine worship.

Most of us remember our first consultations and mine was unforgettable. At the vet school we had learnt all about the Ragwort and Thistles Act, the symptoms of Rift Valley Fever and the air flow required through a pig farrowing unit. However I had never previously met a case of misalliance. Misalliance meaning, in the words of my client, "She's been got at by the dog next door and she needs the injection."

My lack of knowledge was strange considering it is a common enough veterinary problem but then Cambridge set greater store by academic than practical knowledge. Not knowing what injection was required, I made some excuse about needing to get the necessary drug and left the consulting room. I climbed the stairs out of the basement to ask Elisabeth if she knew what I should be doing. This was long before we had veterinary nurses. Practices employed unqualified receptionists to receive the clients, answer the telephone and send out the accounts. I needed advice from my boss so I went to go through the door to the main part of the house where Martin Senior lived with his mother. Elisabeth warned me in no uncertain terms that I was taking my life into my hands.

"What do you think you are doing interrupting my breakfast, boy," bellowed Mr Senior. "Nobody comes into this part of the house without my express invitation and certainly not when I am having my breakfast. Whatever it is, it is unlikely to be fatal so speak to me again when you have finished morning surgery. Now go!"

My memory fails me at this point because, for the life of me, I cannot remember the eventual outcome of that consultation.

The Partners

Martin Senior was 52 years old and, having had four operations on his hips before the age of two to correct his hip deformities, he walked on his hip joint capsules. He must have been in a lot of pain much of the time which accounted for his unpredictable temper. In the first week, I made the mistake of offering to help him down the steps that led up to his house. I got my head blown off in no uncertain terms.

"I'm not a cripple, boy!"

The practice provided veterinary services to Whipsnade Zoo. This was several years before they had their own veterinary staff. Watching Martin Senior easing his way between an adult rhinoceros, weighing over a ton, and a brick wall before giving it an injection was nerve-wracking. Martin was unmarried and lived with his mother above the surgery. We did not know it at the time but, besides his physical disability, he was living with another threat hanging over his head.

His father had died of a dissecting aneurysm at the age of 52 on a bus in Luton. (A dissecting aneurysm occurs when a weakness in the main aorta splits and the patient bleeds out within minutes.) His elder brother had died, at 52 years of age, of a dissecting aneurysm waiting at a bus stop in Dunstable. The previous year, his sister, aged 52, died of a dissecting aneurysm at Victoria coach station in London. Martin Senior was 52 at the time the practice employed me. It was no wonder he appeared cantankerous most of the time. Fortunately he lived for several more years after I left - but probably kept away from buses.

Clive Halnan, on the other hand, was at the forefront of the new scientific veterinary scene. He did all the small animal surgery and had an inexplicable fascination with the dog's anal glands to which he attributed many canine problems. He was a strange man. An example of which was that he kept the placentas of his two daughters in tall glass Winchesters on the top of a cupboard in their dining room. He was undoubtedly clever, but he was also spiteful. He fell out with his partner regularly over petty grievances. The two men were like chalk and cheese.

The Dunstable practice did not teach me much more about veterinary medicine when I was employed than when I was 'seeing practice'. I had hoped that Clive Halnan would be a valuable mentor. Instead, his idea of mentoring was to stick his head round the consulting room door, complain about the treatment I had given to a ketotic cow and ask if I had read the book "Veterinary Diagnosis" by Annie Littlejohn. When I told him I had read the book, he replied "Well, read it again and then come and see me." I read it again but Halnan showed no interest in discussing the case with me at any time later.

He later emigrated to Sydney, Australia where he took up a teaching post at the veterinary school. Whether he took the placentas with him I don't know but they might have been something of a shock to the Australian Customs if he did.

Operating Surgery

On one of the few evenings when I was off duty, Martin Senior telephoned me to come in to the surgery. He needed me to operate on a dog to remove its anal glands. Clive Halnan had booked in the patient but, because Mr Senior had put his clinical coat in his locker, Halnan had stormed out of the practice. I later learnt from Elisabeth Shoemaker that this was quite a common occurrence. Mr Senior did no operating surgery at all except plastering fractured limbs. Hence the call for me to step in.

This was all rather terrifying as I had never operated in the practice before and, while I had seen Clive Halnan perform the operation twice, I had never performed it myself. My previous surgical experience had been two cat spays of the vet school. But Martin Senior had asked me to 'step up to the plate' so I had to do the best I could. I anaesthetised the patient using nitrous oxide, oxygen and ether through a large rubber mask held over the nose and mouth. The gases bubbled through a glass jar containing the liquid ether while a plunger governed the amount of vapour taken up. The mixture of gases then passed through the concertina tubing and the mask. It was rather primitive, but it worked despite the patient struggling violently until the ether took effect.

The next process was to melt candle wax on a small stove and heating a 2ml metal syringe. This melted wax was drawn into the warm syringe and the nozzle inserted into the anal gland duct in the rim of the anus. This whole procedure carried several risks, from considerable haemorrhage to anal incontinence, if things went wrong. The wax solidified inside the anal sac which provided a good outline for its removal. With one finger, protected by a condom, placed inside the anus I incised the skin with a scalpel. Then careful blunt dissection with Mayo scissors isolated the anal sac which was tied off with catgut before placing small nylon sutures in the skin incision. I think the operation lasted about 40 minutes in total at the end of which I let out the very deep breath that I seemed to have been holding in for the previous hour. Eventually a warm feeling of satisfaction of having achieved something I had considered beyond my capabilities later replaced the immediate feeling of relief. It felt good.

The practice facilities limited large animal surgery to the repair of superficial injuries or an emergency Caesarean under local anaesthetic. General anaesthesia of the larger animals was restricted to the veterinary schools equipped with the necessary lifts, winches and state of the art anaesthesia. The only major operations I performed while at Dunstable were two Caesarean sections on cattle. I carried out these under paravertebral anaesthesia of the lumbar spine using a local anaesthetic. This removed all sensation from the flank so I could open the cow's belly and uterus before hauling what was often a 100lb calf from the side of the animal. Throughout all this surgery the cow stood calmly munching hay from the manger in the loose box. I repaired the uterus, muscle layers and skin with a variety of suture materials and both animals made an uneventful recovery.

Throughout my life it has amazed me how an animal's body can heal even under the most unsterile circumstances. In fact I am firmly of the belief we humans have become unhealthily obsessed with cleanliness in our daily lives. Many people are alive today thanks to the improvement in medical technology but how many more people suffer allergies and asthma today compared to a less sterile age?

One operation that has almost disappeared from today's large animal vet's repertoire - removal of impacted baler wire - is known in some parts of the world as Hardware Disease. In the 60s and 70s they bound hay and straw bales with a strong steel wire rather than the plastic or hemp twine used today. Lengths of baler wire would be swallowed by the cow while grazing and get stuck in one of the four stomachs - usually the reticulum. Diagnosis without ultrasound or X-rays can be difficult as the animal simply appears off its food, dull and losing condition. Treatment was by rumenotomy meaning that the largest of the four stomachs was opened via an incision in the cow's flank. The metal would be found by manual exploration of the different stomachs.

The veterinary surgeon in large animal practice had to get "down and dirty" both inside and outside the body. These operations carried out in barns and loose boxes involved the whole farming staff and a successful outcome was celebrated by everyone sitting on straw bales holding mugs of tea. There was no sense of hierarchy - we were just a bunch of friends who had done a good job.

Health and Safety regulations as we know them today did not exist when I qualified. We provide modern vets with a range of protective clothing which puts the rubber boots and body aprons of my early days in practice to shame.

A lot of farm visits involved the rectal or vaginal examination of the livestock. They now carry out pregnancy diagnoses using ultrasound devices. We made the diagnosis by inserting our arm into the rectum of the cow, identifying the uterine wall by touch and then feeling for the amniotic sac through the wall of the uterus. Thus we were palpating our way through three layers of tissue - a further example of 'art' over 'science'. This took a lot of practice to achieve reliable diagnoses but it worked. After a calving, some cattle would retain the afterbirth which required the placental buttons to be detached from the uterine wall before we could remove the retained placenta. This was known as a 'cleansing'. We then placed a large antibiotic tablet in the cleansed uterus to prevent any subsequent infection. A difficult case of placental retention could take as long as half an hour to be sure of eliminating every last fragment of tissue. The smallest residue of necrotic (dead) tissue could cause a severe infection of the uterus, sterility and economic loss to the farmer. The reputation of the practice was on the line every day.

We carried out all these examinations, often stripped to the waist in winter temperatures, using our bare arms. During the Spring flush of grass, the contents of the rectum became a vivid green which stained the skin despite repeated scrubbing with a stiff brush. Shaking hands with a farm vet in the

Spring could be an unnerving experience for some people. Disposable plastic sleeves make socialising much easier today.

In my early weeks in practice I struggled with one particular problem which was hitting the veins of cattle for intravenous treatment. It had not helped that I only took blood from a pet animal once in the 18 months I spent at the Dunstable practice. It was the large animal veins, in particular the main jugular vein, that I found very difficult to hit. Each time I made these repeated failed attempts to hit the vein in front of an unimpressed farmer, the lower my confidence sank. In desperation I rang my original mentor, Roger Massey. He suggested that the milk vein lying under the skin in front of the udder was the size of a small grass snake so why not use that. That did the trick and, after a few weeks of using the milk vein, I had the courage to try the jugulars again. This time I could hit them at the first attempt on a regular basis. It was only several months later during a visit to my family home that I met up with Roger again.

"How's the intravenous work going then?" he asked

"No problem at all, I've even stopped using the milk vein and I am back using the jugular again,"

"Adrian, I'll let you into a little secret. The milk vein, while it is plainly obvious to see, is actually more difficult to penetrate because it is so mobile under the skin. What you needed was a bit of confidence and I knew it would all come right for you."

I owe a lot of my skills to that man who became such a good friend.

One Sunday morning on one of our precious weekends off, Clive Halnan rang me and ordered me to meet him at a particular pub at 12 midday. I was not prepared to drop everything at his whim so I told him we would be busy then but I could meet him, at a different pub, at one o'clock. It was petty, but I felt better for doing it.

On my arrival, and before we ordered any pints, he asked me if Martin Senior had offered me a partnership behind his back. I reassured him that no such offer had even been suggested never mind, offered. His plain anxiety subsided, and we shared awkward half pints of bitter. It was this episode that decided me to stop being the 'rope' between two warring partners and I would look for another post.

Family Life

Leisure time was rather limited. There was always one vet on call at night with another on 'backup'. This meant that we had to be available on the telephone so it was only one night in three we had the evening to ourselves. There were no mobiles in those days. Weekends were assigned in the same way. Each month I had two weekends on duty from Friday night to Monday morning, one half weekend which ran from Saturday lunchtime to Monday morning and one full weekend off from Friday afternoon. Those long weekends 'off' were precious but then, with Kim's arrival in July, we spent our leisure time learning to be parents for the first time which was far more terrifying than being a newly qualified vet.

Camilla, always known to the family as Kim, was born at the Luton and Dunstable hospital on 23rd July 1964 just a few weeks after our arrival at the flat in Dunstable. Jen was some time overdue, so we borrowed Dad's Austin Healey Sprite and, with Jen in the passenger seat, I drove down country lanes with the nearside wheels on the grass verge trying to induce labour. It worked - sort of. She started labour that evening and I drove her to the hospital. Once there, the contractions promptly stopped, and I had to bring her back home the next morning. Another lesson learned - nature will not be hurried.

The hospital induced true labour a few days later. Husbands were not allowed in the delivery suites in those days but I was not going to be put off. I found a doctor's locker room and put on a mask and gown before slipping in to the delivery room to hold her hand. I learned quite a lot about Jen during those delivery hours. She is not a big girl but very strong, both physically and emotionally, brave and she can swear like the most foul-mouthed trooper.

Despite her training as a nursery nurse and attending many baby deliveries and giving advice to new mothers, she found it was rather different when it is your own child. I had it easy. I could escape to work every morning but for Jen it was a full-time job. Her's was a rather lonely life until we met a few friends including Bill and Ann Chennells who remain good friends to this day. There were no disposable Pampers, so we swathed the baby's backside in thick cotton nappies fastened by a large safety pin. We dropped the soiled nappies into a bucket of a vile antiseptic solution called Milton before washing them in a top-loading twin tub washing machine. We then hung them out to dry in the parking area of the flats or on the balcony. We were both very new to our jobs. Mistakes were made, we had our successes, and we were happy.

In the meantime I had a mixed bag of clients to attend.

Chapter 10

Dunstable case histories

I distinctly remember two particular clients in the Princes Street premises. The first was a rather hesitant man who had wandered into the waiting room. Few clients wanted to see the new 'boy'. They wanted the experience of the partners, so I always left the door between the two rooms open. This meant that I could greet any new arrivals before they turned and left. This man had an anxious look about him so I invited him in and asked what the problem was.

"It's the old girl, doctor. She's just not herself after we ran out of her heart pills." Clients often referred to us as "doctor" in those days so I ignored the mistake and asked his name.

"Oh, Mr Harrison ... with Bess," he said. "She don't sleep nearly as well as she did on the heart pills."

"What's her appetite like?" I asked as I rifled through the filing cabinet for the history file.

"Well, she still cleans the plate but she don't enjoy it anymore." I was still searching for the file.

"What's the address, Mr Harrison?"

"Forty seven Chiltern Way."

"Ah, got it," I said, "but hold on, this says sixty three Chiltern Way."

"That's my brother," he said.

There was no sign of this patient's file so I asked what colour the heart tablets were. We dispensed three types of heart pill, a brown heart tonic pill, a red theophylline pill and a white digoxin tablet.

"They're a kind of light blue," he said.

"To the best of my knowledge we don't dispense blue heart pills. How active is she?" I was still trying to get information about the case to make an identification of the patient.

"She just about manages to get out of her bed but she ain't interested in walking very far."

"How old is she?"

"She was seventy three last July."

That completely threw me. It was when he asked if I was new to the practice as he usually saw Doctor Johnson that the penny dropped. He had mistaken our premises for the doctor's surgery fifty yards further down Princes Street. The patient was his wife.

The Ginger Cat

The second patient taught me another valuable lesson. I had been with the practice for about four months during which my confidence had grown. In fact, rather than growing, it bolted so much I was becoming rather arrogant and beginning to believe I was God's gift to the pet-owning public of Dunstable. It was an evening surgery when an elderly couple brought in their large ginger tom cat which had an abscess at the base of its tail. I lanced the boil and cleaned up the surrounded fur before giving it an injection of penicillin. The injection needed to be followed up by penicillin tablets. I handed the paper envelope containing the pills to the gentleman who expressed his conviction that they could not give the cat the tablets.

"Oh, it's very simple," I said. "You push down his lower jaw with the tip of your finger, pop the pill into the back of his throat and massage his throat while holding his mouth shut. Wait for him to swallow and the job is done."

I felt like patting them on the head as they left to make a follow-up appointment in three days' time.

They arrived three days later with slightly ashamed looks on their faces.

"We could not give him the tablet I'm afraid," he said in a low, apologetic whisper.

"Oh, that's ridiculous," I said in all my arrogance. "Give him to me and I will show you."

That cat! It spat, it kicked, it bit, it twisted and clawed but, most of all, it brought me down several pegs and I surrendered by giving it another injection. After the clients left, probably with knowing smiles on their faces, I went to the sink to bathe my wounds but no amount of antiseptic soap would wash away the damage to my pride. I have never forgotten that cat, and that was fifty years ago.

A Highland Cow

As you will have gathered, long weekends off were precious and anything that interrupted them was not welcome. These weekends started at Friday lunchtime and it was on the last visit on one of these Fridays that I attended a Highland cow with a severe case of mastitis. She was a bad-tempered animal at the best of times and even the cowman was wary of her but we got her into the cattle crush where I tied her head firmly to the steel bars. Having confirmed the diagnosis, I returned to the car to get the antibiotic injection. While I was away for those few minutes, the cowman decided that I had tied her head up too tightly and loosened the rope. I returned, not noticing the loosened rope, and went to give her the injection in the neck. At this point she flung her head round and caught me across the bridge of the nose with her wide horn. Once my eyes had stopped streaming with pain and I had mopped up most of the blood, I gave the cowman a colourful piece of my mind - and the injection to the cow.

When I got back to the flat, Jen took one look at me and decided I needed to go to casualty and have my face X-rayed. The idea had been to be having a nice quiet weekend away at a small country hotel but Jen insisted that we should see to my medical needs first. We waited for an hour before being seen by the casualty doctor who ordered an X-ray. This involved another hour's wait before they could find the radiographer. Once he had taken the X-ray I asked to see the picture explaining that I was a vet and used to viewing X-rays. The fracture was plain to see but it was not displaced. However we could not leave until the casualty medic discharged us. This took another hour. He pushed the X-ray onto the wall-mounted viewer and announced that I had been lucky in that there was no fracture.

"So what is that line there?" I asked, pointing at the fracture site.

He looked closer before saying "Oh yes, it is broken but it is nothing to worry about as there is no displacement. If you have any difficulty breathing in the next week come back and see us."

I could have told him that but by that time it was five in the afternoon and various forms of incompetence had wasted a large part of our precious weekend.

The relationship between farmers and their vets is complicated. Each needs to trust the other. The farmer may have accumulated generations of knowledge about his land and his stock and it can take a vet several years to develop only a fraction of this knowledge. You need to know the fields that yield a heavy Spring flush of grass that may render certain cows more vulnerable to metabolic diseases such as milk fever or ketosis. Other pastures prone to flooding may increase the risks of foot rot or liver fluke in the flock of sheep.

The farm workers had their own agendas. They viewed a new vet as fair game. I was on a routine visit to a pig farm to vaccinate the latest batch of piglets. As I climbed into the first farrowing pen the pigmen warned me that the sow could be nasty if anyone approached her litter. In fact she was perfectly behaved while I injected her young family. The pigmen told me the same story about the next litter with the same result. I was not to know they were crying "Wolf" and, as I started on the third litter, the sow made her move to attack. I was lucky enough to be close to the farrowing crate at the back of the pen so I vaulted over the heavy iron bars and put them between me and a furious sow. The pigmen were laughing their heads off until I told them I was not budging until they moved the sow out of the pen. I reminded them that their employer was being charged for my time. That wiped the smiles off their faces and three very apprehensive workers, armed with protective boards, manoeuvred the angry mum to a neighbouring pen.

Disbudding calves

Among the numerous routine jobs we had to do on the farms was the disbudding of calves. Many of the cattle breeds still carried their horns. They sold the cattle at weekly markets where they were held in pens until their auction lot came up. These cattle were often restless. By throwing their heads around they would often catch another animal in the chest just behind the elbow where the external thoracic vein ran close to the surface. The blow from a horn could easily rupture this vein causing an unsightly haematoma (blood clot) on the side lowering its value. For this reason among others, calves had their horn buds removed by electro-cautery. This involved injecting the base of the horn bud with local anaesthetic and then applying the electric disbudder. This instrument looked like a gun with a thick iron ring at the end which, once it was red hot, was placed over the bud to kill the skin around it. Then the bud could be flipped out to prevent any future horn growth. The wound healed quickly over the next week or two.

Beef farmers would buy in a lot of young calves to fatten them up for the butcher's market. All these male calves needed castrating so we might spend a morning removing the testicles from calves of varying age and size. Younger calves were castrated using a strange looking instrument called a Burdizzo or bloodless castrator. This was a clamp applied to one side of the scrotum which cut the spermatic cord with its blood vessels under the skin. I would repeat this on the other side leaving a gap between the two scrotum clamp marks. We used to test the efficiency of the instrument by placing a thick baling twine between a folded paper and clamped it. It would cut the twine in two with hardly a mark on the paper.

94

We castrated older calves using a scalpel under local anaesthetic. Towards the end of one morning's castration when I had been assisting Clive Halnan - he was doing the older calves while I used the Burdizzo on the younger animals - I was getting a little tired after two hours when one calf kicked out at the wrong moment. Its hoof drove the wing nut of the clamp directly onto the end of my amputated left index finger splitting the skin to the bone. (The story of the loss of that finger is another story altogether and nothing to do with my veterinary career.) The end of that finger is painfully vulnerable to direct blows and my blood pressure dropped as the pain shot through my whole body. I had to sit down before I fell down in the middle of a pen of nervous calves. I was in shock so Clive Halnan dressed the finger and told me to go home for the rest of the day.

Whipsnade Zoo

The first time the partners allowed me to visit Whipsnade zoo on my own was to pinion some cranes. I was walking with the head aviary keeper towards the enclosure when he turned and said "You know about cranes, do you, Mr Arnold?"

"Not really," I replied.

"They tend to go for the eyes!"

These first visits to the zoo were slightly scary. The worst were the zebras. They had horribly infected teeth and a vicious bite while, at the other end, their hooves were as sharp as razors. I remember one kicking out in the crush and the hoof struck a corner post which was an old telegraph pole. Later I measured the depth of the cut in the wood as just over an inch or 3 cm to you. Lions were much easier as they were basically lazy. Most of the zoo work was the responsibility of Martin Senior who had accumulated many years' experience treating these exotic patients. I never asked whether my health insurance covered being mauled by a leopard. There were some advantages to our association with the zoo in that, when they had a cull of Chinese Water Deer, they offered us welcome joints of venison – not that either of us knew how to cook it but we learnt by our mistakes.

The Diary List

After nearly a year in the Dunstable practice I was formulating some ideas about what I wanted from my own veterinary practice which I had always intended to set up some time in the future. As an aide-mémoire I made a list inside the back cover of the large diary we each kept in which we entered our daily visits, treatments given, general notes and observations. I headed the list "Things I Will Never Do As a Boss."

After a few months I think there were about twenty items on the list ranging from general courtesy, personnel management and ways of pointing out errors by assistants. I discovered that diary many years later in the attic of our home in Copthorne when we were thinking of moving away from Crawley. It was a salutary experience. As I reviewed each entry, I found that I was trying to explain to my younger self that there were good reasons why I was doing at least 75% of the items I had vowed never to do as a practice principal. The young always think they know best.

Moving On

After more than a year of being the rope between two warring partners, we decided that it was time to move on. The back pages of the Veterinary Record were filled with advertisements for veterinary posts of every type and description - some even intimating that a fluency in the Welsh language would be an advantage. Most general practice positions offered free accommodation, car and telephone expenses for a full day's work at least five days a week with a weekend off once every two or four weeks. Night duties were shared among the practice vets meaning that sometimes one never got to bed before starting morning surgery the next day.

I was tempted by one offer of a post in Grantham owned by a member of the veterinary establishment of the time. Once I got up there for the interview I realised the owner was more interested in veterinary politics than the practice. While the cat was away at committee meetings, the mice, in the form of his assistant staff, played.

After a great deal of thought we settled on the Woking practice owned by Peter Grant. The deciding factor for me was his approach to pain management. At Dunstable there had been no effort made to reduce the pain of the patients apart from the rather primitive anaesthesia. In contrast Peter Grant was an advocate of the judicial use of pethidine to reduce post-operative pain and therefore encourage more rapid healing.

Chapter 11

The Woking Practice

Following a telephone call to Peter Grant, the practice principal, we visited them for an interview. The address was The Corner Hut, Station Approach, Woking, and it was just that - a wooden hut - albeit quite a big hut. There was no car parking except at the side of the road. The main entrance through the waiting room was at the sharp angle of the triangular site while the back entrance was through the wooden fence along one side. It was not the most encouraging of prospects.

Villages, churches and houses give out feelings of warmth, cold, threat, welcome or rejection and the same emotions can be experienced in veterinary practices - especially in the early days of the small general practices which are sadly giving ground to the specialist hospitals many of which feel impersonal for all the cute photos of patients on the waiting room walls.

I can remember little of the interview except that Peter Grant, was keen on pain control and encouraged innovation. There had never been analgesic medication of any kind at Dunstable while Woking provided pethidine and intravenous anaesthesia which was so much more humane than the other practices I had experienced.

I discussed it with Jen for some time before accepting the post of fifth assistant and we moved from a first-floor flat on the A5 to a rural cottage in West End, a small village outside Chobham, about 6 miles from the practice. Peter Grant was on good terms with the property developer who had bought the cottage and the surrounding land but he had no intention of developing the area for several years. This allowed Peter to lease the cottage at a favourable rate until the owner wanted to proceed with the development. Apart from the small border we had in front of our ground-floor flat in Cambridge, this was our first garden! I describe it as a garden but under our inexperienced occupation became more of a wilderness. The practice also provided me with a car, a yellow Ford Anglia estate car. This meant that Jen was not isolated through lack of transport as she could now use the Cortina which we soon changed for a Fiat 1500.

Peter had a few curious quirks about the practice of veterinary medicine. Evening surgeries were a case in point. They started at 5.30pm and went on until we had seen the last patient no matter what time they arrived. This meant that the surgeries would often run on until 9.00pm or later. The reason for this was that Peter felt that, when he first set up the practice as a sole practitioner, his clients had to wait a long time before they were seen. He vowed never to close the door until the last one had been seen. His reasoning was that, as his clients had supported him in the early days, he would not shut them out when the practice became a success.

The Staff

When we arrived at The Corner Hut, I was the fifth veterinary assistant. His chief of staff, Diana Lindo, was in charge of the reception staff and helped by holding wriggling patients and stood by during operations in case we needed something while our hands were sterile. Two other ladies acted as general cleaners, surgery assistants and filing clerks and we used to have several 'Saturday' girls who were usually in their mid-teens and considering a career with animals. There was no register of veterinary nurses until 1965 when the British Veterinary Nursing Association was formed. The term "nurse" was restricted to the medical profession until 1984 before which their veterinary equivalents were known as Animal Nursing Auxiliaries (ANAs). The Royal College approved the first ANA training scheme in 1961.

Having joined the practice as the most junior assistant, within six months I found myself as the senior assistant. The others having left to pursue their careers elsewhere. Peter Grant had quite a high turnover of assistants as he employed newly qualified, single vets who were still finding their career paths by moving from one practice to another experiencing different types of veterinary practice. Being married, Jen and I were happy to settle down in a practice I had faith in. Peter was a good man but, like us all, he had his faults. One of which was his temper.

He had entered into a partnership some 20 years previously but it had gone sour and he had vowed never to repeat the experience. So it came as a surprise when, after 18 months, he offered me a junior partnership. I had got used to his flashes of temper, he had a wide range of experience I could benefit from and the practice was a thriving concern so it seemed a good idea to accept the offer.

There were a few established practices I wanted changed before I signed the papers to which Peter was amenable - but more of that later.

There were two other practices in Woking with whom we had little contact although I had met the junior partner of one of them occasionally and we had always got on well. Late one morning I was driving out of the town to a road accident case in Old Woking when an oncoming car flashed its headlights at me. I recognised the other practice's junior partner's car so drew into the side of the road.

"Adrian, are you on your way to the RTA (road traffic accident) in Old Woking?"

When I said "Yes" he told me not to bother as he had picked the animal up as he was passing. He was taking it back to his surgery. We were exchanging pleasantries when Peter Grant's Rover 2000 drove past sounding its horn as a greeting. The other vet and I eventually went our separate ways.

It was later that evening at the end of surgery that Peter asked me about my friendship with the other practice personnel. It surprised me but told him we were just friendly acquaintances.

"I've always thought it best to maintain a good distance from the other veterinary practices. It could lead to misunderstandings and unpleasantness."

I let the subject drop despite disagreeing with his opinion.

The practice became an ANA training practice at the time I became a partner. We had been employing one a young 16yo girl, Liz Knight, as a Saturday girl, for a year and we encouraged her to train as an Animal Nursing Auxiliary. A year later she passed and, what started as an employer/employee relationship became a close friendship over the years and in the different practices we set up. We are still in touch more than 50 years later.

Mrs Lindo, who had been with Peter for several years before I joined the practice, was in charge of the day-to-day running of the practice, the accounts and client relations. She was the jewel among the 'rough gravel' of the practice.

The practice also offered other services such as training and testing cubs, scouts and, later, Duke of Edinburgh Award candidates. The vets tested the scouts while Diana Lindo tested the cubs. She was a kindly soul who tried to set the candidates at their ease by asking what family pets they were familiar with and then asked simple questions regarding their care. There was one little cub who proved more than a match for her inventiveness.

"Do you have a dog at home?" she asked of the small boy whose feet hung below the large chair.

"No," he replied.

"A cat?"

"No."

"A hamster or a guinea pig?"

"No."

"Do you have a mouse or even a rat?"

In desperation she asked "What pet do you have at home?"

"I've got a goldfish."

Searching around for any suitable question she might ask about the care of goldfish she asked "What would you do if the fish did not look very well?" hoping that the lad would say he would take it to the vet.

"Well, when my goldfish looks sick I tell my Dad and he flushes it down the loo and we get another one."

Once I became a partner, while I was entitled to my share of the profits, we had to provide our own housing, car and living expenses so we bought a small 17th century cottage in Park Road on the outskirts of Woking for the princely sum of £6500. When we left two years later, we sold it for £8500. Domestic properties were normally bought on the back of a mortgage - either on a repayment basis or as an endowment mortgage - and ours formed 90% of the value of the cottage.

The Daily Routine

A more detailed description of the Corner Hut might give a better feeling of the conditions in which the practice worked. The building was entirely constructed of larch-lap wooden slats lined inside with plasterboard and surrounded by a second larch-lap fence. Visiting clients parked their cars at any available kerb space in the roads nearby before entering the front door of the waiting room. A varied collection of wooden chairs provided seating around the sides of the room where the clients waited until one of the reception staff came through one of two doors leading from the central hub of the building. There were no appointments, and we saw clients on a first come, first served basis. The receptionist would return to the larger of the two consulting rooms to retrieve the relevant case history cards. A second door from the waiting room led to the smaller consulting room which later became the dirty operating room, X-ray room and the area where a grieving owner could rest away from the eyes of the waiting room and the hubbub of the practice.

The large central area became the main consulting room in the one corner which benefited from the only window in the room. During the consultation the vet would have his travelling case open on a small table, placed beside the examination table, from which he dispensed the necessary medication. This area also contained four sets of filing cabinets, two desks, a telephone exchange and access to a narrow side cupboard which acted as the main drug storage area as well as a darkroom for developing X-rays. This meant that the room was full of conversations - vet with client, receptionist with a telephone enquiry, two vets discussing a complicated case, all with the boiling sterilizer burbling in the background. After a while we learnt to discount the surrounding noise and concentrate on diagnosis.

We stored several drugs in glass bottles of varying sizes, shapes and colours. Some of these medications originated more than a century previously. Medicines like Fowler's solution which was an arsenic-based compound used as a tonic for cattle since the 19th century. In 1786 it was developed by Thomas Fowler as a remedy for "tasteless ague drop" whatever that was. Other bottles were ridged, or "fluted", which denoted that the contents were poisonous. This fluting meant that we could identify the potential danger in poor light. One I remember was a small green fluted bottle of Tincture of Opium that we used for as a sedative.

The veterinary profession was as enthusiastic about 'purging' as their Victorian medical counterparts. Each practice had its own supply of various laxatives like the powders of the Dunstable practice. Creams to soothe chapped udders, everyday grazes and mild eczemas added to every practice's drug cupboard. It surprised me to learn that one drug we used in the 60s is still available today. Myocrisin is an injectable form of gold (sodium aurothiomalate, if you need to know!) which we used for chronic cases of rheumatoid arthritis. Not only was the injection expensive, it was also painful and I have always had my doubts about its benefits. All this may sound quite primitive until one remembers that medical treatments at the time relied on products such as Andrews Liver Salts, Germolene cream, Ex-Lax tablets, quinine and Coal Tar soap. Simple iodine was the favoured antiseptic of both professions for many years.

At the opposite end of the room, there was a corridor which contained, among other things, coat hangers, large animal surgical instruments, a boiling steriliser and a supply of carrier baskets. It was also the practice loo! There were lockable doors at each end of the small corridor to provide privacy when using the facilities.

Beyond the loo corridor was the kennel area which provided accommodation for about twelve small animals such as cats, small dogs, guinea pigs, rabbits and the occasional budgerigar. Larger dogs were housed in one of three wooden kennels in the limited space outside the back door where they were subject to the vagaries of the prevailing weather. Larch-lap fencing surrounded the whole site to a height of six feet which provided privacy. The address said it all. It was simply a hut on a corner - but it worked. It was a very far cry from the veterinary hospitals of today.

We had a rota for each day of the week showing which vets were on consultation duty, those doing the visits and those performing the day's surgery. All messages, visit requests, phone calls and daily notes went into the large desk diary on Diana Lindo's desk and carried the initials of the person responsible for any necessary action. The vets on the visiting rotas would pick off the calls so they could plan a rational route around the clients. The practice covered quite a large area of about 24 square miles with the furthest client being a dairy farm with a large herd of Friesian cattle in Epsom some 16 miles away.

They called me out to this farm on a Wednesday lunchtime to attend a case of milk fever which required an intravenous injection of a calcium solution pretty quickly if we were to save the cow's life.

This would not have been a problem on any other day of the year but this Wednesday, the first in June, was Derby Day at Epsom. (They moved it to a Saturday in 1995.) I had to battle long lines of race-going traffic to get to the patient in time. The journey which normally took about half an hour lasted just over an hour and a half by which time the cow was in serious trouble. Lady Luck was smiling on us that day and once the intravenous calcium had been given, the animal made a complete recovery.

There would be two or more important items found in the front of a vet's car, an Ordnance Survey map of the larger area and three or four more detailed maps of the neighbouring towns. There were no sat-nav devices back then. You had to rely on your map reading skills and local knowledge. How many people know how to read a map today apart from Duke of Edinburgh candidates, orienteerers and hikers? Can you tell the difference between a railway cutting and an embankment or a church with a steeple on an Ordnance Survey map? The rest of us blindly follow the instructions of an irritating voice behind the dashboard of our cars - and even then we often land up totally lost.

Morning surgery would start at 8.30 and finish by about 10.30 and most cases were fairly straightforward. Every day we all put on a freshly laundered white coat. The 'scrubs' of today were still a long way off. We would bandage injured limbs, lance abscesses and treat upset stomachs with an evil mixture known as Chlor/Bis. (This comprised a mixture of Dr Collis Browne's Chlorodyne (invented in 1848) - a mixture of laudanum which was an alcoholic solution of opium, tincture of cannabis and chloroform - mixed with bismuth, bicarbonate of soda and oil of peppermint.) An injection of what we called "PS/Ben" usually followed.

This was another example of Peter Grant's quirky thinking. His theory was that tissue damaged by infection released histamine. This causes further damage therefore an anti-histamine drug, such as Benadryl, was needed. PS stood for Streptopen, a combined antibiotic of penicillin and streptomycin. The syringe was half-filled with Streptopen then the rest filled with Benadryl, to make up the "PS/Ben", before being injected into the patient. It was common practice in the Woking surgery to combine two solutions in the same syringe. Antibiotics were mixed with steroids injections and vitamins added to iron solutions so that the patients only experienced one stab of the needle. There were no disposable syringes in those days. Our syringes comprised a glass barrel surrounded by a metal frame and a metal plunger within. We would attach a detachable needle depending on the size of the animal. We carried these syringes in a cylindrical metal case which held 2ml, 5ml, 10ml and 30ml syringes. Autoclaves (pressurised sterilisers) came a few years later.

I find it unbelievable that we had no infections at injection sites during the whole time I was there. Eventually these combined injectables formed a sticky sludge inside the syringe and we would have to dismantle it and wash it under the farm tap. What effect this had on the efficacy of the individual drugs I have no idea but it amazes me, even today, that we only sterilised our metal and glass syringes in a boiling steriliser about once or twice a week. Let us just say sterility in the Woking practice was more marked by its absence than its active encouragement.

Don't forget that penicillin had only recently become available to the veterinary profession. Only a few years earlier, Peter had got some of this 'new' drug from some friends at the Weybridge Central Veterinary Laboratory who had found that it was very effective in treating an equine condition known as "strangles". This is a streptococcal infection of the lymph glands of the throat which often proves fatal. Peter took delivery of this dark brown liquid in a glass vial and administered the lot to a group of 8 ponies with the condition. They all made a dramatic recovery. He reported this success back to the technicians at the Weybridge lab who were horrified. They had given him enough of the crude penicillin to treat over 50 horses and he had used the lot on just eight. The main problem with the injection in the early days was that it was extremely painful. There was no gain without pain!

Consultations invariably threw up the occasional difficult client. I remember one lady who was always complaining about our fees. She was one of those ladies whose faintly blue bouffant hair was kept in place by a Hermes scarf. She carried her toy poodle, referred to as "Precious", in a large handbag. One morning she came in, complaining as usual, so I suggested that we only charged her the consultation fee and I would give her a prescription for the drugs. Most of the drugs we used were human medical products, anyway. She was delighted, thinking she could get them on the National Health. She was also a notoriously bad payer so when I wrote out the prescription I added the pharmacy instruction – "Ne. Tr. Sin. Num." I explained that this particular drug was not common and that the only chemist in Woking who might have it was Mr Fox whose premises were just round the corner.

I suggested Mr Fox because he was an old-school pharmacist who would recognise the instruction which was a little-used cod-Latin instruction to the dispensing chemist. The lady left with a broad smile on her face while I waited for the telephone call from Mr Fox. Sure enough five minutes later the call came in.

"Do you really mean what you said, Mr Arnold?" he asked.

"Definitely," I replied, and he thanked me for the information.

The abbreviation, "Ne. Tr. Sin. Num.", translates as "ne tradas sine nummo" meaning don't hand over the goods until you have got the money! A few weeks later the lady in question returned and asked for veterinary drugs instead of the human prescription which she found to be more expensive than ours.

She made no further comment about our fees.

Filing the case history cards was a complicated process. The receptionist would go out to the waiting room and collect the names of the waiting clients and then retrieve their cards from the main filing cabinets. After the vet had seen the client he would write up the case and place it in a cabinet above Peter's desk. Each evening Peter would go through the cards, price them up and place them in another pile for filing the next day. The reception staff put these cards into the Pending cabinet where they stayed until the monthly bills were rendered when they were moved to the Active filing cabinet.

Once a month Peter would go through all the Active cabinet cards and make a list of follow-up notes. These might be a case of a missed vaccination, a fractured leg that had not been re-examined, sutures that had not been removed or a case of severe diarrhoea that had not attended a follow-up consultation. The number of asterisks identified the importance of the query alongside the note. Finally the cards were filed in the TBP file (To Be Paid) until they settled the account when the card returned to the main cabinets. Every morning we allocated the daily visits to the vets not taking morning surgery. To this list of visits we would add some of the more urgent "follow-ups" that were on the planned route of our visits for the day.

In some ways Peter Grant was ahead of his time. A year before I joined the practice Woking station had been put into lock-down following the arrival of a parcel addressed to the practice labelled "Radioactive". The stationmaster, having shut down the station, made urgent phone calls to the practice and the box surrounding a lead canister was removed to the surgery only a few hundred yards from the station. Neither lead-lined gloves nor anti-hazard suits were needed as the radioactive content was a small concave metal disc within the lead container. This we used to treat corneal ulcers in dogs and cats while wearing normal X-ray protective aprons. The stationmaster was not to know this at the time and acted as he thought best when the country was still living under the cloud of the cold war.

What was advanced for the time was the fact that we all had to wear dosimeters that recorded the amount of radiation, mainly from X-rays, we had received in the month. We sent the films inside each dosimeter each month to the Atomic Research Station at Harwell. We never received a negative report during the time we were at Woking.

At the end of morning surgery, at around eleven, the two consulting rooms would become operating theatres when the examination tables became the operating tables. The smaller of the two rooms would become a "dirty" theatre where we treated dental conditions, abscesses and badly infected wounds while the larger of the two rooms became the more sterile, elective theatre for spays, castrations, clean orthopaedic injuries and sterile corrective surgery. We would house the operating cases for the day at the back of the shed in kennels or cages. To say the main consulting room became the 'sterile" theatre was rather an exaggeration when it contained the receptionist's desk, Peter Grant's desk and the four filing systems. It was in fact the hub of the practice. So we might be concentrating on a delicate piece of surgery while there were conversations going on over two telephone lines, the nurse was filing the day's case history cards and casual visitors were knocking on the door to collect their repeat prescriptions.

I mentioned earlier that my father had an exaggerated opinion bordering on veneration of members of the medical profession. Peter Grant had a similar attitude towards the members of any profession (except the oldest!) in that he never charged them a penny for the practice's services. This charitable exercise also extended to his many friends. A deep red diagonal line across the top right-hand corner of the top card identified the case history cards of these favoured clients. My thoughts at the time were that it was his practice and he could do what he liked so long as my salary got paid. This attitude changed when he offered me a partnership but more of that later.

Peter recouped some this generosity by taking the month of March off when he took the practice books home and 'adjusted' them for the eyes of the Tax Inspector. He must have done the 'cooking' of the books quite carefully since they never investigated him for any tax evasion or misdemeanour of any kind.

Those vets on visiting duty would often see over 20 cases a day which would vary from a cat abscess via a colt castration to a calving. The cases would not have been visited in that order because a calving could be an emergency while a colt castration is elective. Milk fever occurs in high-producing dairy cattle usually within a day or two of calving when the blood calcium drops to dangerously low levels. The animal starts with a few tremors before staggering and going down into a sitting position before collapsing on their side. Intravenous calcium must be given as quickly as possible to save the animal's life. We carried 500ml bottles of calcium borogluconate to which we would attach a rubber cap on the end of a long tube. The needle would be inserted into the jugular vein - that's the big one in the neck I had trouble with in my early days. We then attached it to the tube while the cowman held the bottle above his head so that the solution drained into the patient.

Another potentially fatal condition in high-producing cattle is ketosis or acetonaemia. This results from a low blood sugar and requires the administration of intravenous dextrose solution. The cowman could sometimes delay the onset of severe symptoms by 'drenching' the animal with glycerine or propylene glycol. "Drenching" means dosing the animal with a liquid by mouth by inverting a bottle of the medicine into the side of the cheek which induced swallowing..

Other emergencies would include colic in horses, difficult births in many species, road accidents and heat stroke. There were no mobile phones but the reception staff would have a note of the visits being done and they would try to contact us on our rounds if an emergency cropped up.

Vaccines

While the availability of antibiotics was limited, the number of vaccines available for domestic pets was even smaller. We vaccinated puppies at 12 weeks against distemper, which was still sometimes referred to as "hard pad", viral hepatitis and two forms of leptospirosis. The market leader in canine vaccination was Epivax made by Burroughs Wellcome laboratories. It was one of the first veterinary medical products advertised nationally so many clients would come in asking for their pups to be "Epivaxed". Cat flu and feline enteritis could be prevented by vaccination but there were no vaccines available to the smaller species like the rabbit as there are today. Cat flu was still a potential killer of young cats which leads me to an interesting anecdote of the Woking era of the 1960s.

As I have mentioned before the Woking practice premises were "as described on the tin" – a wooden hut with additions.

One of these additions was an area for both boarding and hospitalising cats in about fifteen small cages. One of our greatest fears was an outbreak of cat flu, which is not flu but has a much more complicated name that I won't bother you with. At the first sign of the sneezing symptoms we would have to evacuate the cattery. In fact we had to evacuate everything because we had only one effective method of disinfecting the wooden premises and eliminating the virus, fumigation. A primitive solution - but effective. The process took place once the last client had left the premises after an evening surgery. The vet on duty would collect a stainless steel baking tin and line the base with purple potassium permanganate crystals. With everything in place, and a clear escape route established, we poured a pint of formaldehyde into the tin which we had placed on a heatproof surface in the centre of the 'hut'. We made a quick dash for the back door as the chemical reaction released the formalin gas which spread to every corner and crevice of the building. Standing on the other side of the road you could see the tendrils of formalin vapour oozing their way between the wooden slats of the structure. The next morning the baking tin was empty and distorted by the heat of the reaction and had to be thrown away. As I said, crude but effective.

Other vaccines for the farm animal species were becoming available following the crystal violet vaccine against swine fever and the erysipelas vaccine in pigs. Sheep were beginning to be being routinely vaccinated against the Clostridial diseases of anthrax, tetanus, blackleg and pulpy kidney while poultry got protection against Newcastle disease, infectious bronchitis and coccidiosis.

Puppies, kittens and farm animals were wormed against roundworms and tapeworms although some species of the latter were becoming far less common. This was probably because less raw meat was being fed to pets. Baths and shampoos, used on a regular basis, treated fleas and other external parasites. The sarcoptic, psoroptic, demodectic and other mange diseases were far more common then than they are today.

Operating Surgery

In the early years of my professional life I used to drive past a variety of veterinary practices in Victorian houses, small single-story huts, converted High Street shops and even 16th century merchant's houses. I would wonder at the wide range of operating skills that were carried out within such unprepossessing premises. We would operate from the point of a nose to the tip of a tail repairing eyes, throats, lungs, intestines, fractures of every conceivable bone while correcting malformations of joints and the spinal column every working day of our lives. There were no specialist practices in those early days. Innovative surgery was confined to the teaching schools and highly specialised equine practices in Newmarket. We journeymen general practitioners used what skills we had developed over a lifetime with a remarkable success rate.

Surgery at Woking was still rather basic although anaesthesia was far better controlled than in the previous practices I had seen. We also had recovery kennels instead of any available floor space. Removal of foreign objects was a welcome change to the normal routine of bitch spays and cat castrations. We ventured into the fields of more specific eye and ear surgery and the simpler orthopaedic work. There is something very satisfying about taking something broken or malformed and restoring the patient to full function. Instrumentation was still primitive with dedicated stainless steel veterinary instruments used alongside Black and Decker drills, cabinetmaker's screwdrivers and large bolt croppers to reduce the lengths of intramedullary pins as well as cutting lead clips trapped in the webs of the dog's foot.

A routine operation would start with a sedative, Largactil, and atropine to reduce anxiety and the flow of saliva. The patient would be given an intravenous injection of a short-acting barbiturate, thiopentone, to render the animal unconscious. We would then intubate the windpipe and connect it to the anaesthetic trolley. This would deliver the Halothane, a gaseous maintenance anaesthetic, with oxygen and nitrous oxide gases. Halothane was replacing ether as the maintenance anaesthetic of choice in many practices. Once the patient was stable the operating site would be clipped and sterilised with an antiseptic solution before draping the area and making the first incision. The anaesthetic syringe was left in the vein throughout the operation in case of emergencies and we might use another vein to introduce a saline drip if the surgery warranted it.

Clients are still shocked by the cost of veterinary surgery but rarely think about the reasons for these charges. Take the simple example of an endotracheal tube, used in general anaesthesia for the safe transfer of gases to the unconscious patient. The human anaesthetist has to have access to a certain size range of these tubes to accommodate patients varying between a small child to a large human adult. His veterinary equivalent has to have on hand tubes that fit the smallest kitten to the largest horse. Replacement hip joints vary in size to a certain degree in human surgery but the veterinary surgeon has to be able to replace hips varying in size between a Chihuahua and a Pyrenean mountain dog with the corresponding surgical instrumentation. Not only is there a considerable variation in size of these instruments but the veterinary market is far smaller than the human field so the economics of market size is a major factor in the increased costs.

Then there is the surgical equipment. An anaesthetic trolley in the 1970s would cost about £1000, an X-ray machine about £2000, the operating table another £700 and all that before you start on the instrument inventory. Don't forget my salary at this time was about £1300 a year and the practice paid for my accommodation, car and phone bills. This was when a major orthopaedic operation would cost between £25 and £45 while a Labrador bitch spay would be charged out at about £12.50.

The medical anaesthetist has only one species to cope with while her veterinary counterpart has to consider the needs of differing species. For instance, a cat's vocal chords will often go into a tight spasm if they are touched by an endotracheal tube so a spray of local anaesthetic must be used before introducing the tube. Many anaesthetics of the day, especially the barbiturates, relied upon their redistribution from the brain to other fatty tissue in the body for recovery to take place. Fat patients would come round far quicker than skinny ones which had to rely on the slower process of detoxification by the liver so they developed ultra-short-acting barbiturates for species like the greyhound and whippet.

One surgical technique rarely used outside the veterinary schools was diathermy. This involves the passage of a high frequency current which passes through the patient from the live or Active electrode (diathermy forceps or probe) to the Return electrode. The Return electrode, also known as the indifferent electrode, patient electrode or diathermy pad, was placed under the patient. A foot switch activates the live electrode to coagulate or cut. It was an experimental technique in use when we were studying but several safety issues have prevented its widespread use in the profession today.

One patient that was an unexpected challenge was a pet chimpanzee. It had broken its shin bone in a heavy fall. In spite of the fact that I had never treated an ape before, the practice decided that, since I had occasionally visited Whipsnade Zoo, I was the one to deal with the case. There are many anatomical similarities in human and animal bodies so I treated the chimp as though it was just another breed of dog. At the time we were using virtually the same anaesthetic techniques as the medics so once we had achieved anaesthesia the operation went ahead successfully. Don't think something can't be done until you have considered every angle - apparently complicated problems often have a simple solution.

Dentistry was still very primitive consisting largely of extraction of rotten teeth and the scraping removal of tartar from the others. Frequently the tartar accumulation was sufficient to cover the tooth completely in a grey, brown concrete. Fractured teeth sometimes had to have the remaining healthy roots loosened by a chisel shaped like a gouge before they could be removed. Teeth with two or three roots might have to be sawn into two pieces before they could be extracted. The next few years would see a vast improvement in veterinary dental health care. Dentistry had never featured in the veterinary syllabus of our day so we relied upon continuing education courses and our own wits to improve.

Family life

You may have noticed that throughout this account of my life I have referred to "we" and "us" which occasionally meant one or other of my partners or assistants but, in most cases, it meant Jen and myself. I could never have achieved whatever success I had without her unreserved love and support. We were a team and we still are. She has scrubbed floors, painted walls, washed blood-stained coats, held patients for me and never complained. She also became very adept at making provisional diagnoses over the phone if I was out on a call. "You've got a pyometra on its way to the surgery," she would say when I got in from a previous visit, or "Mrs Robinson's dog's anal glands are playing up again."

Up to this point in our lives we had been the luckiest of people. We both came from stable, happy families; we were very comfortable financially; we owned a lovely home, in fact, our life as a family was jogging along almost perfectly. Jen and I were in love; I was enjoying my work; we had a supportive circle of friends and happy children.

Then, one lunchtime, it all fell apart.

Sophie, our second daughter, had developed a strange cry and showed some bruises on her legs so Jen said she would call the doctor after I left after lunch.

I was just beginning a routine evening surgery when the call came in to the surgery asking me to come in to St Peter's hospital in Chertsey immediately.

"Your wife needs you," was all I was told.

I handed the surgery over to Rees Rogers, the other assistant on duty that evening and leapt into the car. Jen was in a state of shock, sitting in an observation room outside Sophie's room where she was hooked up to a blood transfusion.

"It's leukaemia," whispered Jen through her tears.

The bottom fell out of our world.

All four grandparents were devastated when they heard the news. I rang Mum and Dad later that evening after I got back from the hospital. My father picked up the phone, and I told him we had some news.

"Don't tell me Jen is pregnant again," he said.

He must have wanted to cut his tongue out when he learnt the real news but, bless him, he reacted in the only way he knew how which was to throw money at the problem. He offered all his life savings if it meant a cure for Sophie. I felt so sorry for him then. He had always overcome the challenges that life threw at him by using money but this time it was not the cure-all he wanted it to be.

The day after the diagnosis I drove in to morning surgery where my first patient was a Boxer with pseudo-Hodgkin's disease which is a type of leukaemia. It was hard to keep a neutral expression on my face.

Peter Grant's friend, the senior partner in our medical practice, Derek Milne, had contacts with the Royal Marsden Hospital in Banstead and he got Sophie admitted to the Princess Chula isolation ward. Jen and I shared the business of settling her in by sleeping overnight with her until she was ready for transfer to her own isolation unit. Once she was in isolation we could only see her through a large window. We talked to her by a telephone while there were microphones and loudspeakers in her room. The nurses had to go through air-lock barriers when changing shifts. They passed food through an ultraviolet hatch to prevent any infection getting through. Even her favourite toys were irradiated with ultraviolet light before they went through the hatch. This often resulted in some strange changes of colour in the soft toys.

You must remember that we were a young couple in our late twenties who had never been confronted by terminal disease - let alone that of a two-year-old child. We were still exploring our relationship as a married couple and just about coping with parenthood. The normal life going on around us had suddenly become an alien world but we had to cope with it. Kim needed her parents as much as Sophie. How could we divide our attention?

We existed on autopilot waiting, hoping, praying for signs of remission. Sophie was waxy pale and soon lost her hair. We tried hard to give Kim as much of ourselves as we could but she missed her sister badly. She did a lot of play acting on her own with imaginary classrooms of children. Bob and Florence Conner, our wonderful neighbours at the bottom of the garden, were pillars of strength offering us as much normality as possible. It was a twenty mile, thirty-five minute journey to the hospital every day. Her first remission came after several weeks and we opened a large bottle of champagne when we got her home. She had no hair but she was home and even started nursery school.

Looking back on the experience we both realise that there could have been two outcomes. We could have been burnt to a cinder or tempered to steel in the furnace of our emotions. We were lucky to have been tempered. The practice staffs were wonderfully considerate but we had not had time to form close friendships so we had to rely on each other.

Prior to our wedding, we had spent an hour with our local vicar at Hatfield Peverel, Graham Binnie, on the subject of marriage. His words have remained with us to this day. "A marriage is like an arch. If one pillar falls, the whole structure collapses." It is a phrase that has carried us through both good times and bad throughout our married life. I wish I could tell him what a profound effect he had on our lives.

Dad, bless him, was still trying to relieve our suffering by taking us all on a wonderful holiday in Barbados and Grenada. He was never a 'baby' grandparent - he was much more interested in their achievements later in life - but I have lasting memory of him trying to feed Sophie some form of baby 'mush' with a teaspoon with a silly, satisfied grin on his face. There cannot be many guests who have requested baked beans on toast with chips and tomato ketchup from the Sandy Lane hotel in Barbados.

Chapter 12

Woking case histories

Those vets who were not operating that morning would divide up the list of visits with the monthly exception of one client, Mrs Leveson. She lived in a prestigious area between Woking and Byfleet called Pyrford Woods. Every month she would request a visit by one of the vets for her Pekingese's check-up. This visit was always an ordeal. Everyone dreaded the prospect, so we actually drew straws to decide who was to be the unfortunate visitor that month. She always had a long list of complaints, questions and general inconsequential observations not only about the dog but also on the state of the country. On my first visit to the lady and her pampered pet, I rang the bell and waited for an answer. There was a slight flicker behind the spyhole in the door and a voice asked me to move a little to the right so they could see me.

"Who are you?" demanded an imperious voice from behind the door.

"I'm Mr Arnold, the new vet with Mr Grant's practice."

The occupier obviously put no faith in optics. She put the door on the security chain, opened it a couple of inches to confirm what she had seen through the spyhole and then shut it again. While I waited outside the door, I heard the rustling of newspaper on the other side. Eventually she opened the door fully and invited me in. I was then ordered to stand on the newspaper that covered an area of the highly polished oak parquet flooring. The newspaper was, of course, The Times. I thought this was all a little unnecessary as I had scraped my shoes on the door mat outside but I obeyed. Once she judged me to be in the correct position, she released the patient, named Tricky Woo, named after one of James Herriot's anecdotes, from its boudoir in the sitting room. It raced to greet me by jumping up at my legs while urinating all over my shoes - hence the need for the newspaper. The timid maid, Emily, in white doily and apron, hurried to wipe my shoes before her mistress complained yet again about her inability to perform simple tasks.

The whole household seemed to date from a different era. There was an air of the 1920s about it. The owner led me into the sitting room where I was scrutinised by several generations of Leveson portraits hanging on the walls. She told me to sit in one of two deep armchairs while taking up her position on the chaise longue in front of the French windows. She was a woman in her mid-60s, shrivelled in mind, body and spirit. Once Tricky Woo had settled onto his large silk cushion in his own armchair, she produced a long sheet of paper containing the questions of the month.

I remember the first one vividly.

"My Italian gardener has left me and I am worried that Tricky Woo will catch pneumonia."

Unable to follow the logic of this statement, I asked her to elaborate a little.

"It's quite simple," she said. "Antonio, who was always rather temperamental, took offence at something I said and walked off. He hasn't been back for over three weeks and the grass needs cutting. With the autumn days closing in, there is often a heavy dew in the morning and Tricky Woo's little chest gets soaked. I cannot trust Emily to dry him properly leaving him vulnerable to all kinds of dreadful diseases. If you know of a suitable gardener, please ask him to get in touch with me as soon as possible."

The remaining questions carried on in a similar vein until I escaped after about 35 minutes. On one previous occasion the questions had droned on for so long that Peter Grant fell asleep in the armchair. After being asked the same question three times, he woke up and tried to cover his confusion by searching for a pen he had dropped into the deep upholstery.

Another of the practice's clients was the multi-millionaire, John Paul Getty, who lived a reclusive life at Sutton Place, a Grade One listed Tudor mansion about 6 miles from the practice. A pair of huge wrought-iron gates guarded the entrance to the large estate. On my first visit I stopped the car in front of the closed gates and tried to find a bell, buzzer or other form of communication to announce my arrival. To my surprise and slight apprehension the gates slowly opened despite me not being able to detect any sign of a gatekeeper. As I drove through the open gates down a long empty avenue, I saw farm workers loading hay onto a cart in the distance so I drove over and asked for directions to the house.

"You've come the wrong way," said the rather intimidating foreman. "Turn round and go a quarter of a mile down there and you will see the house on the right. Do not go any further. They do not welcome visitors on the estate."

By this time there was an eerie feel to the whole place, but I found the house which was dark and oppressive. Mr Getty was nowhere to be seen but I was eventually greeted by someone who could only be described as the major domo. Hardly a single unnecessary word was exchanged but I treated the two German Shepherd dogs and made my escape. About a hundred yards from the gates, they

115

mysteriously opened to let me through again with no sign of human presence. I was relieved to get back to normality after such a distinct atmosphere of undefined threat.

A month later I was on duty one Sunday afternoon when the phone rang. A gravelly American voice informed me he was not at all pleased with the veterinary bill he had received for the treatment of his dogs. I explained that the charges were in line with the normal pricing structure of the practice but Mr Getty was not to be placated and his voice deepened into a growl.

"When I was a boy, you vets only knew two dog diseases. One, it was distemper and you couldn't cure it and two, it wasn't distemper and you still couldn't cure it. I don't suppose you've improved much over the years."

He put the phone down before I could defend my profession but at least he did eventually pay the bill. I had heard stories of his legendary parsimony that extended to making his house guests use the pay phone he had installed in the house. It was only when I saw the pay phone in the dark hallway of the house I realised the truth of the story.

The Spider

Not all our patients were run-of-the-mill cats and dogs with the occasional hamster thrown into the mix. There was a ring of the waiting room doorbell one day when I was having a particularly bad morning. My patients were trying to bite me, the clients were complaining about their bills, and my coffee was late. So when a junior nurse went to answer the door of the waiting room and came back giggling, I snapped.

"What the hell is going on out there?" I grumbled.

The nurse shrank back under the unfair onslaught and mumbled that there was someone outside with a spider.

That was it! I had had enough.

I stormed out into the waiting room expecting to find a young schoolboy. Instead I found myself faced by a rather unassuming middle-aged man wearing a raincoat several sizes too big for him, a rain-sodden trilby hat and clutching a cardboard box.

"What's the problem?" I asked.

Nervous, he whispered "It's my spider, doctor." Clients often addressed us as "doctor" in those early days. I could feel my exasperation growing to boiling point.

116

"And what exactly is wrong with your spider?"

"It keeps being sick."

I thought I had heard everything but a vomiting spider was a new one on me so I grabbed the box and pulled off the lid. My eyes popped, my jaw dropped and I took a sharp step backwards. A large tarantula gazed up at me. I quickly replaced the lid. At that stage of my career, despite having treated several different species at Whipsnade Zoo, spiders were definitely beyond me. I quietly suggested that he took it to the London Zoo for specialist assessment.

It was one of the two patients I have ever refused to treat, the other being a full grown rattlesnake owned by a client in Crawley a few years later.

About three weeks later, having finished morning surgery, Mrs Lindo handed me the phone saying that the London Zoo wanted a word with me. The caller asked if I had referred a Mr Robinson with his tarantula to the zoo. Once I overcame my surprise that the owner had taken up my suggestion, the kind gentleman from the zoo informed me that, having examined the spider, they found it to be in robust health. Apparently tarantulas often regurgitate their food, it forms part of the mating ritual. Now I knew about tarantulas.

The Colonel

The work of the practice was split about 70:30 between family pets and farm livestock and the tractor had replaced the working horse on most farms by the late 60s. Only a few enterprises still used horse power such as the nurserymen, Jackmans, just outside Woking. Their extensive nursery beds covered several acres, and they found that their Shire horses damaged fewer plants than the clumsy tractors of the day. Their prize beast was a huge gelding by the name of The Colonel. He moved with a regal pride yet remained a gentle giant - except in one situation.

The farrier shod the horses once a month. He could remove all The Colonel's shoes, trim his feet and attach new shoes to all his feet except the near forefoot but, if he approached that foot with a hammer, nails and a shoe, the horse would go berserk. This was because an inaccurate nail earlier in his life had penetrated the sensitive laminae of the foot causing acute pain. It is a condition known as 'nail bind' and once suffered is never forgotten by the victim. The Colonel was such a valuable member of the nursery stables that we needed to solve the problem.

They set aside a large Dutch barn and layered the floor with about four feet of peat under two feet of straw. The farrier would ring the practice when he arrived at the nursery and we knew then that he would be ready for us in about 30 minutes. When we arrived, The Colonel, with three feet shod, would be standing on the bed of peat and straw waiting for us. We put a large needle into his jugular vein and ran in about 500ml of chloral hydrate which was a common anaesthetic for horses and cattle in those days. After a couple of minutes the giant horse would begin to sway slowly from side to side while we and the staff guided him down onto his right side. This let the farrier to complete his work on the sensitive hoof. There was no pain in the hoof it was only the painful memory of the previous faulty shoeing that demanded the unusual treatment. Forty minutes later, the horse regained his feet and they led him off to his stable to rest for the rest of the day.

Colt castration

Away from the veterinary schools and large equine practices around Newmarket and the other racing centres like Newbury, large animal surgery was limited. In general practice we performed caesarean sections of cattle and sheep, repair of uterine prolapses and general castrations in the most unsterile of conditions. Surgery on this scale was normally uneconomic to the farmer. It was cheaper to put the animal down and send the carcase off for dog meat.

I remember one colt castration I performed in the middle of a field just outside Woking. It had been an uneventful procedure. The animal remained calm with the local anaesthetic working well, and I finished by suturing the skin wound. I was walking back to my car parked at the entrance to the field to get some antiseptic to clean the wound when I noticed an old man leaning on the farm gate.

"Nice job there, boy," he said, chewing on the stem of his pipe.

"Thank you," I replied.

"So what are you doing now?"

"I'm just getting some antiseptic from the car."

"Useless stuff, these modern drugs. In my day we used to pee on the wound. Cleaned it up a treat but I suppose you've got to move with times."

There is some truth in what he said. In the absence of a kidney or bladder infection, urine is almost sterile.

Talking of sterility, one useful first aid tip I have used from time to time over the years, when caught in a situation without my modern equipment, is that clean newspapers are remarkably sterile. The heat from the presses kills most bacteria and then the tight packaging protects the paper during their journey from the print room to the newsagent. They are not completely bacteria-free but they are a lot cleaner than a sweater that has been worn for a day. I have delivered many litters of pups and kittens on newspaper before wrapping them in a potentially bacteria-laden blanket. Unfortunately newsprint processing no longer use hot press machines having moved on to offset printing which does not generate the heat the of the older presses.

Spina Bifida

Sometimes you will find yourself helping the owner as much as their pet. A lovely lady in Old Woking called me out to put down her old Labrador which had terminal cancer of the liver. She worked in a nearby tearoom as a waitress and lived in a tiny cottage across the road. She was remarkably stoical about the whole affair until the last moment when the dog slipped away under the injection and the tears began to roll down her cheeks. I made her a cup of tea while she told me about her daughter who had found that she was pregnant and did not want to marry the father. Her own husband had left her at the end of the war.

To empathise with her, I told her about Sophie's leukaemia and mentioned the phrase "That when you hit rock bottom, the only way is up." She dried her eyes, and I gave her a hug before leaving.

An old adage says you cannot know what someone is suffering until you have walked in their shoes. It was about eight months later that I met her again outside the shops in Woking.

"Hello, Mrs Anderson. How are you?"

"Hello, Mr Arnold. I'm glad I met up with you again because there was something I wanted to talk to you about. Do you remember saying that when you hit rock bottom, the only way is up?"

I felt a chill run down my spine. I said "Yes."

"The only problem with that is that you have to know when you hit rock bottom."

"What happened?"

The spinal shiver got colder.

"My daughter's baby was born spina bifida."

Her words hit me like a punch in the gut so what effect it had had on her and her daughter I could not begin to imagine. Despite the dreadful news she was quietly accepting of the situation and, this time, she gave <u>me</u> a hug. You never know what might be waiting around the corner but try to be prepared for it.

Aspirin Cat

Ill-informed first aid can create unexpected problems. For instance, not enough cat owners are aware than aspirin is poisonous to cats. One client called me out one day describing their cat as "doing a wall of death round the living room walls." As I stood in the hallway of the house, the owner had not been exaggerating. The shuddering sound of the living room door as the poor cat thundered around the walls of the room confirmed her description. She explained that it had been limping for a couple of days so she had given it an aspirin tablet. By now the cat was showing the worst symptoms of salicylic acid (aspirin) poisoning.

The first problem was to catch the animal. I waited until it passed the door and quickly entered the room before closing it again. I felt somewhat dizzy trying to follow the cat round the walls of the room when I saw a possible solution. The client had furnished the bay window with heavy curtains. I waited until the cat approached the window and pulled the curtain into its path. The curtain fell off the rail, and I wrapped the struggling cat in its folds. Once wrapped in the curtain I transferred it to the travelling cat basket in the car and returned to the surgery. I dosed it with activated charcoal before giving it a sedative and an intravenous drip. Genetically the cat does not have the enzymes necessary to eliminate salicylic acid and despite continuing treatment for a few days the cat died of aspirin poisoning. Despite your best efforts you will not win them all.

Injection allergy

Another elderly lady taught me a few valuable life lessons. She was a spinster who lived just the other side of the railway line from the surgery. Having lost her fiancé during the war, she spent some 15 years nursing her mother until her death. Then her father fell ill and required her care for the rest of his life. She had lived on her own since her father died five years previously leaving her only her cat for company.

From time to time the cat required some basic treatment - the occasional abscess, mild episodes of tonsillitis or worried by ear mites. The one treatment that the lady would not allow was injection. It had shown such a dreadful reaction to an injection several years previously that she was determined it would never suffer such trauma again. This was not much of a problem since abscesses can be lanced, infections treated by antibiotic tablets and ears treated with drops after cleaning. It just meant that recovery took a little longer.

However, one form of treatment demands an injection. This is vaccination, and the owner refused point blank to allow vaccination of her beloved pet. Early vaccinations had been painful and there had been a few adverse reactions to those first vaccines. Those occasions were behind us by this time but she was adamant that her cat was 'allergic' to needles.

There was a severe outbreak of cat flu going around the town and I pleaded with her to allow me to vaccinate her cat. There was no way she would relent! However, after a long discussion I persuaded her to allow me to give the cat 1ml of sterile water to prove to her that the 'allergy' did not exist.

Within a minute of administering the sub-cutaneous injection, the cat went into shock and it was only after two further injections of emergency adrenalin it began to recover. I can't explain it but she knew her cat better than I did and I had learnt another lesson.

While we were waiting for the cat to recover, she asked me to put a sixpenny lump of coal on the fire. (Six old pennies were worth 2½p.) I guessed at the value of one medium sized lump of coal and put it in the grate.

"No!" she shouted. "That's worth at least a bob. Get a smaller one." (A bob was one shilling or 5p.)

With her income being so tight, she could cost each lump of coal. Too many people today know the cost of everything but the value of little. She had to eke out the most value from her limited resources but, although very poor, she lived a contented life - unless I tried to stick a needle in her cat. The "poverty line" was lower in those days when poverty meant just that. Poverty today seems to imply a lack of affluence - but I am getting grumpy again.

The injured swan

121

Calls can come in at any time of day or night. Most out-of-hours work was justifiable while some were trivial. These trivial night calls were a different matter. It was just before two in the morning when the phone rang beside my bed.

"Is that the veterinary surgeon?" asked a particularly refined voice.

Still half asleep, I confirmed that I was the vet on duty.

"I think I may have injured a swan when driving home this evening. I heard a bump as I was approaching the Victoria Bridge and this swan ran off and lay in the ditch beside the road. When I tried to approach it, it hissed at me so I must have injured it. Would you mind going out to see if you can help it in any way?"

"So where are you at the moment?"

"Oh, I'm back home in Pyrford Woods."

Remember Mrs Leveson in Pyrford Woods? This lady could have been her twin sister and Pyrford Woods was 5 miles away from the Victoria Bridge. What was I to do? The odds were that the bird had either died or flown off. No-one would know whether I went or not, except me. But I knew I could not sleep unless I satisfied myself that I had done all I could.

So I was not in the best of tempers when I arrived at a gravel pull-in beside the bridge over the canal. To my surprise there were three other cars parked in the lay-by, the occupants of which were shepherding the swan onto the canal. As I approached the group, the bird shook its long neck, took a few steps across the water, spread its magnificent wings and headed north towards Staines.

One of the 'shepherds' asked me what I was doing there at that time of night. I pointed up at the disappearing swan and said "That's my patient!" It was at this point that whole affair descended into farce because a police patrol car swung onto the gravel, scattering small stones in our direction. The officer got out saying what I had been waiting to hear a policeman say all my life. He actually said "Evenin' all. What's all this 'ere then?"

I explained the situation to the officer who burst out laughing. I pointed out I did not appreciate being called out at two in the morning to see my patient well on its way towards Heathrow.

"No. I can understand your feelings, sir," he said, trying to hide the broad grin on his face, "but you don't know our side of the story. We had received a call from a passing motorist concerning a suspicious gathering at the Victoria Bridge. We thought you might be a bunch of anarchists!"

To my surprise, I did get some more sleep that night. It was probably the effects of a clear conscience.

While on the subject of night calls, there was another night call which fell between the two categories of serious and trivial. Again I was fast asleep when the bedside phone shattered my dreams with an apologetic lady on the line.

"I'm so dreadfully sorry to call you at this time of night, Mr Arnold, but I am in a real quandary."

"What's the problem," I asked.

"It's my Cavalier spaniel, Jodie, She sleeps in my bedroom every night. I know I should have had her nails clipped before now but I sent the carpet away for dry-cleaning yesterday. Now Jodie will not stop pacing around the room clicking her nails on the floorboards. I just cannot sleep!"

It might seem odd but I went and clipped the dog's nails. You may think I was pandering to a silly client who should have known better, but I would only have lain awake half the night wondering whether I was doing the right thing in refusing to go. There was also the chance that the practice reputation would grow because of the owner repeating the story around her circle of friends.

Another unusual request for a visit came at about 8.00pm on a summer's evening.

"You're not going to believe this," said the caller "but my Corgi's skin won't stop moving. It's rippling all the way down its back. He looks none too happy either."

It was only half a mile away on a council estate and the owner appreciated my arrival. He led me through to the kitchen where the patient was looking distinctly miserable in its bed. We enticed him out of the bed onto the kitchen floor and I laid a gentle hand on its back. As the owner said, it was rippling. Not only that, it was hot, so I tried to part the hair to get a closer look. To my horror, the skin split revealing a seething mass of maggots lying just below the surface. Very carefully I tried to assess how far the maggots had invaded under the skin of the back and realised that almost the whole area from the base of the neck to the base of its stumpy tail was affected.

It was the worst case of fly strike I had ever seen which needed urgent radical attention. Fly strike is a condition where parasitic flies, like greenbottles and bluebottles, lay eggs on soiled hair or open wounds. After hatching, the maggots bury themselves in the dog's fur and eventually under the skin, feeding off their flesh. It is much more common in sheep but can affect any furred animal. It took months of tiny skin grafts to restore a vaguely normal-looking coat.

Road accidents are often the subject of night visits. Even late in the evening quite a crowd can gather around an injured animal in the road which only adds to its distress. On arrival at the scene I try to persuade the onlookers to move back while I get a muzzle on the dog or a blanket around a cat to prevent injury by the frightened animal. Having muzzled the dog, the next action is to prevent further injury and escape so I needed a lead. If none is immediately available, ties, belts, stockings - we can use all these items to prevent an injured dog from escaping from the crowd of onlookers.

On a previous occasion a car had hit a German Shepherd dog and broken its right thigh bone but, before I could get to it, the terrified dog raced back into the road only to be hit by a car coming from the opposite direction. The second collision broke its left shin bone. The adrenalin of fear and shock is a powerful analgesic (painkiller) and even with two broken hind legs the dog ran just under three miles on those damaged legs. I calculated this by using a map measuring wheel on the large Ordnance Survey map of its route.

Telepathic dog

Not all owners are correct in their analysis of their pets' behaviour. One evening at a BSAVA conference in Birmingham I was having a drink with the animal behaviourist, Dr Peter Neville, who told me the tale of his 'telepathic' dog. He had been visiting a friend, and they were just finishing their supper in the front room when his friend mentioned that his dog was telepathic.

"Your dog is not telepathic," replied Peter.

"Watch," said his host. "I will move out of this chair and turn right out of the door to go to the kitchen. She will get up and precede me to the kitchen."

"OK," said Peter. "Show me."

Sure enough, the dog got up from under the table and turned right to the kitchen. He returned to his chair.

"Now I will turn left to the front door," said the owner and once again the dog got up and turned left.

Peter thought for a while then asked his friend to get up and go in random directions while he watched the dog. Within five minutes, Peter said "I've got it!"

"What do you mean 'you've got it'?"

"Don't tell me where you are going. I will tell you."

His friend rose from the chair and Peter told him, without hesitation, he was going to the kitchen. He tried various other directions and each time Peter got it right.

"How the hell did you do that?"

"I watched your dog lying under the table. He was looking at your feet, so I did the same. It is an uneven number of steps from your chair to the doorway where you make the turn so, to turn left, you start off on your right foot and vice versa. Now I want you to step off with your right foot and turn right to the kitchen."

The owner of the dog almost fell over his feet in the attempt. Not everything is as inexplicable as it would appear - conversely, it often seems that the more we learn, the more we realise how little we know. As a vet you sometimes have to resort to philosophy.

There are other times when you have to think laterally to solve a behavioural problem. One client asked me about his dog that had recently become terrified of entering a small sitting room in the house. There was no obvious reason for this change in behaviour but, when I visited the house, the dog was obviously reluctant to cross the threshold to the room. I spent time questioning the family about this change in the dog's behaviour before the teenage daughter mentioned that they had put the dog in the room several months ago when they were having a firework party. The dog was frightened of fireworks so they chose this particular room because it faced away from the garden and the dog could not see the fireworks. Since the dog's behaviour change seemed to date from that time, I looked around the room for anything that might have spooked it. The small room had two armchairs, a coffee table in front of the fireplace, a couple of pictures on the wall and a mirror over the mantelpiece. There were two brass candlesticks on either side of the mirror but nothing of a threatening nature. The dog stood in the hallway outside the open door looking nervous when a thought crossed my mind. I was looking at the room from my height of six feet. The dog was much lower to the ground. I went down on my hands and knees, took another look around the room and the answer was there in front of me. The windows faced away from the garden but the mirror reflected a small corner of the back lawn. Asking where they had let off the fireworks they said it had been that particular corner. The dog had seen the flashes reflected in the mirror. I closed the door so that the dog could not see what I was doing. Then took the mirror off the mantelpiece and placed in on the floor facing the opposite wall.

Would my theory work?

I opened the door again and offered the dog a treat from my pocket. He looked at me, then at the open space above the mantelpiece, before creeping into the room and taking the treat. He was not frightened of the room. It was the mirror that terrified him.

Sometimes you can work out an answer but at other times there seems no explanation for an animal's behaviour. One couple had a rescue Greyhound bitch which bit every light bulb she could get at so they had to rely on candles and recessed lighting. The only exception was one central ceiling bulb in the main living room. Eventually even this bulb fell victim to the dog's obsession. A visitor was standing under this ceiling bulb when the dog leapt onto his back and shoulders to crunch the bulb and plunge the room into darkness. We never sorted out this behaviour. Like people, some animals are just plain weird.

Foot and Mouth Disease

Sometimes we are a little too clever for our own good. The case of the outbreak of "foot-and-mouth disease that wasn't" is a case in point. A farmer asked for a visit to examine one of his heifers that was off her food and not looking too good. The farm was on my route of visits that morning so I added it to my visit list. The farmer met me at the house and led me to a loose box behind the milking parlour where a Friesian heifer stood looking very forlorn. After examining most of the body, sounded the chest and taken her temperature I opened her mouth to find three medium-sized ulcers inside the lower lip. A slight shiver ran down my back as I lifted a hoof where I found more small ulcers. These were the classic signs of foot and mouth disease. The UK had been clear of the disease for ten years but there was always going to be a new case eventually. Was this the one? The shiver got colder.

My lecture notes on the disease flashed in front of my eyes as I tried to remember what my next action should be. I put the farm into quarantine using my legal powers as a Veterinary Investigation Officer. Then I got the staff to lay thick banks of straw across every entrance to the farmyard and soak them in strong disinfectant. I told everyone they were forbidden to leave the premises and called the Divisional Veterinary Officer. He instructed an investigation team to get to the premises as soon as possible. This was about 12.30 - the time when most of the staff had their lunch. So I had to suffer their hostile looks and disgruntled comments for the next two hours until the ministry team arrived.

To my astonishment they drove their car straight over my carefully constructed disinfectant barrier. Two men got out; one them sniffed the air and said "It's not foot and mouth."

"So can we go and get some lunch at last?" asked the spokesman for the staff glaring at me with outright hostility.

"Oh, yes, of course you can."

I was left speechless. It was several minutes before I regained my voice and demanded how the hell he could dismiss a diagnosis of foot and mouth disease without even seeing the patient.

"It's the smell, you see," he said as I led him to the loose box. "You're too young to have seen a case of foot and mouth but it has a particular stench which, once smelt, is never forgotten."

He examined the heifer before saying, rather kindly, "I agree it looks just like it, doesn't it? You did quite the right thing, bearing in mind your lack of experience with the disease, but this is probably a mild virus infection showing similar symptoms. Sorry, lad."

I was not welcome at that farm for at least six months afterwards.

Breaking the partnership

I had been flattered by Peter Grant's offer of a partnership bearing in mind he had not had a partner for twenty years and I jumped at the opportunity while there were a few changes I wanted applied to the new business. Peter used to treat his friends free of charge but I asked that we should charge them normal fees when seen by other members of the practice. He was happy to agree to this suggestion. He was more reluctant to alter his position on not charging other professionals in the town but again he accepted my conditions. The final request was that he should stop the practice of doctoring the books before the yearly tax return. He was unhappy about this saying it was the only way he could maintain his standard of living. I pointed out that a good accountant could probably save him more money through legal channels than he could by clandestine, and illegal, measures. Reluctantly he agreed to end the practice, but it was this that finally broke the partnership two years later because he did not keep his word on this matter.

After two years I was becoming very unhappy with his continued fiddling of the books which, if discovered, would implicate me, as a partner, in his tax evasion. Jen and I had long discussions about all the implications of breaking the partnership and we discussed the situation with Dad who had extensive experience in tax law. Finally, we concluded that, despite our affection for Peter, our situation with Sophie's treatment and the uncertainty of the future, we had to break the partnership.

Joan, Peter's wife, was the first person I told of our decision because she had been so very supportive of us both.

"Adrian," she said. "I love Peter dearly but could never work with him. Don't worry, I understand completely and you have my blessing for what it is worth."

It was worth a great deal.

The solicitor who had drawn up the original partnership agreement was a senior partner of Hempsons, one of the most prestigious 'professional' firms of solicitors in the city. He summoned me to appear at his office the next week. Peter had told me not to mention the tax fiddling issue to the solicitor which rather tied my hands.

The tall, stern man ushered me into his dusty, leather-lined office in the heart of London under the shadow of St Pauls. Then he began his onslaught.

"You young men think you can sign a binding document one day and tear it up the next. Well, I am telling you now that this will not happen without a severe financial penalty being applied."

I felt like an errant schoolboy in the headmaster's study. I tried to explain that Peter Grant was breaking the law and that several friends and members of my family had advised me to have no part in his actions.

"So, what is he doing? Nobbling horses? Signing false documents? Rustling sheep? What?"

"I'm afraid I have given my word to Mr Grant that I would not disclose the problem to you."

"Never heard such nonsense in my life! Partnerships should be open and based on trust and anyway, I don't believe you."

"Believe me or not," I said. "It is the truth."

"You may consider it to be the truth but I will recommend that you forfeit a third of your payment into the partnership for breach of promise."

This was going nowhere except downhill, fast, so I tried a different approach.

"Let me give you an analogy as an example of the problem."

His silence encouraged me put my case allegorically.

"Let us suppose that I am a young driving instructor who has been offered a partnership in a driving school. The principal has always carried out his lessons at 40mph, rather than the legal 30mph, because it meant he could get in an extra two lessons a day and increase his profit margin. My father, who is a policeman, tells me that legally the business is breaking the law and I could be held responsible for my partner's actions and possibly lose my licence to teach. Unlikely but possible and not worth the risk to my career and he advises me not to enter into the partnership."

The solicitor leant back in his chair and steepled his long fingers together in front of his face.

"So he _is_ nobbling horses - or sheep - or greyhounds - but you are not going to tell me. Is that right?"

"It's nothing like that but I am bound by my word to Mr Grant that I would not divulge to you my true reason for breaking the partnership. I'm sorry."

The solicitor sat in silence as he weighed his thoughts. The entire world seemed to have stopped in its rotation as we sat opposite each other waiting for time to move on. Even the long case clock in the corner seemed to have slowed its movement. At last he lifted his head, looked me in the eye and said "Very well. Against my better judgement I will recommend to Mr Grant that he should refund you your full partnership payment."

He stood up, and I went to leave when he held out his hand which I took. His firm handshake came with words that live with me to this day.

"Mr Arnold, I treated you badly when you came into this room for which I apologise. You are an honourable young man and I am glad to have met you. However, I am afraid you will have to tell Mr Grant that I shall no longer be handling his legal affairs. Good day."

As I walked back to the Tube station, I had no feeling of victory but more of regret that my regard and friendship for Peter had come down to a legal decision made by a stranger. It was time to move on and the next day I gave Peter my three month notice of leaving. He understood my reasons and appreciated the fact that I had kept my word about his tax affairs so our remaining time at Woking was amicable.

From time to time during our training, Paul Scammell and I had talked about the possibility of us setting up our own practice. He was more interested in the farm animal side of practice while I preferred the challenges of small animal surgery. We thought we had the makings of a good team. Following qualification, when I felt more qualified to fly to the moon than practice veterinary medicine, we both went our separate ways. While he went to a practice in the Peak District in Derbyshire, we went to Dunstable followed by Woking but we still kept in touch.

At the time of the break-up of my partnership with Peter Grant, it turned out that Paul was looking to make a move from Derbyshire so things fell into place for us to fulfil our earlier ambition and set up our own practice.

Chapter 13

Setting up the Crawley practice

Looking back, we must have been mad to leave a secure job for an uncertain future with two young children, one of whom had a potentially fatal disease. Even today I cannot imagine what strength it demanded of Jen to encourage and support me to follow the dream of setting up our own practice.

Paul, Jen and I spent many hours marking in veterinary practices with blue stickers on a large Ordnance Survey map of South East England. Sophie was under treatment at the Royal Marsden Hospital at Banstead in Surrey so we needed to be within striking distance of the hospital. Analysing the rash of blue spots covering the area we shortlisted three possible candidates - Totteridge in North London, Milton Keynes which was about to become a "New Town" and Crawley, an established New Town with further potential for development. We spent precious long weekends reconnoitring the three locations. Totteridge was too expensive, Milton Keynes would take several years to develop while Crawley was closest to Banstead and developing rapidly. There was only one small practice in the town which was mainly served by a large practice 5 miles away in Horley.

We spent several weekends visiting the town, chatting with local people in pubs, talking to shopkeepers and local post offices before deciding that the town would benefit from another veterinary practice. Jen and I put our house in Woking on the market. We had bought it for £6500. House prices were taking off and we hoped we might get £10,000 for it but we eventually sold for £8500. We had already committed ourselves to the purchase of a larger house in Copthorne on the outskirts of Crawley. Then we needed a property we could convert into veterinary premises.

One of the first options was a shop with a parking forecourt for five cars. We asked the town's chief planning officer about the possibility of getting planning permission for the change of use. He offered us an appointment in his office on the top floor of the Town Hall. Paul and I arrived to put our case for the need of another practice in the town pointing out that the shop premises had off-road parking.

"That is all very well for owners of small pets such as cats and dogs," he said. "But what about when the shepherd needs his flock of sheep treating? How were they going to be accommodated?"

We could not believe our ears at hearing such a stupid question and we both laughed slightly.

"You may laugh," he replied, rather put out by our amusement. "You don't seem to realise the consequences of the inconsiderate use of the roads in the town. Last year we had the annual visit from a travelling circus which advertises its arrival by holding a small parade through the town. After a few hours they needed a rest and stopped for a cup of tea at that cafe down there." He pointed out of the window.

"Come and see for yourselves. Look! Down there - the lamp post. That is where they tied up the elephant that was leading the parade - and it is a No-Parking zone!"

We gave up at that point and looked for other premises in the hope that the full planning committee had more common sense than the planning officer. We found a detached property with a large front garden we could convert into a car park and our application was eventually approved. We were now the proud owners of two properties in Crawley and our house in Woking; a bouncy 4-year-old and a 3-year-old with leukaemia; no water and missing floorboards in our Copthorne home and no income.

Life was a bit hairy for the next few months.

Not only did we have to convert the practice property to function as a surgery but we had to equip it. Drugs were easy, we set up an account with a veterinary distributor and put in our order but equipment was a different matter. Surgical instruments are expensive especially if they are designated solely for veterinary work as the market is so much smaller. In one of the many adverts at the back of the Veterinary Record we found offers of second hand surgical equipment. We did a lot of research finding the best prices for the standard instruments. This led us going up the East End of London to meet a shifty character wearing a pork-pie hat and pencil-thin moustache. He was a trader in hospital equipment. When we arrived at the front of his warehouse, there was a hand-written note informing any visitors he would be back in half an hour. How long the notice had been there was unknown, so we sat in the car and waited. In 1970, the Biafran War in Nigeria was ending, and the trader had been away negotiating a large order of surplus hospital beds for export to the beleaguered country.

He invited us in to the dusty warehouse where heat-sealed instruments hung out of filing cabinet drawers. If Aladdin had been in the surgical equipment trade, this would have been his cave.

We knew there would be some tough negotiating because we were on a tight budget so I had taken a few precautions before we got down to business. I had found some very competitive prices for three particular instruments - Allis forceps, Gillies needle holders and eyelid retractors. I opened the negotiations by asking his prices for each one of these instruments.

"17/6d for Allis forceps? You must be joking. No! I can let you have them for twenty-five shillings."

"What about Gillies needle holders?"

He pulled out a cabinet drawer and showed us a pair of Gillies made by Allen and Hanburys still in their protective wrapping.

"Perfect condition. Never been unpacked. Lovely piece of kit. Two quid," he said.

"Sorry. I can get them for 32/6d."

I thought I saw the first suggestions of a softening in his face and asked about the eyelid retractors. He let out a long sigh and offered another £2 for the instrument.

"Twenty five bob," I said. (A bob was a shilling, twelve pence in old money and 5p in today's currency.)

"OK. OK. OK. Why don't we say 18/0d for the Alliss, £1/10s for the needle holders and 27/6d for the retractors?"

I had played my last card but we were now playing on the same field. We explored the rest of the warehouse. Eventually we came away with almost a full inventory of surgical equipment, a hydraulic base of a dental chair which we would adapt to a consulting table and an old WWI military field X-ray machine together with its operating manual. The manual was a piece of history in itself in that several photographs showed British soldiers wearing puttees, a type of gaiter, outside an army bell tent of the First World War.

We bought the X-ray machine on the basis it passed the safety test we would have carried out before we completed the purchase. As far as I remember it was a Phillips Mk. 2 machine, so I rang the company and asked if they could send a testing engineer to verify the safety of the machine.

"What model would that be, sir?" the receptionist asked.

"A Phillips Mark two," I said.

She laughed in a kind of deprecating way before telling me that Phillips used Arabic numerals to denote their machine, not Roman. "So that makes it a Mark eleven," she said.

"No, it is an Arabic two not a Roman two."

"My God!" she said. "That is a really old machine. I'm not sure whether we have anyone still left who can remember that model. Give a moment and I will ask the repair department."

She came back about five minutes later to say one of their old engineers, who had just retired, still remembered the model and he would be happy to come down and run the necessary safety checks. So it was about two weeks later just after lunch that he arrived at the surgery. We led him through to the consulting room where we had installed the machine and as he entered the room, he threw his hands up in excitement.

"Oh, just look at it," he said. "That is a work of art."

He opened his large bag of tools and dismantled the control box. "Just look at that," he said, pointing out the ancient brown insulating paper surrounding the various elements inside.

"They just don't make them like that anymore. This is not just an X-ray machine it is a thing of beauty."

He spent the next three hours adjusting, testing and cleaning before pronouncing it safe and fit for the purpose for at least another ten years. As he was packing up, we asked him how much we owed him,

"Not a thing," he said. "I haven't had so much fun in years. If anything I owe you for the pleasure you have given me."

Another problem was that we had to use trays of developer, stabilisers and fixers to develop the x-rays in an improvised darkroom under the stairs all of which took time. Fortunately we had become friendly with many of the medics in the town and the radiographers offered us the use of their automated developing machine at the hospital. We would trundle the plates down to the hospital which was only five minutes away where they would be developed and dried within minutes instead or hanging up to dry in the under-stairs cupboard at the surgery. We did blot our copybook on two occasions when we left the hospital with the wrong x-rays which resulted in a call from the hospital asking if we had one of their images because they had one of what might be a cat but certainly wasn't one of their patients. It all added to the varied tapestry of their day and they were never that fussed by our occasional lapses.

As mentioned previously, we rendered all veterinary bills as a single figure under the heading of "To Veterinary Treatment", there was no itemisation or break-down to show how the final figure had been calculated. Paul Scammell and I were determined to bring the profession further into the 20th century and one of the ways to accomplish this was to hand a detailed bill to the client after every appointment, operation, laboratory test or visit. The way we could do this was by using Scribe cartridges. These were grey plastic boxes about the size of a paperback novel which held packs of duplicate invoices with a sheet of carbon paper in between. The invoice sheet itemised the charges under about eight or ten headings such as Consultation, Visit, Drugs, Operation, X-Ray, Laboratory, Hospitalisation and Other with the Total at the bottom. The owner kept the top copy while we kept the pink under-copy for our accounts.

When I informed our very traditional accountant of this idea, he nearly exploded with apoplexy.

"My God, you'll be giving away Green Shield stamps next."

It convinced him that we were dragging the reputation of the veterinary profession into the gutter alongside other 'trades people'. Despite his deep misgivings, our clientele warmly welcomed the idea.

While we were about the business of innovation, we offered consultations by appointment. We allowed ten minutes for each appointment but if it was likely to be a short procedure like suture removal or post-operative check-up we would shorten them to five minutes while we would allocate potentially more complicated cases a double appointment. This allowed us to control the flow of patients through the surgery and car park instead of coping with a scrum of people and their frightened pets when they all arrived at the same time which often happened at the beginning and end of free-for-all surgeries in the past.

The plan was for Paul, who was still single, to do locum work while Jen and I converted the Crawley property and set up the practice which meant that we had some cash coming in. As soon as we got planning permission, I got a phone call from Richard Gover, the vet in Horley, offering me a job of escorting some valuable thoroughbreds to South America by ship. The owners would completely fund the trip and it would take about 3 months to complete as we would have to supervise the settling-in period once we got to South America. It was a blatant attempt to lure us away from establishing a competitive practice and I turned it down.

Paul would spend two weeks doing a locum job then come home to the flat above the surgery where he had a week off to recover. Locums were worked hard by their temporary employers to get full value for their money. During this time I would run the new practice with the help of a young receptionist who enjoyed working with small animals. Once Paul had recuperated, I would take a week off to recharge the batteries after which the routine would start all over again.

After 6 months I got a letter from Liz Knight, the nurse we had trained in Dunstable, who had moved to become the head theatre nurse at a prestigious veterinary hospital in Surrey, to ask if we had a job for her. She said she had liked working with me at Woking and was looking for a change. I had to turn her down at the time because we did not have the income to support her higher salary. Two years later I contacted her again to see if she was still interested in working for us. As a result she joined the practice, married her landlady's son and moved with him to Aberdeen - all within the space of about 5 years. She did a lot of babysitting for us at the time and we became great friends. It was several years later that her husband died of leukaemia and, when I was setting up the Colchester practice, I wrote to her again, expressing our sympathies for her loss. I asked her whether she was looking to make a new start in life by coming down to East Anglia and help us grow the practice. She accepted the offer and stayed with us for ten years during time which she met and married her second husband, David. They still live just outside Colchester to this day.

The early practice

While Paul was away doing the locum work, I ran the practice in Three Bridges Road. When I say "ran the practice", it usually consisted of sitting and waiting for some unsuspecting client to wander through the door while passing the time trying to make a model boat. That boat has never been finished and still lies in dusty abandonment in the roof of our garage to this day.

When we finally opened the practice, we had been unable to sell our house in Woking; we were committed to further mortgages on the practice premises and our own home, Oakmead Lodge, in Copthorne, Sophie undergoing chemotherapy - and no income. I can remember the first payment I made into the practice account was for 17/6d (87½p) of which 12/6d was for a tub of poultry antibiotic powder. As I waited in the queue at the bank counter, the bank manager, a tall Yorkshireman, was standing at the back talking with one of his staff. He recognised me and curled his finger and pointed to his office round the corner. My heart sank into my boots. Our overdraft was close to its limit, as well as three outstanding mortgages with the bank - the National Provincial as it was in those days. I crept round the corner expecting the worst when he flung open the door.

"Come in, Adrian, lad, Have a seat."

Clutching my paying-in book I sank into the chair and braced myself for the worst.

"Ow's business?" he asked in a jovial tone.

"Bit slow to start with," I said.

"Well, that's only to be expected. Don't worry, things'll improve. Just you wait and see. Anyway, what I've brought you in here for is to tell you one of the best jokes I've heard in years. I thought you would be a man who enjoys a good joke."

I could not believe my ears. I can't even remember the joke but, about once a month after that, if he was free, he would give me a nod to meet in his office and exchange jokes. Unfortunately that kind of bank manager has long gone to the counting house in the sky. He later proposed me for membership of the Crawley Rotary Club which helped to raise the profile of the practice. I say 'raise the profile of the practice' because any form of advertising was seriously frowned upon in those days.

The Royal College of Veterinary Surgeons had very strict rules regarding the advertising of veterinary practices. The size of the brass plate in front of the practice was strictly proscribed. They were not allowed to be larger than 15" by 8" and they even specified the wattage of any lighting of the plate. This was in complete contrast to the advertising practices in America.

During our trip across North America in 1960 I can remember driving down the eastern side of the Rockies and seeing a bright light 40 miles away on the outskirts of Denver. As we got close enough to read the giant neon sign, we realised it was advertising a veterinary practice in the city. Limited companies were not allowed to be veterinary practices let alone run them because only individuals entered on the Royal College Register could legally practice veterinary medicine.

On the subject of advertising, Richard Gover, the Horley vet who offered us the South American trip, later reported us to the Royal College for bringing the profession into disrepute by advertising. The local newspaper had approached us asking if they could do an article on the life of a local vet. We agreed with the two provisos. There should be no names or other forms of identification included in the article and that we had full editorial rights over the piece before it went to print. We thought we had covered all the bases.

We had not considered the possibility that the newspaper would ignore the last condition and print the article without consulting us. It was not a small column but a full two-page spread. There was nothing we could do about it and, even if we had seen the article, we would have made very few changes. Despite these best efforts to avoid any suggestion of advertising, we received formal notification from the Royal College that we were under preliminary investigation for malpractice.

If they had found us guilty, they could have struck us off the register and we would have lost our livelihoods. These investigations take a long time so we spent a very anxious six months wondering whether we had a future in the profession. In the end the disciplinary board accepted our sincere intentions of showing the profession in a favourable light and went so far as to congratulate us on our promotion of the profession. Richard Gover's argument had been that the article mentioned a practice run by two "young vets" which identified us because the other neighbouring practices had vets of varying ages. We pointed out that only our bona fide clients would have known our ages and therefore we could not be guilty of advertising to any but our established clientele.

In an interesting follow-up to this story, Richard Gover asked me to appear as an expert witness on his behalf several years later. He was the defendant in the Reigate Crown Court in a case of malpractice. There were two witnesses called for the defence, myself and Brian Singleton who was President of the Royal College. It had been Brian's practice that Liz Knight left to join us in Crawley several years earlier.

It was a case involving the treatment of a simple fracture of a collie's leg. A high-powered QC from London had been brought down to present the defence case. Their arguments revolved around the meaning of the term "simple". In everyday conversation, "simple" suggests straightforward or uncomplicated but it has a very specific meaning in orthopaedics. There are three common types of bone fracture - simple, compound and comminuted. Compound denotes a fracture in which the bone has broken the skin; comminuted describes a bone that has broken into several pieces while simple shows that the bone has broken into two pieces - it does not imply an easy, or simple, repair. A shin bone broken in a straight line can be one of the more challenging orthopaedic operations. The broken surfaces will not stay in perfect line, always trying to slip away from each other. One can reunite a jagged fracture line like jigsaw pieces. Trying to repair a straight-line fracture is like balancing two rulers on top of each other. Despite the insistent questioning by the QC for half an hour I was able to hold my ground, and the Recorder judged in our favour.

Practice Routine

Morning consultations started at nine o'clock after we had checked any overnight patients in the hospital kennels. One of the challenges of veterinary medicine is that you never know what clients will present you with next. Cats may have huge abscesses which may contain as much as 150ml of pus or irritable ears because of mite infestation; the odd hamster off its food may follow dogs with vomiting and diarrhoea or a goldfish with a fungal problem. They were all grist to the veterinary mill. Morning surgery usually finished at about 10.30 in time for that vital mug of coffee before we started the operating list.

As mentioned before, I am always prepared to learn from anybody who has more knowledge or experience than me. That includes many people. I cannot begin to list them all but, as an example; we became friends with Robin, a dentist in Crawley, who had kept reptiles as pets for several years. We had little or no knowledge of such animals so I was happy to ask him for advice when presented with the occasional lizard, snake or a chameleon. We also needed to learn a lot more about the advances in dentistry that had taken place since we graduated. The vet school taught the rudiments of tooth extraction and clumsy de-scaling of gross accumulations of dental tartar but little else.

We allocated a full morning's operating to dentistry to which we invited Robin. He demonstrated a few techniques such as root canal work which, previously, would have meant tooth extraction. We anaesthetised the patients, intubated them and applied a gag which held the mouth open. The differing anatomy of a dog's head to that of a human fascinated Robin.

"They've got flip-top heads!" he said. "I love it! It makes life so much easier."

After three sessions we became so much better at dentistry, putting our previous clumsy techniques to shame and resulting in far less discomfort post-operatively for our patients.

By this time our repertoire of surgical procedures had expanded quite a bit. We now had ultrasonic tooth scaling machines to remove the plaque and tartar below the gum line as well as rotary drills to polish the cleaned teeth. We had become adept at the surgical correction of various eyelid deformities such as entropion which is when the eyelashes turn in on the eye and ulcerate the cornea.

Study of human plastic surgery techniques allowed us to remove much larger skin growths and mammary tumours without leaving vulnerable scar tissue. New orthopaedic techniques allowed us not just to pin fractures but to screw and plate the more difficult injuries. We were also improving our techniques of ligament replacement and repair. General practice had not reached the stage of prosthetic implants yet but early work in this field was being developed in the teaching hospitals and the emerging specialist practices.

By this time we were neutering various species, performing mastectomies, tumour removal, eye removal for glaucoma, and anterior cruciate repairs. Popliteal resection for hip dysplasia, corneal ulcers, barbed wire tears, airgun pellets, and tortoise shell repairs were all becoming common procedures while open chest and spinal surgery had been added to our surgical expertise.

Those not on the operating rota for the day would be out visiting housebound patients. These visits were becoming less frequent with the increased ownership of private cars. Vet's vehicles are notoriously smelly at the best of times but the worst visit was always to collect an injured tom cat which invariably sprayed the upholstery with its distinctive stink. No amount of scrubbing, bleaching, disinfecting and even professional valeting would remove the lingering memory of that journey.

We would follow lunch by more visits and the afternoon consulting session. We may have held a general practice meeting of the staff if there was a lull before evening surgery which ended at about 7.30. At the end of the day we make our way home hoping for an undisturbed evening.

A Vet's Day

I can remember the bedside phone going off at what seemed to be about 5.30am on a winter's morning and making a grab for the handset that I knocked off the bedside table. Once I had retrieved the phone in the dark the voice on the other end was very faint.

"...Ss th ... vet??" came from a distant voice. I mumbled a reply as I was fumbling for the bedside light.

"Could you speak a bit louder I can hardly hear you?"

"Is that the vet?" The voice was decipherable but still very quiet.

"I can hardly hear you," I said.

"I'm talking at the top of my voice," came the reply. By this time I had found the light and turned it on which solved the problem - I was holding the phone upside-down.

"MY CAT'S BEEN RUN OVER," the lady's voice boomed down my ear once I had the phone the right way round. By this time I was wide awake. I apologised and explained the problem to the caller who lowered the volume and explained the situation. I promised to be with her as soon as I could get dressed but, in the meantime, asked if she could she get the cat to the surgery where I could treat the injuries much more efficiently.

The injuries, although apparently dramatic, were only superficial and I could patch the cat up once it had overcome the initial shock. A few hours in one of the recovery kennels would be enough to allow the cat home again. By this time it was getting close to 7.00am, and I had to make a decision. Should I drive the six miles home, eat a quick breakfast and rush back to open the surgery at 8.15 or stay at the surgery, make myself a strong mug of coffee and catch up on some paperwork? I decided on the latter. There were always bills to pay, reports to write up, condolence letters to send and monthly budgets to calculate so a quiet hour meant that I could get ahead of the day. The day's operating cases would arrive at about 8.30 so I would be ready whatever the day held in store.

The first patient to the morning surgery was a large boisterous black Labrador which dragged its diminutive owner into the consulting room at a full gallop, banged into my knees, and sat with its tongue hanging about three inches out of its grinning mouth. The owner had to collect herself and her wits before her breathing returned to normal.

"So what's the trouble, Mrs Alexander?" I ask.

"Well, he's not quite himself, doctor." Notice the "doctor" again. It is a reliable indicator that this consultation will not be 'run of the mill'.

"What's his appetite like?"

"Well, it's all right, but he eats it as if he doesn't want a second helping."

"Do you ever give him second helpings?"

"Oh no! Never! He's too much of a handful as it is."

"What about exercise?"

"He will fetch a ball but he brings it back with that look in his eyes which seems to say 'Don't throw it quite so far next time'".

No, I am not joking. This is an accurate record of our conversation.

I check his temperature, listen to its chest, check any signs of anaemia, feel its abdomen, look for early signs of dehydration. All to no avail. The dog glistens with health and vitality so what am I to do? I can't tell her that there is nothing to worry about because she is plainly anxious about the dog's health. However, it is a poor veterinary surgeon who cannot find something slightly wrong with an animal which needs no expensive treatment but justifies the owner's concern. Sure enough, on opening the salivating mouth, I notice that one tonsil is marginally larger than the other which, to us humans, would mean an insignificant itchy throat, and requires no more treatment than time. It reassures the owner and who leaves happy knowing that all is right in the world.

One client presented my partner, Paul, with a potentially baffling case when he was in practice in the Peak District of Derbyshire. A young lad walked into his surgery, plonked a glass jar full of small twigs on the table and announced that it was his stick insect and he was a bit worried about it. The veterinary curriculum at the time did not cover the diagnosis and treatment of insect diseases so Paul played for time and tried to identify the patient. After a few minutes of unsuccessful examination of the jam jar, a small voice from the other side of the table said "Mister ... I fink I've brought my spare jar."

There are other times when the client can mislead you quite innocently. I called in the lady owner of a rather sad-looking mongrel which was usually a bundle of excited activity.

"What's the problem with Sam," I asked.

"He's constipated."

The dog looked up at me with doleful eyes as I ran through a general examination. The most obvious discovery was that, rather than suffering from constipation, it had a nasty case of enteritis. His intestines were empty, thickened and uncomfortable. I could not call the owner a liar so I had to get the true information by a roundabout route.

"What colour are his motions, Mrs Jefferson?" I asked.

"Oh, I haven't seen them. It was my husband who told me that Sam was constipated."

"Is your husband in the waiting room?"

She nodded, so I opened the door and asked Mr Jefferson to come into the consulting room. He had been busy reading the Racing Post at the time.

"I gather you think Sam is constipated," I said.

"Nah, he's got the runs, 'asn't he."

"You told me he was constipated," muttered the wife.

"No, I didn't."

"Yes, you did."

"You got it all wrong, woman," said the exasperated husband.

Eventually I stepped in and explained that Sam was suffering from inflammation of the intestines and was therefore more likely to have had diarrhoea.

"There. I told you so. I said he'd been straining the whole time," said the husband.

What had happened was that Mrs Jefferson had heard her husband say the dog had been straining which she had interpreted it as constipation. They both left in a huff, each blaming the other, after I had dispensed Sam's medication together with some dietary advice.

Another incorrect assumption by clients is what I call the "pinched foot" syndrome. Dogs and cats are not fond of having their feet held too tightly. This applies particularly to dogs so, when the animal limps, the owner feels the foot of the affected leg. The dog then pulls its foot away and yelps. Therefore, the owner deduces the pain is somewhere in the foot.

'It ain't necessarily so' as the song says.

The dog may have sprained its elbow or shoulder and, when it pulled the foot away, it wrenched the upper joint causing pain and thence the 'yelp'.

The commonest misdiagnosis by the owner is identifying the lame leg. When an animal goes lame, it limps along with its head going down with each step. The owner associates the drop of the head with the lame leg whereas it is almost invariably the opposite limb that is affected. The owner notices the downward nod of the head but misses the upward lift of the head to take pressure off the bad leg. Always get them to take the animal outside and get them to walk it in the car park as you watch the patient. It is more than likely that the owner has diagnosed the wrong leg. Don't forget that they are not trained vets.

The morals of these stories is firstly not to believe everything the owner tells you but also that advice is often more beneficial than any medication. Use both whenever necessary.

Don't show fear to owners - they think less of you. I can remember an assistant vet we had at Woking, Rees Rogers. He was a nice guy only about two years younger than me but he had a fresh face and dressed in a schoolboy manner with a blazer and creased grey flannels. Despite his limited experience he was a good vet, but the clients were not keen to see him. I could not work this out. All right, he looked young but then most of us did then so it must have been something else.

I was in the main consulting room which was open plan with Peter Grant's desk, Diana Lindo's desk, the telephone exchange and all the filing cabinets around the walls when I noticed him consulting with the owner of a bad-tempered Springer Spaniel. The dog snapped at him and he jumped back in surprise to avoid the bite. It was then I saw the look in the owner's eyes - one of contempt bordering on disgust. Any vet subconsciously knows that a patient might have a go at them. After all, they are nervous and often in pain and attack is an effective mode of defence. Rees's action was perfectly understandable but his movement was exaggerated. Instead of moving a hand or his head out of the way he moved his whole body backwards which gave the owner the impression he was afraid of animals. This was a completely unjustified judgement but true to this owner. Later on that day I had a word with him about it, explaining that if he could train himself to move just the threatened part of his body out of the way, he would avoid giving the false impression of apprehension. He took several months to overcome what is a natural reaction, but he managed it and became much more popular with the clientele and a much better vet.

There are situations when all the self-restraint in the world cannot protect you. A few weeks later Rees was called out to a pub in Ottershaw to examine an aggressive Dobermann. The owner was very proud of the fact that it was a potential 'killer' and he had asked me previously if I knew of a 'killer' bitch so that he could breed a litter of 'killer' dogs to guard the pub. I ignored the request but had warned Rees of the dog's aggressive nature. On his arrival at the pub it was after the lunchtime opening hours and the front door was locked. There was no response to his knocking, so he went round to the back and let himself in through the large delivery gate. The next thing he knew was that he was lying on his back in Woking hospital with several bite wounds and a mild case of concussion. The dog had attacked him from behind the door and knocked him flat on the ground where his head hit a stone. It is easy to say with hindsight that he should not have entered the premises without the

144

knowledge of the owner but he had a busy visit schedule and wanted to get to the patient as soon as practically possible. The pub landlord was later prosecuted for not keeping a dangerous dog under control but life is full of "what ifs" and it would be a very dull life if we kept our eyes firmly fixed on Health and Safety regulations and Risk Assessments. Mind you, there were no such things back in those days; we tended to rely on common sense which just occasionally let us down.

The end of the day does not signal guaranteed time for relaxation. One Christmas Eve coming back from the midnight service I was greeted by my parents, who were spending the holiday with us, saying that a distressed owner had just called to say that his dog had been hit by a car.

Who takes their dog for a walk at 12.30am on Christmas Day morning?

Well, I'll tell you. Train drivers coming off their last shift, nurses getting home after a very long day, long distance truck drivers just making it home for Christmas - these and many other working men and women work long and unsocial hours and, it they are unlucky enough to have their dog run over in the middle of the night, who am I to complain?

I used to set myself a challenge on these night calls to see if I could get from home to the surgery without passing another vehicle on the road. Even at two, three or four in the morning I never achieved my goal. The best I ever got to was two cars at about 4.30 in the morning on the four miles between our home and the Crawley surgery on my way to a dog having an epileptic fit.

Chapter 14

Clients and patients

Even in the 70s we had a fair amount of paperwork to complete. There were the tuberculin testing reports for the MAFF, the maintenance of the DDA (Dangerous Drugs Act) records, VAT returns and all the financial records of the practice. Modern practices are almost overwhelmed by the required Governmental demands for data of every kind involving the employment of dedicated book-keepers. We also had our own patient records to maintain. We kept case notes on 8" by 5" index cards and, as they became full, additional cards were added by Sellotaping the tops of the cards together. This meant that a full history of the patient was always available. We added the treatment charges on the right-hand side. Most of the entries were a mixture of longhand interspersed with acronyms such as CBC, PTS, PUO and ACL which were universally recognised by the profession. Others were restricted to the individual practice such as NAF (nothing abnormal found), QAR (quiet, alert, responsive) and ADR (Ain't doing right). Every practice had their individual dictionary of acronyms.

Then there are those that should definitely be kept "in house" like the one my partner was liable to use - PITA - meaning "pain in the arse". These are normally tucked away in the small print of the history but there was one evening surgery when it nearly landed me in a lot of trouble. A particularly demanding lady came into the consulting room where I listened to her problem. After examining the animal, I left the room to collect a drug from the store at the back. I left the case history card on the work surface beside the examination table. When I returned found her leaning over the table and twisting her head to read the card.

"Oh, Mr Arnold! I did not realise you kept such detailed case histories of your patients. I had completely forgotten about that ear infection last year. But, tell me, what do the letters PITA mean?"

Standing out large and red on the top history card, they could hardly be missed. I had to think very quickly before saying "Mrs X (I forget her name), you are one of our more valued clients and the abbreviation means Pass It To Adrian."

A very satisfied smile spread across her face while I breathed a sigh of relief and made a vow to strangle my partner later.

Sometimes, if a consultation had included a conversation about a client's family, I might make reminder notes to myself for future use. These personal comments might include such events as the

16yo son taking 'O' levels, the camping holiday in Scotland or that the client's mother not well. They meant that next time the client came in I could ask after their family which made the consultation more personal and the client would feel that bit more special and I could make a better diagnosis. An experience we all appreciate from time to time.

Occasionally I would enlist the help of the owner if their pet needed attention out of hours. The nursing staff needed their rest time as much as we did and if the client was willing, I was happy to accept their offer of help.

One such situation happened early on a Christmas Day morning when I got a call from the actor, Peter Vaughan, who played the hard man, Grouty, in the sitcom Porridge. There was nothing 'hard' about Peter who was one of our kindest clients. His dog had been chased through a barbed wire fence by an uncontrolled aggressive German Shepherd. It had suffered multiple tears across its body as it tried to escape the wire. All the injuries were fairly superficial, but it was covered in blood by the time we met at the surgery. He readily agreed to act as my theatre nurse. We anaesthetised the patient before cleaning the wounds and suturing the various tears across its body. After the operation was over, we sat and chatted over cups of coffee waiting for the patient to recover from the anaesthetic before we returned to our respective family Christmases. I think I removed about 30 sutures ten days later when the wounds had healed. Despite his 'hard man' image on the screen he was a pleasure to know.

Another celebrity from a few years earlier was not so easy to deal with. Russ Conway was a client of the Woking practice and occasionally called on us to treat one of his cats. He had won a DSM in the Navy at the end of the war and became a talented pianist with over twenty chart topping hits. Hiding beneath his show business success, he was a troubled man having to conceal his homosexuality at a time when it was still illegal. The first time I visited his home he offered me tea - or whisky if I preferred a real drink. He ushered me to a sofa and sat beside me to explain the current problem with his cat. As the story went on, I found his hand resting lightly on my knee. After a few more minutes the hand moved up and down my thigh while he kept an innocent smile on his face. Before matters became more complicated, I suggested a diagnosis requiring a drug I had in the boot of my car. This gave me an excuse to extricate myself from an embarrassing situation. I can remember him standing at the front door waving goodbye in the rear-view mirror with a sad smile still on his face. Despite escaping what might have been an awkward situation, I felt rather sorry for him.

The Eagle

There were times when I took the children with me on weekend visits. Small children can become quite stern in their manner if they feel a little apprehensive. I am reminded of this when I think of an emergency call I got one Saturday afternoon. Jen was off shopping with Kim and she had left me in charge of Tam, who must have been about five and Hamish, two. The call came from a client who rescued injured birds of prey and either nursed them to release back in the wild or give them a protected environment. One of his eagles had slipped its jesses, which are the leather ties round a hunting bird's legs, and attacked a falcon in another enclosure tearing the skin on its back.

On the way there, the children asked various questions about the patient in question.

"What's an eagle, Daddy?" asked Tam.

"It is a large bird of prey which sometimes attacks other smaller birds like the hawk it has attacked this time."

"Hawk? That's a funny name," said Tam. "How big is an eagle? Is it bigger than a hawk?"

"There are lots of different eagles. Some are the size of a big crow while others, like the golden eagle, may have wings that are six feet across."

"What do eagles eat? Do they eat grass?"

"No, they eat small animals like mice and shrews and rabbits. Golden eagles will sometimes carry off baby lambs."

This last remark caused her jaw to drop followed by a thoughtful silence.

Arriving at the home of the client, I left the children in the car outside while I attended to the patient which was a small merlin. The bird was perfectly calm under its hood. While the owner gently held its body, I injected local anaesthetic into the torn skin and stitched it with fine catgut. The whole operation took less than ten minutes at the end of which I asked the owner if I could bring the children in to see the birds. He was only too happy to agree, so I went out to the car to collect them.

"Would you like to come in and look at the birds?" I asked.

"Is the eagle in there?" asked Tammy.

"Yes, Tam, but it is perfectly safe."

An anxious look of doubt crossed her face. "I'd rather stay here, Daddy."

I picked up Hamish to take him in to look at the birds.

"Are you taking Hamish?" asked Tam in a horrified voice.

"Yes, as I said, it is perfectly safe."

"Well, keep a jolly tight hold on him," she told me in very stern terms.

I think she had visions of the eagle carrying Hamish off over the rooftops of Crawley. I led Hamish into the house where the owner brought in the eagle on his gloved wrist. The leather hood over its head fascinated Hamish who pointed in excitement at the bird saying "Birdie got a hat on! Birdie got a funny hat." It was a very relieved Tammy who saw us emerge from the house apparently unscathed.

Horse work

Night visits can be difficult in urban areas with intermittent street lighting. But when you get a request at two in the morning to attend a wounded horse in the middle of an isolated field divided by strands of barbed wire, you need a powerful torch as well as the car's headlights. The distraught owner had called to say three geldings from a neighbouring field had chased her mare through several sections of barbed wire. It was Spring when hormones flowed stronger even in castrated ponies. She was tangled up in a web of wire and bleeding badly. Just before she rang off, she mentioned the mare did not like men. It all sounded as if I had something of a challenge ahead of me.

Driving across the muddy field, I found the owner trying to reassure the terrified mare that all would be well. Twisted strands of barbed wire wrapped the poor animal so tightly that they prevented even the mare's strongest efforts to escape. Her struggles only tore the skin even deeper. I was lucky in that she had collected a small collection of friends and neighbours to calm the pony down. A couple of the small paddocks had rudimentary shelters and the only lighting available came from the car headlights. Unfortunately there was no way that the horse would allow a man anywhere close enough to cut away the wire, never mind repair the multiple tears to the skin.

One of the many items found in a vet's car boot would be a set of casting ropes. Using a complicated system of a loop round the neck and further loops around the lower limbs, we can bring the animal to the ground and then truss it up to allow treatment to begin. This is easier said than done and none of the onlookers knew how to help when a voice piped up from the back of the small crowd. "Would you like a casting team, mate?"

I could not believe what I was hearing but it was music to my ears. For many generations local blacksmiths used to call on a group of friends to cast a difficult horse. I had thought those days had gone with the horse-drawn carriage. It turned out that the caller had been a blacksmith but had converted his skills to repairing cars. He was still in touch with his casting team and, sure enough, within 40 minutes, six burly men appeared out of the night. I was giving them instructions when one of them laid a gentle hand on my shoulder and suggested that I stood back while they got on with the job. Each man knew his position and his task so within a few minutes the horse was lying quietly on the ground and I could get to work with my wire cutting shears. It was about two hours later that we untied the horse and led it to a dilapidated shed with something like 60 or 70 stitches in her sides. The casting team all came and shook my hand saying they had never had so much fun in the past 30 years. Great teamwork.

Equine work can vary from the mundane to the highly specialised. As general practitioners in a semi-urban environment, our work largely comprised the former. Returning to the surgery after lunch one day I found the one visit not claimed by other members of the team - the pony case! It was a few miles away, so I took the opportunity during the drive to make a mental analysis of our average horse owner. She would be aged between 12 and 15. Being in hock to her parents to the value of about £100 for the cost of the undistinguished pony, she could only graze it on tin cans, broken glass and barbed wire in a local paddock. She could meet me there anytime between 1.30pm and 2.15pm on a weekday or after 5pm on a Saturday and she could pay off my bill at about 50p a week. It was at this point I decided that we could do without our equine clients.

If you think this might be an exaggeration I can recall one Welsh pony stabled in the garage of a semi-detached council house in Gossops Green, Crawley where the only grazing available was the patch of grass at the back of the house about half the size of a small tennis court. To my mind, doting on a pony stabled in the middle of a council estate borders on cruelty.

In Crawley we had no farm clients. It was a semi-urban environment and those few remaining farms had used the same veterinary practices for generations and were slow to change allegiances. There were several horse owners with a variety of equine patients from the three day eventers through the fashionable hunter to the child's pony. Paul Scammell suffered an unfortunate incident involving a horse visit when he was on duty one weekend. The terrified owner of a New Forest pony had called him out to rescue the animal which had fallen through the rotted wooden cover of a septic tank in the field. The pony was about six feet down thrashing about in a deep pool of slurry. Having called the fire brigade, they were only too happy to supply slings and lifting gear but they baulked at having to get down and dirty in the pit to attach the slings to the terrified animal. They left it to Paul to get into the pit. He stripped off as many clothes as he could while preserving his decency from the growing crowd of onlookers and climbed down into the slurry chamber. Having attached the canvas slings around the terrified animal, the firemen - they weren't called firefighters then - hoisted it to safety to the applause of the onlookers. When we met on the Monday morning, he was still not best pleased at having to take four baths to remove as much of the staining as he could.

Not quite on the subject of horses, but closely related, was a call out to meet the new owners of a pregnant donkey at a field occupied by four other donkeys at 4.30pm on a Saturday afternoon. I arrived about 10 minutes early so had time to lean on the five-bar gate and watch the donkeys grazing the paddock. When the owners eventually arrived I asked them which donkey was theirs.

"That one over there with a red head collar on," the excited owners replied. Unfortunately I had bad news for them.

"I'm afraid it's not pregnant," I said.

"How can you tell from this distance?" came the shocked reply.

"Because no pregnant donkey urinates from that area of its body which that one did ten minutes ago."

Someone had sold them a male donkey - albeit a rather woolly one.

The Rabies Case

On some days veterinary life is anything but normal. One of those days started quietly one Thursday morning when I was taking morning surgery in Crawley. The telephone rang, and the receptionist put the call through to the consulting room. It was the Crawley Police station. In those days of more policemen and fewer vets we got to know each other over the years and, this time, it was the desk sergeant, Dave Griggs.

"Morning, Mr Arnold. We've got a case of rabies here at the station. Can we bring it round to you?"

"No, you certainly cannot!" I said. "I'm not having a certifiable disease on the practice premises. Dave, just tell me you have got a sick dog but do not mention the 'R' word."

"Well, I'm sorry," he said, "but this is the nearest thing to a case of rabies I've ever seen. You should see it. It's staggering about, rolling its eyes and a whole load of saliva is pouring from its mouth."

"Dave, if you mention rabies one more time you will regret it, believe me. I will have to report it and lots of public health legislation will kick in. None of which will do your career much good. Just tell me you want me to look at a sick dog."

"Honestly, Adrian, it really does look like rabies."

"You've done it now, Dave. I will have to report this to the DVO." (DVO meaning the Divisional Veterinary Officer.)

"So can I bring it round?"

"You can bring it in a police van so long as it is firmly secured inside the van. You must park outside on the road. Do not, and I repeat 'Not', under any circumstances, come into the car park."

Ten minutes later, after I had notified the DVO of the reported case of rabies, a police van pulled up on the road outside the surgery. Two constables opened the back doors to reveal a salivating, incoordinate, wild-eyed German Shepherd dog in the back of the vehicle.

"How long have you been chasing that dog round Three Bridges?" I asked.

"Oh, about 20 minutes," said one. "Anyway, how did you know we had found it in Three Bridges?"

"Because that dog's name is Prince, he has got severe arthritis in both hips. He's 14 years old. I've been treating him for the past six years and to the best of my knowledge he has never been out of the country. He hasn't got rabies, he's totally exhausted and frightened."

"So that's all right then. We can leave him with you and you can get him back home."

"No-o-o - it's not as easy as that. As I told Dave Griggs, I have reported it as a case of suspected rabies and an emergency investigation team are already on their way from Guildford. You have to take the dog back to the station."

As soon as the investigation team arrived at the police station, the full might of bureaucracy came into force and they put the whole building into quarantine. They allowed no-one either in or out.

One man, who had only dropped in to ask for directions, was held in the station until they lifted the quarantine four hours later. They brought a mobile police incident van over from Horsham. They passed telephone wires through the window to maintain communication with the public. I presumed that poor Dave was getting a roasting from his superiors for the chaos that had descended on the station.

By this time we were well behind with the day's work so, leaving the others to catch up with the consultation clients, I set off on the round of visits. It was about 3.45pm by the time I got back to the surgery, and Liz, the receptionist, told me she had been fielding calls from the editor of the local newspaper editor. His last call finished with the threat that if I hadn't contacted him by 4.00pm he would print what he had got on the rabies story. Once I had a cup of coffee in my hand, I gave him a call.

"Oh, thanks for ringing back. What can you tell me about this case of rabies?" he said.

"First of all, it isn't rabies but, more importantly, I want you to tell me what you were going to print if I had not got back from my visits in time to make this call?"

"That doesn't matter now I've got you on the phone?"

"It matters to me," I said. "Please read out what you would print and then I'll tell you what I know."

He huffed and puffed a bit before reading out the proposed article in which he had got several facts about rabies completely wrong. I could just about forgive him his lack of veterinary knowledge, but he had got the name and address of the owners wrong as well as the name and sex of the dog.

"Doesn't accuracy mean anything to you members of the newspaper profession?" I asked. He was a little unhappy with that comment but thanked me for the more accurate information.

I have had a questioning belief in reported news ever since.

Gypsy Foal

Sometimes a simple request for help can have unexpected consequences. One Sunday morning I got a call from an anxious motorist. He had seen a badly injured foal in the middle of a field where a group of gypsies grazed their animals but there was no-one else about to help. When I arrived at the field, I found the foal, barely a week old, suffering multiple injuries which looked as though they had been caused by being stamped on by a much heavier horse. I was almost certain that the culprit was the large stallion standing in the corner of the field away from the other horses. Both hind legs and one foreleg of the foal were broken with the fractured bones protruding through the skin. There was only one kindness I could perform which was to put it out of its misery. Since there was still no sign of the owners, I loaded the body into the boot of the car.

Throughout the day, news of the injured foal spread like a wildfire, and we became inundated with calls from concerned animal lovers. The eighteenth call was different. It was from the gypsies who had returned to find their foal missing and they were angry. Threats of lawsuits followed arguments about whether the injuries could have been repaired. I offered to let them come down to the surgery to view that extent of the injuries to the foal. That only resulted in the threat of "Oh, don't you worry, mate. We'll be down and you will regret it."

The call ended with promises of violence towards me and my family.

I have spoken before about our good relationship with the local police so I rang them to say I thought someone had threatened me. Nothing further happened until the next morning when I arrived at the surgery to find the wooden railing along the front of the property smashed into pieces to form a pile of firewood in the middle of the car parking area. Gazing at this potential bonfire were two policemen.

"Mornin', Mr Arnold. We gather someone has threatened you with GBH," said the first copper with a slight smile on his face. "Well, we are here to provide protection - armed if necessary. We thought a machine gun up on that corner of the building with a missile launcher on the other side would do the trick!"

This light-hearted banter reduced any remaining worries I had to normal. After a cup of coffee we decided that the gypsies had probably done their worst and putting it all down to experience was the most practical course of action.

Surgical Triumphs and Disasters

When I first considered veterinary medicine as a career it was operative surgery that attracted me more than the medical diagnosis. There is something very satisfying about taking something broken or deformed and putting it right. As Roger Massey once said to me "In medicine, your patients get better in spite of what you do whereas, with surgery, they get better because of what you do." There is a certain element of truth in this and it took a few years in practice for me to appreciate the challenging detective work needed to make a medical diagnosis before treatment could begin. Veterinary patients will tell you the truth, nothing but the truth but not necessarily, the whole truth. The owners, on the other hand, are very adept at misleading you both intentionally and otherwise.

To the best of my recollection I have only lost two patients on the operating table. Others have died later but only two during the actual surgery. The most painful loss was that of one of our own dogs. Mippitt, our corgi, was in difficulty giving birth to her first litter because the size of a deformed monster pup was preventing its passage through the birth canal. She was a lovely dog who came from a long line of champions bred by one of our best breeder clients in Woking. Their only drawback was a dangerous vulnerability to anaesthesia. These were the days when we induced anaesthesia with barbiturates and maintained it with a mixture of nitrous oxide, oxygen and Halothane. We did not know it at the time but it was an extreme sensitivity to barbiturates that caused the problem.

The operation all started off perfectly normally, and I delivered three healthy pups together with the monster. I had just finished closing the muscle layers when she suddenly stopped breathing and despite all our attempts to resuscitate her with artificial respiration, intra-cardiac adrenalin and heart massage, we lost her. Many years later more sophisticated induction anaesthetics replaced barbiturates and increased the safety margins in veterinary surgery.

Jen and I hand-reared the three surviving pups by feeding them every two hours. (I say 'Jen and I' but it was invariably Jen who took on the responsibility.) We kept two, Butch and Dumbo, and sold Billy, the third pup, to our next-door neighbours but the whole episode knocked my confidence badly.

The Hamster

On a brighter note there have been some very satisfying successes. Towards the end of a morning surgery in Crawley, a kindergarten teacher brought in a young hamster which had been dropped by one of her pupils. She was almost certain it had broken a hind leg and, sure enough, a gentle examination confirmed a fractured femur (thigh bone).

"Is there anything you could do about it?" she asked rather apprehensively.

"I'm afraid not," I replied. "We do not have the equipment never mind the expertise to repair such an injury."

"Oh dear! Little Jimmy will be heartbroken."

Something in me relented, and I suggested that she left the hamster with me and I would think about the problem. With morning surgery finished and, drinking my mug of coffee, I had an internal conversation with myself.

'What would you do if it was a cat?'

'I'd pin it - but I haven't got a pin that small.'

'Yes, you have. You could use a hypodermic needle.'

'But the tissues are so small I wouldn't be able to see the structures well enough.'

'You've got a jeweller's eyeglass at home you could use that.'

'What about the anaesthesia?'

'Your partner is a brilliant anaesthetist so leave that problem to him.'

So we got on with it. It all went like a dream and I had the great pleasure in phoning the teacher and telling her the good news. I can remember that we charged the school 17/6d (87½p today). But my true payment arrived about ten days later when a large manila envelope thudded through the letter box. Inside were seventeen letters from the kindergarten class thanking us for our treatment of Snowy, the hamster. The best one came from Jimmy who wrote 'Dear Mister Vetman, thank you for mending Snowy's leg. I promise I won't drop him ever again. Love from Jimmy.'

It was worth its weight in gold that letter.

Some surgery is dramatic while other procedures are simple but relieve a lot of suffering. Several times I have been presented with a dog carrying a hind leg as if it was broken. Often we can put this right by using simple manipulation because the cause is a dislocated knee cap or patella. By stretching the leg out straight and gently easing the knee cap back into the groove of the femur it restores the leg to normal much to the delight and astonishment of the owners. Unfortunately this kind of magic rarely lasts. The original cause of the dislocation remains. There has been some stretching of the ligaments and the groove is too shallow to keep the patella in place. It is a hereditary condition which affects several small breeds and needs more complex surgery to correct permanently.

The owners of another patient thought I performed a piece of surgical magic on their Jack Russell. They had brought it in for euthanasia as it was dragging a huge tumour along the ground so much that it had become torn and infected. It rather surprised them when, after examining the patient, I said I thought I could remove the growth. It was in fact a very large lipoma which is a benign fatty tumour which rarely, if ever, spreads to other parts of the body. Some animals have more than one lipoma lying under the skin. After we removed the tumour, we weighed it. It touched the scales at 14 pounds. We then weighed the dog which now weighed in at 12½ pounds. In effect we had removed the dog from the tumour. It left the surgery somewhat light-footed.

The real question was why had the owners left it so long before taking it to a vet? The poor animal must have been dragging this rotting, infected mass around for months if not years. It turned out they had delayed bringing it to the surgery because they were certain I would tell them that there was nothing I could do and the kindest course of action would be to put it to sleep. This was an example of the fear that many people have of cancer, the big "C".

We all know many forms of cancer are fatal but our innate negativity prevents us from seeing the thousands of people who have made full recoveries from the condition. Not all cancers are the same, pancreatic, bone and liver cancers still have poor prognoses but, despite huge strides are being made in the humane treatment of many other forms of the disease, we still dread the word.

One of the most difficult questions I was often asked is "Could you have done something if we had brought him/her earlier?" Take the example of mammary tumours in the dog. In many cases we can remove these at an early stage, without questionable radio- and chemo-therapies, resulting in a full recovery.

The important words here are "at an early stage." If they are left alone, mammary tumours will continue to grow and spread to other parts of the body rendering the chances of any form of recovery almost nil. So when I am asked that question by the owners of a 9-year-old spaniel bitch who had seen a small growth grow larger and finally spread to the lungs, how should I answer that question?

The honest answer is "Yes. If you had brought her when you first noticed the lump, I would probably been able to save her life." But these people are grieving, there are tears running down their cheeks, they cannot string two or three words together without choking. Do I rub salt in the wound with the honest answer?

I can't.

I reply in dishonest platitudes to remove some of their grief and tell them the outcome was inevitable. Unfortunately, this well-meaning dishonesty has repercussions.

Perhaps a couple of years later they may be having supper with some friends who ask them what the vet said about their dog's cancer because their own dog is showing a small lump on its tummy. "Oh, he said there was nothing he could have done." So it denies another pet potentially life-saving treatment because I tried to be kind and not tell the truth.

The Iguana

I have mentioned previously that the consulting vet cannot anticipate the species of his next patient. An evening surgery in the Crawley practice demonstrated this fact perfectly when a gentleman brought in a long cardboard box containing a medium-sized iguana.

"So what's the problem?" I asked.

"She's off her food. Won't eat a thing."

I should confess at this point that I know little about iguanas despite reading Zoology as a Part 2 at university. But I had a look at the conjunctivae, the lining of the eyeball and its socket, and they seemed nice and pink. Stethoscope sounds from the chest suggested no problems there but, when I felt the abdomen, the intestines were obviously empty. Because food has to go in through the mouth, I opened its jaws and there was the problem staring me in the face. A large, perfectly round, tumour was pressing the tongue hard up against the roof of the mouth preventing the passage of any food. Being perfectly round and smooth, the chances were that the growth was benign so if I could remove it the problem should resolve itself. I showed it to the owner who asked if I could do anything about it.

"I can try," I replied not quite knowing how. "Leave it with me and I will have a think about it."

The problem was that I had never anaesthetised an iguana before so I looked the subject up in the textbooks. These informed me that there are two methods of anaesthetising iguanas - either by using Halothane by mask, our usual anaesthetic, or by putting it in the fridge overnight. We tidied up the fridge sufficiently to accommodate the reptile and left for the night.

The next morning we were relieved to find the patient still alive, stiff as a board but breathing very slowly. My partner wafted a mixture of oxygen and Halothane towards the rather wooden victim while I prised open its tight jaws. A small scalpel blade run round the base of the tumour allowed it to pop out quite easily looking like a white table tennis ball. Small catgut sutures repaired the lining of the mouth and the job was done. Iguanas are cold-blooded creatures and its heartbeat had slowed dramatically in the fridge so there was hardly any blood loss at all. We put it back in its cardboard box and placed it on the central heating boiler. By mid-afternoon the patient had recovered sufficiently to tuck into a small meal of lettuce leaves and a few grapes.

Another challenging piece of surgery had a very different, and sadder, end. The owner, a man of about thirty five, brought in his daughter's pet rabbit which had been shot in the back by some idiots with an air gun. We admitted it and X-rays showed the pellet embedded in the spine where it was pressurising the spinal cord causing paralysis in the hind legs. The owner asked us to try to remove the pellet hoping the paralysis might resolve itself. Initially, the operation was technically a success, but it still took three days before we saw voluntary movement return to the hind legs. Every evening the owner had visited the rabbit after work to look for improvement and it delighted him to see early signs of progress. He had purposely kept his daughter away for fear of upsetting her even further if the operation failed. After a week the hind legs were getting much stronger despite marked incoordination but we had hopes that, in time, this would also improve. The rabbit seemed comfortable and eating well so the whole family came to see the patient after surgery on a Saturday morning. The man and his daughter were happy to see the progress but there was a completely different reaction from the mother.

She turned on me and accused me of prolonging cruelty to her daughter's pet and insisted that we put the animal down immediately. Husband and daughter turned to her in shock but, for all their arguments and pleading, she was adamant until, reluctantly, the husband agreed to his wife's demands and we put the rabbit down. I felt completely gutted as the parents left with their daughter in floods of angry tears. To this day I am still not sure where the law stands in a case of this kind.

Scary Times

Most occupations carry the risk of injury. The emergency services are an obvious example but even the office commuter can be run down by a drunken driver and the veterinary profession is no different. One can take reasonable precautions to avoid injury but there will always be the danger that comes out of the blue. I could describe my work at Whipsnade Zoo as potentially dangerous but, with the experience of the keepers and the heightened sense of awareness, most accidents could be pre-empted and therefore avoided.

During a visiting session one ordinary morning in Woking I attended a large hunter gelding called London at the military stables in Brookwood. The lady owner had noticed some early signs of lameness. She led the horse out of the loose box into the yard and turned him to face me. Without warning, the horse reared up and flashed his near side hoof past my right ear. Even today I can still feel that wind as it whistled past my head and just caught my shoulder. The owner seemed unsurprised by this attack. She simply turned to the animal and said "Naughty London! Mr Arnold does not want to play this morning."

On other occasions you will be aware of potential danger. It was at one lunchtime when the police called me out to attend a house in Old Woking where the owner's dog was preventing her from entering the property. On my arrival I was met by two officers who were both looking a little shaken. One of them had had his uniform sleeve torn to large shreds. It hung over his hand which was bleeding rather freely. First things first, I cleaned up his wounded hand and applied a simple dressing before suggesting that he took himself off to hospital. It was only after I had finished applying this first aid that I noticed the owner of the dog. She was a diminutive lady who I recognised immediately as a client and realised what the problem would be. This lady owned a very large Pyrenean Mountain Dog over which she had no control. Put plainly, it was a vicious animal. She had been out shopping in the town and the dog had prevented her from coming in the front door by snarling, barking and baring its teeth. She had called the police for help. After suffering injury in their attempts to capture the dog, they decided that they needed professional help and called me.

This situation required a certain amount of forethought and planning. My theory was that the dog was defending its territory and that it would be at its most aggressive at the threshold to the property. If I entered the property without the dog's knowledge, it might show less aggression if it found me inside the house. Nice in theory but would it work in practice?

There was only one way to find out.

By this time a small crowd had gathered on the pavement so I persuaded two of the onlookers to go round to the back and hammer like hell on the back door to attract the dog's attention. Once I was sure it was barking loudly at the other end of the house, I slipped in through the front door and called it by name which was, rather inevitably, Samson. My only protection was my veterinary case which I held in front of me as a shield. The dog came bounding through the house towards me and

160

my adrenalin levels went through the roof. Showing every sign of an impending attack he eventually stopped about three feet in front of me - but he did stop. That was the first part of the problem solved but there was still a long way to go.

For all my planning and forethought, I had forgotten to take a lead in with me. I would have to deal with that problem later after I had calmed the dog down. In a quiet but firm voice I spoke to Samson telling him how good he was; how well he had guarded the house; that his owner missed him; assured him I would not hurt him and every other reassurance I could think of. After five minutes I was in danger of running out of things to say and there was no reduction in his aggressive behaviour. I recited every bit of poetry I had ever learnt, every song, ballad and hymn that crossed my mind. It even got to the point when I was telling him nursery rhymes. Slowly, ever so slowly, he calmed down, and I began to hope I could win this battle of wills. After some twenty minutes I called through the front door to the owner.

"Mrs Jamieson, where is Samson's lead?"

"It is hanging on the hook on the back door," she replied.

This meant I had to get past the dog to get to the back door. This took another fifteen minutes of monotonous talk to the dog but I slowly moved past the huge animal which took up most of the floor space in the small hall. After another 10 minutes I had got the lead on him and led him out of the front door.

The owner and I had agreed before my entering the house that it was time to put the dog down as it was a danger both to her and other people. Once outside I passed the handle end of the lead between a cast iron drainpipe and the wall of the house. Then it was just a matter of pulling the dog's neck hard against the solid pipe so he was in no position to bite me. Then I gave him a lethal injection of pentobarbitone directly into the heart. He was dead within seconds and I began to breathe normally for the first time in over an hour.

Danger will comes when you least expect it and especially if you are tired. At the end of a long day and an even longer evening surgery an owner asked me to examine his dog. I had met this dog before and knew that he was quick with his teeth. I told the owner to keep a firm grip on his head while I went to take its temperature. As I lifted its tail, it turned and bit me through the hand.

"I told you to keep a good hold on his head," I muttered through gritted teeth.

"What's your problem? It's only a bite. I thought you vets got used to getting bitten."

No! Getting bitten is not something a vet gets 'used to.!

There will be other times when you know the job will be scary before you start. Another night call came from the police at about ten on a wet November evening. Someone had reported a dog injured on the main railway line just outside Colchester. Could I meet the attending officers at the Ipswich Road rail bridge? We lived about 8 miles away at the time so it took a while to reach the scene. A large Golden Labrador had slipped his collar and run down the embankment just before a train came down the main London line and hit him. We could see the dog from the bridge about 150 yards down the track. One of the coppers offered to lead me down the steep slope of the railway cutting with his torch. Slipping and sliding our way down the steep slope to the track, we found the dog with one hind leg almost completely amputated and in considerable pain. After giving it a heavy dose of Pethidine to dull the pain, I got a temporary pressure bandage on the leg. The gap between the track and the embankment was narrow, so the policeman carried my case while I staggered after him with the dog in my arms. We were about 20 yards short of the slope up to the bridge when the Norwich to London express came hurtling past us. We both pressed ourselves hard against the muddy bank to avoid the suction effect of the passing train. It was a scary experience, and it took time before our adrenalin levels lowered sufficiently for us to complete the climb up the bank to the car.

Veterinary surgeons' cars were invariably filthy both inside and out from transporting injured and sick patients inside and decorating the external bodywork with every conceivable form of mud, slurry, straw and other unmentionable excrement while visiting isolated farms. This case only added to the mess in the back of the car but, I am pleased to say that, after amputating the injured leg, the dog made a complete recovery to enjoy life for many more years.

Glaucoma dog

Sometimes we have to make very difficult decisions like telling an owner that the moment had come to put their beloved pet out of its misery. This can be even more of a problem when that pet is the last remaining link to a late partner. It hurts like hell but it may be the last kindness you can do for the animal - to relieve it of its pain and suffering.

At other times you can get it wrong. One such case was a middle-aged Beagle dog which had developed glaucoma in the left eye. Treatment for glaucoma at that time was limited to using medication to delay its progress but eventually increasing pain in the eye demanded surgical removal of the eye. Unfortunately, glaucoma in one eye almost always predicts the development of the same condition in the other eye at some future date. It is a hereditary condition in a number of breeds. In this case palliative treatment no longer controlled the pain, and I removed the eye. I warned the owners of the likelihood of the other eye being affected in the next year or two.

It was about a year later when the owners presented the dog with glaucoma in the right eye and, despite diuretic therapy, the condition quickly deteriorated and I had to recommend euthanasia.

"Please, Mr Arnold, would you remove the eye? We are both sure that even being blind he can still live a happy life."

"You cannot ask me to do that," I said. "I understand your grief but I have to consider the dog and I believe he would suffer too much with the inevitable blindness."

The debate went back and forth for about 10 minutes before I relented but with conditions. I agreed to remove the second eye on the condition that the owners signed a letter dictated by me. This said that they agreed to allow me to assess the dog's quality of life within 6 weeks following the operation. Then if, in my opinion, and my opinion alone, I felt that the dog was suffering I had their written permission to put it down. They agreed to the compromise.

I could not wait the full 6 weeks and I called at their home, unannounced, 4 weeks later. The lady answered the door and greeted me with a smile.

"Freddie! Come and see Mr Arnold."

The dog came bounding round the corner, banged into my legs with his tail going like a paddle on steroids. Having met me, he dashed off and came back with a tennis ball which he dropped at my feet. This was one seriously happy dog. The owner invited me in and told me they had invented a game for him. She took me into the dining room and tossed the ball into the forest of chair and table legs. The dog raced in, barely touching any of the woodwork, and retrieved the ball.

"That is wonderful," I said.

"Oh, no! That's not the game. Give me a hand to move the table around."

We pulled the chairs out and turned the table through 90 degrees before replacing the furniture. All the time the dog's front legs were pumping up and down in excitement. The owner then

163

threw the ball into the new arrangement of the table and the dog dived in. He crashed into every piece of wood in his way, but he found the ball and brought it out. After about eight retrievals the dog had identified the new layout of the furniture and hardly touched a thing as he collected the ball. Freddie taught me a great lesson that day - that there are few situations that are totally impossible. Since that day whenever I have faced a problem I think of Freddie. He lived very happily for another 5 years.

All night work

Even if I got a couple of evening or night calls I could count on getting some sleep during the rest of the night but there have been about half a dozen occasions when I never got close to our bed. All but one of these calls involved births of some kind or other - usually canine. One such case came in at about ten on a November evening just as we were thinking of turning in. The caller was one of our breeder clients whose Basset Hound bitch was having some whelping problems.

When I arrived at the house, the breeder led me by torchlight down the garden to the whelping shed at the bottom. It was a well-built and waterproof building with its own heating system. The bitch had whelped four pups over the previous three hours but was tiring and there were several more pups left to come. Having examined her and finding no obstruction in the birth canal, I gave her an injection of oxytocin. This is a naturally occurring hormone which increases uterine contractions reducing the mother's need to strain quite as much. Sure enough, the fifth pup arrived five minutes later. So we settled down on the floor with a cup of coffee and waited for the next arrival. This one came forty minutes later a little before midnight. The bitch was not distressed, but she had almost given up straining. A further examination followed by another injection resulted in puppy number six.

It was at half-past two in the morning when we were finishing our fourth mug of coffee that a knock came on the door of the whelping shed and the owner's husband stood in the doorway in his dressing gown. Still half asleep, he told his wife that her Weimaraner bitch had begun labour in the kitchen. She was three days earlier than expected. He then went back to bed. By this time the Bassett had delivered the eighth pup but the effects of each subsequent oxytocin injection were getting weaker. I was contemplating the need to get her back to the surgery and deliver the remaining pups by Caesarean.

To cut a long night short, I left the house at 7.30 the next morning to grab some breakfast before starting morning surgery. The Bassett had delivered nine puppies with one still to come, the same number as the Weimaraner had produced in two hours. Having finished morning surgery, I went back to deliver the tenth Bassett pup leaving the breeder with nineteen puppies on her hands.

Airline work

Crawley was heavily dependent on nearby Gatwick airport for its economic health and there were the odd times when even we vets benefited from work coming from the airport. The first time they asked us to do veterinary work for the airline industry was when Caledonian Airways asked us to update their animal loading manual. Caledonian was an independent charter airline which operated many flights both to Europe and across the Atlantic. Each airline had its own loading manual which was a very weighty document running to hundreds of pages that had to be kept up to date at regular intervals. We learnt that it was unofficial practice among the airlines to share the information in their respective manuals. So Pan Am would get hold of a copy of the British Airways manual which they had copied from Lufthansa who had previously copied it from Air France. So one children's game of musical chairs mutated into another, Chinese Whispers. The end result was that lot of the manuals made little sense.

Caledonian wanted to revise their animal loading manual. We agreed to look into the problem and the executives invited us to their Gatwick office where they presented us with their current manual. They asked us to give them some indication of how long the task would take. We said we would call them when we had read through the document. On returning to the surgery it only took us about twenty minutes to realise that the manual in its current form was a load of useless rubbish bordering on the absurd. During the transposition from one manual to another by non-medical staff, drug names had been so badly copied that they could not be found in any pharmacy. We thought "Petaline" probably meant Pethidine but we could not be certain and there was certainly no sign of Petaline in any pharmacopoeia that we consulted. Then there was the problem of the vaccines and antiserums listed in the medical pack. Were they kept in a fridge on the aircraft? Because, if not, after a couple of transatlantic flights they would be of no more use than tap water. We learnt that only a few passenger jets carried a fridge. One of which was a VC10 but Caledonian flew mainly BAC One-Elevens or Boeing 707s neither of which had refrigeration facilities..

Finally, the recommended size, quantity and type of bandages, swabs and other dressings would only have treated a small cut on a spaniel's leg never mind an injured horse. Having read through most of the paperwork we rang the airline to say the manual would have to be completely re-written.

"Could we do it in two days because that was when the manual was due to go to the printers?"

We told them there was no way we could complete the job within two days. So they went ahead and printed the old information anyway. We just hoped that the specialist livestock carriers took greater responsibility.

The Illegal Kitten

The next call to the terminal was from the airport police on a Saturday afternoon. They had confiscated an illegally imported kitten that some tourist was bringing home from a holiday abroad. The media was full of ill-informed rabies stories and the police wanted a Veterinary Inspection Officer (VIO) to attend the case. A policeman met me at the main entrance and escorted through to the departure area. The tourist had smuggled the kitten in from Spain and had spent two days in London before catching a return home to the States. An observant Customs officer had noticed the animal wriggling under the passenger's sweater and called the police.

The kitten was in a very sorry state. It was very thin, anaemic and covered in the scabs of mange over its head and neck and spreading further down the body. This type of mange is highly infectious and there was no assurance that it was not carrying other diseases. The owners were not prepared to pay the costs of quarantine and prolonged treatment so I had to put the suffering animal down. There remained the problem of the body.

No-one at the airport was prepared to take responsibility for its disposal so the police decided that, as the VIO, the responsibility was mine. To prevent any contamination, I asked for four thick plastic bags in which to wrap the body. The only bags they could find were those from the duty free shop. I was being escorted from the departure area by the policeman when he got an urgent call on his radio.

"Sorry, sir," he said. "I've got to take this call. Can you find your own way out?"

There was little I could do except agree so I found myself walking through the Customs Hall carrying a duty free wrapped article which caught the eye of an observant Customs officer.

"What have you got in that bag, sir?" he asked.

"You really don't want to know, officer."

"I'm afraid it is my job to know. Please unwrap the package."

"I'm sorry I can't do that. These bags contain the body of a dead cat."

He thought I was pulling his leg and became even more officious until I persuaded him to call the police to verify my story. It took about half an hour to locate the policeman who confirmed my version of the events. I finally got it back to the surgery where I locked it away for the local veterinary investigation centre to remove the following Monday.

Bad debtors

For most of the years when I was in practice there were no debit cards and few people carried an American Express card. Quite a few of our clients did not even own a bank account. They lived from one week's pay packet to the next. Only about half the accounts were paid within the month. Payment at the time of the consultation was a rare event. As a result, bad debts were a recurring problem.

We sent out three consecutive monthly accounts before deciding whether to take any action over a debt. If the amount was worth it, the first action would be to make a list of the worst debtors, cancel an afternoon surgery and drive round the area visiting the non-payers. This was almost invariably a fruitless exercise as payments were rarely collected. It was no coincidence that, in Crawley, so many bad debtors lived in at an address named Crook Close.

The range of excuses stretched from the mundane to the unbelievable. First, they would tell us they would come in and pay the bill the next day. They never did. Then, we had got the wrong address and their name wasn't Smith, it was Jones or that the Smiths had moved away three weeks ago. Next, it wasn't their dog it was their husband's, and he was away on an oil rig and finally, they had never owned a dog or cat in their lives so it couldn't be them.

One woman used the last excuse denying ever having owned a cat never mind the one we had put down for her. In this case there might have been an evidence trail. Whenever we euthanased an animal, we always got a signature on a consent form. So, on returning to the practice, I asked Liz, the receptionist, to go through the consent form file to see if we had a signed form from this lady. Sure enough, there it was in black and white.

167

I went back the next day but, before ringing the doorbell, I carefully folded the paper form so that only the signature was visible. When she opened the door, she looked at me curiously and said "Didn't I see you yesterday?"

I ignored the question and showed her the signature. "Is this your signature?" I asked.

"Yes, but what has that got to do with you?"

I unfolded the form showing the consent for euthanasia. "Then why did you sign this form when you told me yesterday you had never owned a cat?"

"Oh, THAT cat!" she said, before adding "I'll come in and pay you tomorrow."

She never did.

Having had little success with a personal visit, we had to decide whether to go to stage two which was to take them to court. Since this involved further expense we only took this route if the amount was significant. After a few weeks we would be informed of the court's ruling that the debtor had undertaken to pay off the bill at something like five shillings (25p) a week. If we were lucky, we might receive one or even two payments before they stopped. The final recourse was to send in the bailiffs. This cost even more money and usually resulted in the bailiffs reporting that there were insufficient goods to cover the debt. At this point we gave up with gritted teeth.

It is very difficult to deny pet owners treatment for their pets even when you know the likelihood of payment is slim. It may even be illegal but I am certain it borders on the unethical. I joined the profession as a vocation. I am saddened that today many members of my past profession seem to view it more as a business from which to make a large profit. But, not having seen the figures of these practices, I may be maligning them.

Some bad debtors are simply con merchants. For several weeks I had been treating a Labrador cross brought in by a nice man who brought the dog in on behalf of his disabled flatmate. He kept on forgetting to ask the dog's owner for the money to pay the bill promising to bring the money the next week. I felt that, since he was being the Good Samaritan, the least I could do was to go along with the situation. My suspicions began to grow after I had been treating the dog for six weeks with no payment forthcoming. Eventually I suggested that, since he was the last patient of the particular surgery session, I would drive him and the dog back to his flat where the owner could pay up. He agreed to the idea so we all got into the car. After driving for about five minutes towards the other side of Crawley, he turned and said "OK, you've got me. I don't have a flatmate. The dog is mine."

He had taken me in and I felt a fool.

It so happened that we were passing Crawley police station at the time and I had an idea.

"I am taking you into the police station on a citizen's arrest," I said.

That shocked him and he pleaded for leniency quoting unemployment, end of marriage, death in the family and almost anything else he could think of. I pulled into the police station car park where I suffered a fit of compassion and told him to get out and walk home while I drove back to the surgery.

It was a few weeks later when I was visiting the police station on another matter and I got to chatting to the desk sergeant. I told him about my idea of making a citizen's arrest. He pondered for a while. "That's an interesting point," he said. "He was committing fraud against you so, yes, you could have made a citizen's arrest. What is more interesting is that there is no bail allowed on a citizen's arrest. We would have had to keep him in the police cells until his case came up before the magistrates - and that might take weeks."

Chapter 15

Assistants and locums

Once the practice began to grow Paul and I decided that we needed an assistant to help with the increasing work load. We had mixed luck with our assistants. First, we had to provide them with accommodation so we bought a two-bedroom flat on the far side of town. We supplied a car and another inventory of equipment for visiting patients. We had to equip them with the captive bolt pistol for the euthanasia of larger animals, forceps to stem serious bleeding, lots of bandages of varying sizes and rolls of cotton wool. All this, on top of their salary, made for a considerable financial commitment. Some of our assistants were appreciative while others took too much advantage. One Irishman held regular drunken parties through the night irritating his neighbours who complained to us. When he left, Jen and I cleaned up the flat and found it in a revolting state with excrement on the floor and sheets bundled up around piles of vomit in the airing cupboard.

Our best assistant was our first, Judy Townsend. She had worked for a time in small animal practice in Canada and we took her on as a blind date but one which worked out happily until, after a few years, she left to join her fiancé up in Lancashire. Apart from some of the temporary locums, Judy was the best assistant we employed at Crawley. She was intelligent and caring. She adopted a stray cat called Filth, the ugliest cat you could ever imagine, who accompanied her up to Lancashire.

The next assistant who still comes to mind was Felicity, known as Flick. She was a shy girl whose leisure time was taken up by the devoted care she lavished on her two German Shepherd dogs she kept in the flat. She and I were taking evening surgery one night when I had to collect an antibiotic from the pharmacy at the back of the consulting rooms. Suddenly, an explosive argument erupted from Flick's room with heated words flying back and forth. I decided to leave the matter alone until we had finished the surgery session when I went into her room. She was sitting at the desk writing up her notes.

"Flick, what was happening in here about 20 minutes ago?" I asked.

She burst into a flood of tears.

"Come on. What's the problem?" I asked as kindly as I could and got one of the saddest replies I have heard in my life.

"My problem is" she said, as the tears ran down her cheeks, "that I don't like people,"

170

"Flick, that is so sad," I said. "But, if that is the case, you are in the wrong job. General practice is all about people. You are a good vet and there are plenty of career choices available to you that don't involve such close association with the public. There is research, industry or other lab work - but you are obviously unhappy in general practice. You need to change the direction of your career."

She later found work in a commercial laboratory.

Assistants were long-term employees but when Paul or I took a holiday, we would engage a locum in the same way he had worked in the early days of the practice. During the main holiday periods, these locums came at a premium, costing as much as £100 a day on top of their keep and accommodation. So the cost of a fortnight's family holiday which might be nearly £2000, would increase by that amount again when locum costs were added. Despite the cost we became friends with many of these itinerant vets who would step into the breach during holiday periods.

These locums came from Australia, New Zealand, Holland and South Africa working their way round the world, gaining experience before settling down to a permanent post. By this time Crawley was a four man practice and there was a constant demand for locums. Two Australian girls used to visit us regularly during the summer to fill in for staff on holiday. Robyn McKay came over to earn enough cash to play her trumpet, tour the country and play competitive hockey at county level. Her compatriot, Liz, divided her time between veterinary locum posts and leading extreme tourist trips like a double-decker bus journeys travelling from London to Kabul across unpaved terrain and various deserts. On the last trip they punctured their last spare tyre in a desert in Iran. They solved the problem by getting the carpet weavers of the area to seal the damaged tyre with silk threads - a repair which lasted for another 450 miles.

Another locum, John Birley, who had worked for us on two occasions, rang me in bed at about eleven o'clock one night having taken a locum post in the suburbs of London. He was in a quandary and seeking advice. That afternoon he had arrived at a practice which he had agreed to run during the sole practitioner's holiday. On his arrival his employer was standing on the front doorstep with his suitcase already packed. He told John that evening surgery would start in half an hour. He would find everything he needed in the consulting room and he would see him on his return in two weeks' time. Normally, a locum is at least given a tour of the practice and its facilities but, on this occasion, the vet got into his car and drove off.

Once John had explored the premises, he found that there was only one bottle of antibiotic, Streptopen. There was one pair of scissors, a scalpel handle with a couple of blades and two pairs of Spencer Wells artery forceps. He was horrified and felt he should report the owner to the Royal College for malpractice. What should he do?

"John," I said. "You have contracted to act as locum to this man so you cannot renege on that agreement. What I would suggest is that you order the bare minimum of drugs and surgical instruments you need to carry out your work and then decide whether to report him after you have finished the job."

I did not hear from him for a few years when he contacted me again on another matter. I asked him if he had reported the vet he did the locum for.

"No," he said. "His clients plainly loved him for all his limited veterinary expertise and I did not have the heart to take him away from them so I left it alone."

These locums were not just in it for the money or the travel experience, some of them were truly altruistic like one Australian, whose name I wish I could remember. He had been treating a blind client's guide dog which was suffering a critical bleed from a tumour on the spleen. The dog was too weak to survive the anaesthetic, so we contacted two German Shepherd breeders who agreed to let some of their dogs to donate blood. We collected several blood transfusion kits from Crawley hospital and began the transfusions. This had to be given slowly throughout the night. So the client and the locum spent the night on the kennel floor playing chess beside the dog. It was all very makeshift, but it worked and we successfully removed the spleen the next morning. I would love to say it all ended happily, but the dog died six months later of secondary tumours in the liver.
You can't win them all.

Continuing Education

By this time there were three of us in the practice, Paul, myself and Judy Townsend, our assistant. Discoveries and experience were expanding our knowledge of every aspect of daily life especially in the realm of veterinary medicine. This meant that, to keep up with developments, we needed to take time out to attend conferences, seminars and other teaching courses to keep up to date. Each of us undertook to attend at least one, if not, two continuing professional development

(CPD) events every year. One year it might be lectures on skin problems; the next, eyes; another, orthopaedics - they all kept us abreast of the rapid development within the profession. Later on there would be seminars on business management, legal obligations and workplace safety. As with all such training courses, their quality varied across a wide spectrum from inspiring to useless. Today CPD is demanded of all practices wishing to be registered as being up to the required standard.

One of the highlights of a small animal vet's year is the annual British Small Animal Veterinary Association (BSAVA) conference. This is held at one of the major conference centres such as Olympia, Brighton or the NEC in Birmingham. These conferences last for four days and offer a huge range of opportunities for further learning by lecture or demonstration, catching up with colleagues spread across the country and viewing the enormous trade fair which offers the latest in veterinary technology.

The Colchester practice had become one of the first practices in the country to have gone completely computerised and I was invited to give lectures on the subject at these conferences. This resulted in the foundation of the short-lived British Small Animal Veterinary Computing Association to which I was elected President. This meant several visits to other practices who were considering computerising their businesses. I think I learnt more from them than they did from me.

Chapter 16

Life outside the veterinary practice

Family Life

Both Kim and Sophie had attended the local primary school, the Franciscan Convent School, half a mile down the road from our home. One of us escorted them across the busy A264 road with its heavy commuter traffic to East Grinstead. Once across the road it was safe for them to make their own way to the school where they spent many happy days under the watchful eyes of Sister Bonaventura and Sister Annunciata. One day a school friend of theirs brought in a bone he had found in a neighbouring field. The sisters being unable to identify the discovery, Kim volunteered my services to provide the answer. It was the lower jaw of a pig.

Over the next few months, this game developed into a competition among the pupils to see who could bring in the strangest bone. Each evening on my return from the surgery there would be a small collection of bones waiting for identification. It was like a Finals examination all over again!

The girls were often happiest when playing with the animals around the house although I am not sure whether the feeling was always reciprocated. They learnt how to 'hypnotise' our small flock of six chickens. You tucked their head under a wing and, holding them in both hands with the head under the wing facing down, rocked them from side to side for a few minutes. When put down they would remain in that position for several minutes - apparently hypnotised. Our cat nearly jumped out of its skin one afternoon when it came out of the back door to be confronted by six inert chickens blocking its path.

As a 'reward' for being hypnotised, the hens would be placed on the back of the girls' bikes and cycled round the house while they clung on desperately. The hens lived in a mobile coop in the garden but they were all killed one night when a fox broke through the wire mesh. Cunning-but-cute Mr Fox has never appealed to me following that wholesale slaughter.

By this time we were employing veterinary nurses who we sometimes called out to assist with night or weekend calls. There were other times when all I needed was an extra pair of hands while dealing with an injured animal. The children seemed keen to help when I was on weekend duty. In the early days Kim spent a lot of time washing syringes while Sophie re-arranged all the change in the cash drawer. One weekend Tam and Hamish offered to help me with a post mortem of a dog. The pet had gone missing three days previously and had been found dead in a nearby wood. The children were both fascinated until I cut open the abdomen releasing a cloud of pungent gas. Hamish tells me he remembers passing out at that point while Tam simply said "It doesn't half stink, Daddy."

It turned out that someone had shot the dog in the chest with an airgun. The children became almost immune to the sights and smells of veterinary practice while hauling black plastic bags containing dead bodies to the deep freeze waiting for collection. Life and death became familiar subjects of conversation which did nobody any harm.

Hamish has accumulated several memories of which I have no recollection. Memories of me removing a tumour from a koi carp or hospitalising various jays in the stable at the back of the house. Jays are not the most common bird and I have no idea how to anaesthetise a fish and I would have thought the memory of him passing out beside the post mortem table would have stuck in my memory. Memories can be strangely elusive and we all remember things differently. All I can say is that we had a lot of fun as a family even if the circumstances were sometimes gruesome.

Breaking the partnership

As the practice grew Paul and I began to have our differences about the future direction of the business. He was happy with the three-man practice we had established while I wanted to expand the practice. Crawley was growing at a steady rate with new housing developments enlarging the town towards the west. Since we were to the east of the town, I was a little anxious that Horsham, only seven miles further west was also developing. There was a real possibility the Horsham practices may develop branch clinics on the far side of town in competition to us.

We debated this problem for at least a year until we decided that I would buy Paul out of the partnership and run it as a sole principal. Crawley had been good for both of us especially as Paul found his wife, Sue, among our clientele but it was time for us to go our separate ways. He went into the Ministry of Agriculture, Fisheries and Food (MAFF), now known as the Department for Environment, Food and Rural Affairs (DEFRA), where he worked in the Dorchester office.

Why do those in positions of power or authority feel the need to change the names of large organisations? British Airways became the dull, BA; the Post Office tried to become Consignia; Age Concern had to become Age UK while most polytechnic colleges have fulfilled their dream of becoming universities. Forgive me, these are just the grumblings of the grumpy, old man I fear I am becoming.

My first job was to find a senior assistant to replace Paul. This turned out to be David Clare. Not only did he become a very good friend, he also married our receptionist and eventually bought the practice from me when we moved to Colchester - but that was all a few years away.

After Paul left, the practice expanded to a four vet enterprise with five ancillary staff so David Clare and I established a branch surgery on the other side of the town as the original premises were becoming overwhelmed. In the middle of all this expansion my father threw an awkward spanner into the works.

Having reached the age of seventy, he decided it would be tax efficient to retire to the Isle of Man where he and my mother had done their courting and where we had spent our early childhood holidays. To take full advantage of the tax benefits, he could not continue running the farm business although he could keep ownership of the land. Please don't ask me to explain the intricacies of this financial manoeuvre because taxation law is a foreign country to me.

The upshot of these decisions was that he wanted me to go into partnership with his farm manager, John Payne, as a sleeping partner, while keeping a family eye on the business. The farm at Ulting in Essex was seventy miles away from our home and practice in Sussex but, having discussed it with Jen and David, I signed the partnership agreement.

Up to this point Dad had run the farm along experimental lines but it had generated little profit. At our first meeting John Payne and I decided to improve the profitability of the farm by eliminating some of Dad's 'vanity' projects and improving the general business practice. Within two years, three things happened that were to change our lives. First, the farm began to show a healthy profit; second, I developed an interest in farming and third, I came into a bequest which enabled me to buy a small local farm to add to the acreage still owned by Dad. The original farm was over-staffed and over-equipped so adding another 150 acres almost next door seemed a sound business investment.

Once every six weeks I would leave home at 5.30am, drive the seventy miles and arrive for breakfast at seven when the farm work was beginning for the day. John and I had known each other for twenty years and we had become good friends. He had the farming knowledge and experience while I could ask the stupid questions that sometimes challenged the established way of farming and occasionally led to profitable ideas.

As my enthusiasm for farming grew, so I questioned my role in the veterinary practice. I was thinking perhaps Paul Scammell had been right all along. Up to about two or three years previously I felt I knew 75% of my clientele by name and character but recently I realised that I knew less than 30% of the people who visited the surgery. The practice was in danger of becoming impersonal.

Over the next two years we had many family discussions about the future before deciding to move up to Essex. We would be closer to the farm while setting up a new practice. David Clare was happy to buy me out over five years which gave us an income while we established ourselves in East Anglia.

Having taken the decision to move, Jen and I set about short-listing potential towns for the new practice which included Ipswich, Sudbury and Colchester. Ipswich did not appeal to us. Sudbury was a small market town with an established practice while the three Colchester practices were all south of the town which was expanding to the north. We just had to find suitable premises for conversion to a veterinary practice.

Chapter 17

The Colchester Practice

It took over 18 months to find and convert a property to suitable veterinary premises in Colchester. We finally settled on an old vicarage within a quarter of a mile of the station. It had various advantages - the rooms were all of a good size, being close to the station it was easy to give directions, the three other practices in the town, except for one small branch surgery in a shopping parade, were all on the other side of town and it had garaging for three cars. Two of the garage spaces were integral with the house which we could incorporate into the veterinary premises while the third was a 'temporary' Marley shed. By taking this down it allowed access to the back garden which would become the car park. The original French windows to the garden offered a direct entrance to the main living room which would become the waiting and reception area. Jen and I spent most evenings preparing and painting the various rooms while employing plasterers, electricians and flooring contractors to complete the more technical work. I would describe myself as a "don't Do It Yourself person".

Walls had to be re-arranged and decorated; floors needed waterproofing while box seating in the waiting room would provide useful long-term storage space. An internal phone system, surgical equipment, pharmacy shelving and improved lighting all took time, effort and money but all this activity got the word about in the local area that a new vet practice was on the way.

As we did in Crawley, having decided on the premises, I wrote to each of the three existing practices in the town informing them of my intention to set up practice in their town. To say that their replies were varied would be a marked understatement.

From one, I received no reply at all while the second offered me an immediate partnership in his practice. It was the third practice that gave the finest response. It was a mixed practice that specialised in poultry medicine run by the senior partner, a South African, by the name of Howard Hellig. His letter ran as follows - "Dear Mr Arnold, we resent your coming but welcome to Colchester, yours sincerely,"

As a result of this letter we met for a pub lunch to discuss the veterinary potential of the growing town. He conceded that there was room for another practice and it would not impinge on the area of his clientele.

We were to meet again a few years later to discuss the growing problem of bad debts. We compared our respective lists of major debtors only to find that the same individuals appeared on both lists. There was one publican who owed us both a considerable amount of money so we decided to get our own back in an original way. We booked a table for lunch at the pub, ordered the most expensive dishes and wine and, when the bill arrived, told him we would deduct the cost from his outstanding accounts with our practices. We left with a smile on our faces while his jaw dropped towards his large waistline.

The mobile phones available at the time were heavy bricks and the reception was unpredictable. The first commercial mobile phone was the Motorola DynaTAG 8000X which offered 30 minutes of talk time, six hours standby and could store 30 numbers. It also cost over £2600. It would be several years before they became the essential accessory of today. We had to rely upon the tried and trusted method of contact between the surgery and the vet using the clients' phone numbers.

In the early days of the Colchester practice I had few clients, but I needed to visit the farm in Ulting, about 15 miles away, from time to time. I installed a Pye Telecommunications radio in my Austin Metro with a base station at the surgery which enabled us to maintain contact even if I was away from the premises. It was not the most satisfactory arrangement, but it was better than nothing. Even when we decided that mobile phones were a practical alternative, mobile coverage was still very patchy. Signals from different phone networks varied from place to place and since the practice now had four vets who lived in different localities around the town, it was a matter of making the choice that best suited everyone. Even then the phones needed to be stood upright at home to receive the signal. A phone lying down would miss a call and therefore a client's goodwill.

Family Life

The life of a veterinary general practitioner should be a vocation to care, not just for their clients and patients but also for their family - and themselves. Without the support and encouragement of Jen at my side I would never have achieved any success as a vet who, eighteen years after retirement, can still take pride in the continuing success of the two practices we set up all those years ago in Crawley and Colchester.

Once the children had graduated to secondary schools Jen investigated outlets for her own energies away from home and family. Having qualified as a children's nurse from St Christopher's College in Tunbridge Wells, she took a job in the premature baby unit at St. Thomas's Hospital in London and then worked in a Dr. Barnardo's home before taking up a post as the nanny to a family in Stock. Her brother and sister had enjoyed rather prestigious public school education thanks to various generous benefactors and scholarships but there were few financial resources left from a vicar's stipend to provide such education for an unexpected third child. Not that there weren't compensations in her family life. Of the three children, she probably became the closest to her parents. Known as Jenny Wren to her loving father who she used to tease unmercifully, it may have been through him she gained her broad altruistic streak.

She attended a course of lectures in the opportunities offered by voluntary work such as the RNIB, Marriage Guidance, Magistracy, Samaritans and other similar organisations. Our marriage was so strong that this may have been a contributing factor in her final decision to train as a Marriage Guidance Counsellor. This took the best part of two years and involved several weekend courses at the central college in Rugby. Confidentiality is essential in both veterinary medicine and marriage guidance so it came naturally to both of us to maintain the anonymity of our respective clients. Having qualified from Crawley, she continued her marriage guidance work in Colchester - even when some expensive management consultant company decreed that they should change the name to Relate. By the time she retired she had helped hundreds of couples over the course of twenty-five years. As with so many other organisations, Relate was becoming more and more bureaucratic and less personal so she looked for a different outlet for her considerable talents. She found another career on the local magistrates' bench in Sudbury.

Within a few years many of the smaller magistrate courts were being closed so that 'local' justice, the cornerstone of the magistracy service, fell by the wayside. In the end, the only magistrate courts left in Suffolk were in Ipswich and Bury St Edmunds with the local magistrate associations amalgamated into an amorphous body of strangers. The old local annual dinners held in local restaurants were supplanted by prestigious evening gatherings at impersonal Town halls. She maintained all these voluntary contributions to society while raising a family of four and making a wonderful home.

Many people tried to persuade Jen to train as a Chair of the bench but she was much happier, and more effective as a questioning 'winger', as they called the subsidiary magistrates. Chairpersons had to follow all the rules. Jen is not a follower of rules. After her capacity to love, her greatest strength is her innate common sense. As an example, the rules governing the appointment of new magistrates stated that "common sense is not an attribute to be taken into account when considering an application to become a magistrate." As a magistrate, Jen would have to hear cases where the defendant was guilty in law but a victim of society leaving her feeling unable to dispense justice.

Despite all these contributions to the community, Jen has always put family first. We are a team. If she had a late evening marriage guidance appointment with a male client, I would sit in the waiting room of the offices as a chaperone while doing practice paperwork.

Both our professions would take an emotional toll on us from time to time but we always had each other for support. Some of Jen's clients had horrendous memories of wartime evacuation. Some hosting families treated the evacuees as slaves.

Thankfully we have always had our family to restore us to normality. They were regularly quite rude to us and it was only when they became polite that we knew there was trouble ahead!

While writing this book I have asked our children for their own memories of life with a vet, marriage counsellor and magistrate for parents. Their memories are fascinating but neither Jen nor I have many recollections of the stories they came up with. This is not strange because if three siblings got together to remember an event thirty years ago, their memories would invariably contradict each other.

Kim remembers me leaving the locum's Morris 1100 in the practice car park for her to collect when she came home on the train at the weekends only to find I had left two teaspoonsful of petrol in the tank.

Hamish put my father in his place wonderfully on one occasion. He had mentioned that he was going up to Covent Garden with a few school friends, both girls and boys.

"Girl friends, heh!" he said with a slightly lecherous wink.

"No, Granddad. Just friends who happen to be girls!"

I was proud of him at that moment.

We were not quite so happy to get a reverse charged telephone call from him in Darwin airport at three in the morning saying he had run out of money on his gap year travels.

Tam was the one who got into scrapes of one kind or another. Not that the other two didn't get injured from time to time but they all got used to me reassuring them that, whatever it was, "it was all perfectly normal." Blood pouring from a cut wrist damaged by a piece of broken glass in the long grass, a fractured arm from falling out of a tree or faces cut by shards of glass from a broken windscreen - "It was all perfectly normal." The phrase has long been a feature of our family vocabulary.

The phrase reminds me of the time when Tam contracted appendicitis in about 1990. I visited her in the old Colchester hospital after the operation and found three large blood splats on the floor at the entrance to the ward. They were still there three days later! The ward was so short-staffed that she had to wheel her two drip stands to the loo in the corridor. Not a lot has changed in the NHS since then. They hung the patient's notes at the end of their beds so took I the opportunity to read them when she was asleep.

They discharged her after four days. She had only been in her own bed at home for less than an hour when Jen and I heard her shout "Mum! Dad! I've broken open!". Sure enough the skin wound had split releasing a small amount of pus so I tried to reassure her that "It was all perfectly normal" although it was anything but normal.

The GP came and took swabs, dressed the wound and prescribed antibiotics. After another five days there was no sign of improvement and I took matters into my own hands. As I have said before, nobody abuses my family or staff without consequences. I rang the consultant surgeon's secretary to tell her I was bringing my daughter in to have the wound repaired.

"Oh, you can't do that," she said. "He's doing a rectal clinic."

"I don't care if he is doing an ENT clinic, I am bringing her in now."

We sat in his waiting room for some time before the extremely irritated surgeon called us in.

"I don't care to have my clinics invaded by people who think their problem is more important than others," he said.

"You may not consider my daughter's case to be unimportant but I consider that her present wound breakdown is the result of careless operative technique."

As a consultant surgeon, he was not used to being addressed in such a manner and he bristled with anger.

"And what exactly leads you to that conclusion, Mr Arnold?"

"Because the infection has been identified as E. Coli, an intestinal bacterium, and that her appendix had burst before the operation began. This suggests that the abdomen was not flushed properly at the end of the operation."

"Ah," he smiled benevolently. "That is where you are wrong. She did not have a ruptured appendix."

"Then I suggest you take a careful look at her notes," I said quietly.

I had already seen the entry of "appendix rupture" in her notes when they had been hanging off the end of her bed.

He flashed the pages of her notes back and forth in his irritation before finding the relevant entry when he went silent for a few minutes. The atmosphere in the room was distinctly Arctic for the next half an hour as he repaired the infected wound under local anaesthetic.

It would have been nice to have had an apology but Tam and I were just happy to get back home. Recovery was uneventful after that.

Computerising the practice

Establishing the Colchester practice was a little easier than setting up the Crawley business despite doing it on our own instead of with a partner. We had the benefit of an income from the Crawley practice to tide us over the early months although the lack of a partner meant that I was on duty 24/7, 365 days a year for the first two years. That is not completely true because after six months, I persuaded a veterinary practitioner, John Waller, to hold the fort for me on Wednesday afternoons and evenings.

Veterinary practitioners were a curious breed. They had no academic qualifications from any vet school. However, if they could show they had worked for seven years or more in a veterinary practice, the Royal College would admit them to what they called the Supplementary Veterinary Register. John had worked for many years in his father's practice but had never been accepted by a veterinary teaching school. He could deal satisfactorily with most veterinary situations apart from major surgery. He could repair a skin wound under local anaesthesia. Should anything more serious arise, he could always contact me or admit the patient for treatment the next morning. Business was light in those early years and I had a lot of spare time on my hands but you could never relax completely knowing the phone might ring at any time. So the few hours off duty that John afforded me were very welcome.

I employed a young girl, Angie, as a receptionist. She had no nursing training but she would help by holding patients, answering the phone, making appointments and taking the money. The financial side of the practice took up more and more of my time using handwritten ledgers every evening. I decided to get a computer to take some of this load off my shoulders. The first machine was one of the early Apple computers - before they became Apple Macs or Mackintosh - and it boasted twin floppy disc drives. In those days floppy discs really were 'floppy' comprising a thin magnetic disc enclosed by a cardboard cover which had to be quite gently inserted into a 5" (12.7cms) slot. The drives were labelled A and B. We have lost those drive letters today relying usually on a single drive, C.

There were no specific software programs for veterinary practices but several for general accounting which suited my needs perfectly. It made reconciling bank statements a breeze compared to the laboured hours I had spent previously with pen and paper.

It was about four years later that dedicated veterinary programs arrived on the market. The first ones were designed by computer engineers who had no concept of the needs of veterinary practice. Many of these companies went to the wall leaving a lot of practices disillusioned by the idea of computers. Fortunately, I found a company, Business Data Systems (BDS), established by a vet in Edinburgh, John Robertson. He had seen the need for computerisation in the profession and knew what was required. He employed software engineers to write a program that the practising vet needed. He lent me a machine to experiment with for two weeks before deciding to buy when I realised that computers would play a significant role in business generally and veterinary practice in particular.

However, there was a major hurdle to overcome - acceptance by the staff. By this time the practice employed an assistant vet, two part-time receptionists and a veterinary nurse, none of whom were keen on a computer in the practice. Their over-riding fear was of "breaking it" so I explained that if they could break the loaned computer, there would be no point in my buying it. They took this up as a challenge and I soon found them sneaking up to the office trying to disable the machine. They had a few early, minor successes but I found that I could easily reset the machine. Eventually they accepted my decision to install the system even if the acceptance came with an air of lingering suspicion.

It took time for the system to bed down with monitors in the waiting room, both consulting rooms and the study upstairs. I mailed all our clients explaining our conversion to the new computing system while assuring them that any mistakes were our personal responsibility and not that of the new system.

Most of the staff took to the system well. But one nurse, Sue, married to the local RSPCA inspector, lived in dread of approaching any keyboard. She felt that every time she touched the keys something seemed to go wrong. She was developing a real phobia of the whole system. I managed to solve the problem by offering to pay her £1 for every time she managed to "break" the system. This brought a smile to her face, and a renewed enthusiasm for her work while the number of computer crashes gradually diminished and each one of us learnt by her mistakes.

The programs were not perfect and about every 6 weeks I had to install the latest update to correct errors that were being discovered by the increasing use of the system throughout the profession. The staff dreaded these updates because they invariably needed a few tweaks to return the program to full working order. Each update would arrive on a large tape cassette I would load up after an evening surgery. Over the next few days I would have to ring the company's offices in Edinburgh with the latest problem. This involved the engineer, Tom, talking me through lines of code and altering characters and symbols to repair the error.

Our first unexpected success came one Saturday afternoon when I was called out to the surgery by a passing motorist who had injured a stray red setter. Once I had examined the dog which was only suffering minor injuries, I admitted it to the hospital kennels. There was no identification on its collar and red setters have few identifying marks so I tried a computer search for a male red setter of about 5 years of age and living the nearby area. Much to my surprise it came up with two possibilities - one living 5 miles away but the other only half a mile away up the Mile End Road. I rang the owner's number and when the man answered I identified myself and asked him if he had Sammy with him.

"He's in the garden," he said.

"Can you actually see him?" I asked

"Well, not actually. But he was here half an hour ago. Why do you ask?"

"Because I think I have got him here in the surgery,"

He put the phone down to look in the garden. "I can't see him so you may be right. Can I come down now?"

Although bruised and scratched, Sammy was thrilled to see his owner arrive to collect him.

Computers can do things we ordinary mortals would take ages to achieve but, as we all know to our cost, they are not infallible.

One evening surgery the assistant consulting in the other room came through and told me that his monitor had gone on the blink. I tried various keystrokes and checked the connections before suggesting that he completed his consultations in the back surgery. Once the last clients had left, I set about trying to solve the problem.

It turned out we had admitted a tiny 8 week old puppy for observation in the kennels. The receptionist had taken pity on it and brought it through to sit on her lap behind the reception desk. When she stood up to deal with a client, she placed the pup on the floor. The main computer hub lay beneath the desk and from it, ran all the cables to the various monitors throughout the premises. The puppy was attracted to these 'worms' and began to chew through the cable. Having identified the problem, it took time to run a fresh cable to the consulting room monitor. Fortunately, the pup suffered no ill effects much to the relief of the receptionist.

Computer monitors were not the flat screen viewers of today. They were small, rounded boxes looking like the TV sets of the day. There were no Windows or iOS operating systems. The programs used languages such as Basic or Fortran and text appeared in a basic Courier typeface in either orange or green on a black background.

Chapter 18

Costs and bad debtors

Owners have always complained about the cost of veterinary medicine and I believe they have well-founded reasons today but I will discuss that particular problem later. There are valid reasons why veterinary medicine is costly which are largely unappreciated by a public. They are used to going to the doctor, attending a hospital appointment and undergoing an operation without having to reach into their wallets or purses. The NHS is financed by taxes and subsidised by government.

Whenever there is a road accident involving a family, the emergency services attend to the human casualties. The police close off the road while the Fire Service cuts open the vehicle when they are lifted out of the wreckage, placed on stretchers, carried off to the local hospital where they are X-rayed, had blood taken for analysis, sedated, anaesthetised, surgically repaired and hospitalised - all on the NHS.

In the back of some of those vehicles involved in the collision are probably a few family pets trapped in the wreckage. Who deals with them? It is the vet. The vet who has to provide the "ambulance" (her car covered in blood), the hospital ward (kennels), the X-ray machine and darkroom, the laboratory, the theatre, instruments and nursing staff. I am sorry but these facilities do not come cheap.

There is also the cost of drugs. Compared to the medical market, the veterinary one is tiny so drugs specifically developed for animal use are expensive.

The veterinary licence for a drug, I was told on good authority, can cost the pharmaceutical company upwards of one million pounds. Before this legislation, there were many drugs which only benefited dogs or cats or horses, only cost a few pence each and were remarkably effective. But they became uneconomical if the company had to provide research data to support the application for a licence and therefore they were quietly removed from the marketplace. Two examples spring to mind - Prednoleucotropin and Mysoline.

Prednoleucotropin is a combination of the steroid drug, prednisolone, discovered in 1955 and an analgesic, cinchophen, which was formulated as far back as 1887. It had two invaluable properties. It effectively relieved arthritic pain in dogs and each tablet cost the client less than 2p each. The disadvantages were that it only worked in dogs - many clients used to ask me if they could have some for their own arthritic pain having seen its effects on their dog. However, it did not have a veterinary licence. The company decided that the cost of getting the necessary veterinary licence far outweighed the likelihood of any residual profit and withdrew the drug.

Mysoline, manufactured by ICI, had been a recognised human anti-epileptic medication for many years and the company got a veterinary licence for the drug. Unfortunately, it is far less effective in canine epilepsy compared to the previous treatment of the condition with phenobarbitone which was also very much cheaper. However the Veterinary Medicines Directorate states that human drugs which do not have a veterinary licence cannot be used if there is already a drug already licensed for a condition. Most vets in general practice in my day knew that their patients responded far better to 'phenobarb' than Mysoline but we were prevented from dispensing the better drug by bureaucratic legislation.

Bureaucracy brings me to another piece of incomprehensible stupidity. In the early days of my career we dispensed tablets in paper envelopes until Health and Safety came along. When Paul Scammell and I started up the Crawley practice, we dispensed tablets and capsules in plastic pots with child-proof caps. We attached a self-adhesive label with the necessary instructions to the container. The regulations specified certain mandatory items of information which had to be included on the small label. These were - the name, address and telephone number of the practice; the name and address of the owner and the name of the patient. Instructions for the use of the medication were obviously necessary while the only optional piece of information was the name of the drug. This meant that if a child accidentally swallowed some of the dog's tablets the emergency doctor had to ring the vet's surgery, often out of hours. The duty vet then had to rush to the surgery to find the relevant case record to establish what drug they were dealing with. All this wasted valuable time in an emergency situation. Quite how many committee meetings were needed to draw up such ineffective legislation I cannot imagine.

There was an NHS warehouse in Witham just a few miles down the A12 from Colchester. I dropped in one day and spent a very profitable hour with the manager of the depot. He could provide me with swabs, cotton wool, dressings, suture material, disposable instrument packs at a fraction of the cost I was paying to my veterinary suppliers. As a result we could make considerable savings on our day-to-day items before the authorities stepped in and put an end to the association. These costs are the reason why veterinary bills seem to be unnecessarily high but the problem is made worse by the bane of our veterinary practice life - bad debtors.

Bad Debtors

Poisoned Cat

The other major cost to a veterinary practice is the wage bill - not just for the permanent staff but for temporary locum staff to cover holiday and sickness absences. One August Bank Holiday Saturday I was called out to a cat whose owner had not read the instructions on a can of flea spray. Instead of applying a light spray the owner had soaked the poor animal in a powerful organophosphorus compound called Nuvan Top. By the time I arrived the cat was salivating, trembling and had suffered its first fit - all symptoms of organophosphate poisoning. I got the animal into a carrying cage after giving it a large dose of atropine. During the journey back to the surgery it urinated through the cage onto the front passenger seat. Fortunately, it was a female cat not a tom which would have stunk the car out for weeks. Once back at the surgery I was transferring it from the travelling cage to the kennel when it turned and sank its teeth into the knuckle of my left hand. Such injuries are part and parcel of a vet's life so I washed it thoroughly and doused it in an antiseptic solution before applying a plaster to the wound and thought nothing more about it.

It was at the family lunch on the Monday that I noticed that my hand had swollen and Jen asked me if I had seen my colour. The family turned to look at me.

"Dad, you do look a bit queer," one of them said.

Apparently my face had turned a pale shade of green. To cut a long and rather boring story short, they admitted me to Colchester hospital where the surgical houseman tried to lance the abscess that had developed within the knuckle. Three days later the wound was still discharging pus, and I was feeling rather strangely light-headed. I had got septicaemic meningitis. The infection had got into the bloodstream and travelled to the brain.

So what has all this got to do with the costs of running a veterinary practice? The weekly turnover of the practice was about £1500 a week. The infection left me unable to work for ten weeks. This meant that I had to use a locum vet at a cost of £100 a day, provide accommodation and rent a car for him while I slowly recovered. Vets don't get sick pay so our income was severely reduced that year. To rub salt into the wound so to speak, the owner of the cat never paid their bill while others still complained about the costs of veterinary treatment. This was back in the 1980s when veterinary medicine was a vocation rather than a business.

Garden Centre Debtor

One bad debtor episode that sticks in my mind involved a lady customer who ran a small garden centre on the outskirts of Colchester. She brought in her dog for treatment one morning where she had been seen by our Australian locum, Robyn Mackay. At the end of the consultation, Robyn presented her with the itemised bill of something like £7.75p. The lady took it through to reception, slapped a £5 note on the counter and walked out saying that £5 was about all the consultation was worth, leaving both Robyn and the receptionist rather lost for words. They only told me about this episode at the end of the morning surgery.

A cup of coffee and a little thinking time later I had a planned course of action. The next day I visited her garden centre, picked up a plant priced at £7.50p, gave her a £5 note and began to walk out.

"Hey, hold on! You can't do that," she said.

"Why not?"

"Because it is priced at £7.50p."

"Which was the about the same price my practice charged you for veterinary attention yesterday and yet you decided the value of that treatment as £5. Please do not come back to my surgery expecting to receive any further veterinary treatment."

I left the plant on the counter, collected the £5 note and walked out with a smile on my face.

The Widow

One consultation of which I am probably most proud had little to do with veterinary medicine. Mr and Mrs Anderton normally came in together with their two Cavalier spaniels. He always wore a regimental blazer with a crest, a pencil-thin moustache and a brusque military manner. He may have achieved the rank of corporal in an undistinguished military career, and he was a bully. Rather than speaking, he barked. She maintained a subservient position about two paces behind her husband and never spoke. So it was rather a surprise when she arrived at the surgery alone one afternoon.

When I called her into the consulting room, she burst into a flood of tears. I got her a chair and sat her down.

"What's the problem?" I asked. Both dogs were looking perfectly healthy as they wandered round the room.

In a tearful whisper, she said "I can't pay your bill."

"Oh, sod my bill! What's the matter with you?"

"My husband died suddenly of a heart attack a month ago and he had sole signatory rights on our bank account. I've got no money and I owe so many people who have lent me cash or let me put things on account. I don't know where to turn."

Putting an arm round her shaking shoulders, I said "You don't need a vet, you need an accountant."

"But I don't know anybody like that. My husband dealt with all our finances. I don't even know if he had any life insurance. Have I got any money in the bank? How much do we still owe on the house?"

The poor woman was at the end of her tether.

"It just so happens I know an accountant friend who deals with just your sort of problem," I said as I handed her a tissue and reached for the phone.

When his secretary answered I asked to be put through to my friend.

"David, I've got a lady in my surgery who needs your help urgently."

I explained the bare bones of the problem and asked him if he would see her if I put her in a taxi and sent her round to the office. He immediately agreed, and I asked my receptionist to get a cab for the distraught Mrs Anderton.

"But what about the dogs?" she cried.

"You can leave them here with me and collect them once you have seen my friend, David. Don't worry."

About three hours later, a completely transformed woman returned to the surgery. She seemed to have grown two inches, her head was high, her eyes were bright, and a smile beamed from her face. That consultation was one of my most successful and I still remember it with a grin on my face. The dogs were very pleased to see her back too.

Defence of Staff

I sometimes feel an affinity for Professor Henry Higgins in My Fair Lady when he says -

"An average man am I, of no eccentric whim, who likes to live his life, free of strife, doing whatever he thinks is best for him - well, just an ordinary man. BUT..." let an abuser in my surgery and all hell will be let loose.

Where is all this whimsy leading to? To an ordinary afternoon surgery when my receptionist passed a blank history card through the hatch to my consulting room. The name of the client was one of those mid-European surnames in serious need of a few vowels - something like Styczynski. It was the spelling that rang a distant bell in the back of my mind. I asked the receptionist to join me in the consulting room and asked her to search through the 'dead' files for a client of the same name.

She returned a few minutes later holding a card slashed across by heavy red lines. The notes read 'This client is NEVER, EVER to be seen by this practice again' and gave the reason. Some four or five years earlier he had had been extremely abusive to the reception staff, and I had given him his marching orders.

By this time, the waiting room had filled up with clients and patients so it was with a lot of pleasure that I opened the door and called out "Mr Styczynski?"

An undistinguished man, holding a cat box, threaded his way past the other clients.

"OUT!" I said, pointing to the door.

"What? Me? ... Why?"

"Because, some years ago, I told you never to return to this practice after you had been thoroughly rude and abusive to my staff. It is an attitude I will not tolerate. So go."

I am not ashamed to say I had a satisfied smile on my face as he slunk out of the door with the applause of the remaining clientele ringing in his ears.

Reception staff in any walk of life, whether it is banking, hospitals or veterinary practice, are the front line of the business. They are the ones who create the first impressions, good or bad. They are also the first in line for complaints and abuse. In the vast majority of cases, the fault lies further up the command chain over which the reception staff have little control. This is where the responsible principal should step in.

I learnt this lesson first from Peter Grant in Woking. On the rare occasion that an operation or other procedure went wrong, he always took responsibility despite the fact that the error may have been caused by an inexperienced assistant or nurse. He would visit the client personally, not over the telephone or by letter, and accept whatever anger and abuse the client chose to throw at him. I have tried to protect my own staff in the same way ever since.

There is one other situation when, I believe, it is the responsibility of the boss to step up to the mark. That is with dangerous patients. I have had to deal with a few hundred potentially dangerous situations and a lot of adrenalin has flooded my system over the years - but, as principal, it was my job. I cannot pretend it was easy, and I had to work myself up into a state of mind which said to the patient "It is either you or me - and it ain't going to be me!" Dog catchers, heavy leather gloves and large thick blankets were among the articles we used to subdue these unappreciative patients but most useful of all was a determined state of mind.

Veterinary cancer therapy

It is my belief that the public's firm conviction that veterinary fees are unnecessarily high is sometimes the fault of the profession itself.

Cancer therapy is a case in point. In 1994 our year had its 30th anniversary reunion at the vet school. I can remember the pride with which the clinical director, showed off the new oncology suite which offered almost every conceivable form of cancer therapy. He related the case of one 10-year-old greyhound which had suffered an aggressive osteosarcoma (bone cancer) of the lower jaw. Having removed the lower half of the jaw, they treated the animal with intense radiotherapy and concurrent chemotherapy at a cost exceeding £9000. The dog could only lap liquid food clumsily following the surgery. I remember asking him how long the dog had lived following the original surgery. The answer was "over nine months". This reply rather horrified me when I thought of the pain and suffering inflicted on that animal in the name of "healing" science. Quite an animated discussion followed for the next half hour during which he mentioned another couple who routinely transported their pet rabbit once a week from Scotland for aggressive radiotherapy at £500 a session.

I gave up at that point. He and I differed in our opinions but that did not jeopardise our friendship. Despite this difference of opinion it was a wonderful weekend and gave us all the chance to catch up with each other's lives since qualification.

Since that time, costs and therefore fees have increased at such an alarming rate that even the upper ranges of pet insurance policies often fall significantly short in providing cover for veterinary attention - treatment that, in the past, they would have covered in full.

Chapter 19

Retirement

Looking back at our class of 1964, most of us had gone into general practice with Mike in the West Country; Ken in the North East; Dick into an eminent Newmarket equine practice while Dave went out to Southern Rhodesia where he has been trapped in Bulawayo since independence. John set up practice in Scandinavia; Paul remained with the Min. Of Ag. - sorry, it's DEFRA now - after leaving Crawley and Neil practiced in Torquay before retiring to France. Dave Revell died too young of leukaemia while Richard Dyball and Alan Findlay followed academic careers. Both landing up as directors of studies at Clare and Churchill colleges, respectively. Caroline established her own veterinary pathology practice while May Lim took up a senior post in the Singapore Veterinary Service. Only one, Bill, left the profession to farm in Scotland but perhaps he had had enough of veterinary life since he followed both his parents into the profession.

By the late 90s I had taken a less active role in the practice, maintaining the paperwork and working part time as a consulting vet. One morning when I arrived to take a morning surgery, I was walking through the hospital area when I noticed a lively Springer spaniel in one of the kennels.

"What's the Springer in for, Vicky?" I asked my theatre nurse

"Tests," she replied.

"What tests?"

"The lot. Andrew has brought it in for everything - full blood workup, biochemistry, ECG, ultrasound and X-rays."

Andrew was our latest assistant, three years qualified, who had the potential to be a good vet, but he was still at the learning stage. Not being too happy with this shotgun approach, I decided to discuss it with him after morning surgery. He was just finishing up his notes of the morning session when I joined him in the consulting room

"I see you have got that Springer in for tests," I said. "What's wrong with it?"

"I don't know so I brought it in for testing."

"What are the symptoms?"

"Well, the owner just said he was not well."

"Was it eating? Had it been sick? Any cough? Has it got a temperature?"

All questions answered in a quiet, apologetic voice, "Don't know."

Not only had he failed to get a history, he had failed to carry out any of the simplest examinations preferring to let the laboratory do the work for him. It wasn't his fault, he had not been taught properly. He had never learnt the adage that "laboratory tests do not make a diagnosis, they are there to confirm or deny a diagnosis." We may be entering the age of robotic surgery but we were still a long way from robotic diagnosis.

In the meantime, bureaucracy was spreading its slow paralysis throughout everyday life and the life of a practising veterinary surgeon. There were more and more forms to fill in, boxes to tick and reports to be generated. Common sense was being replaced "risk assessment" and thinking "outside the box" was considered rather dangerous. The fun of not knowing what challenges would face you each day had gone. Replaced by clock-watching, form filling and a background apprehension of negligence suits, I had had enough.

All this is not to say that I have not enjoyed and taken pride in the large part of my professional career although some of the highlights of my career had little to do with my professional expertise.

It was in the early nineties I suffered the first bouts of depression. The Colchester practice had grown to a four-man practice and was providing a reasonable income. Our family life was great without tensions of any kind so there was no obvious cause of these episodes of illogical anxiety, fear and physical trembling. If I was to be honest when someone asked me how I felt my answer would have been "I feel stupidly vulnerable to something I cannot identify." Everyone suffers depression in their own particular form. It is not a feeling of being "down", it runs so much deeper and more physical than that. To be told to "pull yourself together" only tells me that the speaker has no concept of true depression.

Put simply, it is a bugger.

The GP having diagnosed depression prescribed a variety of antidepressant medications some of which had distressing side effects while others only 'coloured' my life a uniformly dull grey. The doctors referred me to various psychiatrists, psychologists, behavioural therapists and, for a time, they put me under the care of the mental health team at Addenbrooke's hospital in Cambridge.

Between episodes, I was my normal outgoing self without a serious care in the world but I could descend into a black pit of despair without warning. I say 'without warning' but that is not completely accurate because Jen could see a 'blip', as we now call them, coming about 48 hours before it hit me. I found out later that two of my Cambridge year colleagues had also suffered episodes of depression. The veterinary profession in the 60s and 70s was close to the top of the list of suicidal professions although it has slipped down that list in recent years. I have known three colleagues who have taken their own lives during my career.

I will not bore you with the pharmacopeia of anti-depressant medications to which I have been subjected over the past twenty-five years. Just let me say that, between us, Jen and I have learnt how to cope with the condition and we can live our retirement years happily with only the occasional 'blip'.

But it took its toll on my role as principal of a busy practice and standards slipped - not because of any incompetence or laziness by the staff but the quality of my leadership was faltering as was my pride in my chosen profession. My immediate problem was that I could not predict when the depression would strike and render me unable to fulfil my practice rota responsibilities. Paperwork could always be postponed to a later date but booked appointments wait for no one. It was not fair to keep asking the staff to cover for me at short notice so the prospect of early retirement loomed. My depression was one factor, but I realised that I was losing a lot of my enthusiasm for the work. For over thirty years I had taken pride in offering a personal service to my clients many of whom had become good friends but the 'art' was fading from the work and being replaced by a faceless 'science'.

Life after Practice

Having taken the decision to retire, I sold the business of the practice to my senior assistant, Vivian Long, but kept ownership of the two premises the rent of which would provide us with an income in our retirement. Since that time I have maintained an active and friendly relationship with the practice for the past nineteen years and, even now, I am greeted with a cup of coffee whenever I drop in for a chat even though, since that time, Vivian has also retired and the practice passed on to her assistant, Charlotte.

There were regrets of course. One cannot devote a large part of one's life to a profession without some feelings of loss. But I still had several good years left in me so Jen and I had to decide how I would move on. As I have mentioned previously, I have always had an interest in computing, albeit self-taught, and it was obvious that, while the young were comfortable with keyboards and mice, their parents and grandparents were out of touch with the developing technology. Some had been to evening classes with little success as they sat at a different machine each week. This must have been like learning to drive one week in a Mini, the next, an Astra and later, a Renault Clio. As well as the practical issues, they all had different needs and interests so there was an opportunity to offer one-to-one tuition in their own homes. A small notice in the local parish magazine attracted several local clients. There was no curriculum. I taught them what they wanted to do - emails, search engines, Facebook, photos - anything and everything.

This led to teaching at Age Concern in Colchester and running a class for the University of the Third Age. My pupils kept asking if there was a useful instruction manual for the use of a home computer by the older generation. Searching the libraries, I found that all the available manuals, except one, were written in American English with weak American humour, scattered with acronyms and 'computer speak'. The one British exception took three pages to explain the wiring of a three-pin electric plug. There was obviously a niche in the market to provide a guide written in plain English, seasoned with the odd dash of British wit and avoiding any form of technical language.

After my first few local lessons I realised that within ten minutes of finishing a lesson many of my pupils had forgotten more than half I had taught them. They needed written referral notes on the subject under instruction. After a year I had notes on most of the common computing queries stored on a CD which I took with me to each lesson. At the end of the session I would print out the relevant notes and leave them with the client for future reference.

I gathered this material together and used it as a basis for a computing instruction manual. More in hope than expectation, I sent a proposal form with the first three chapters to John Wiley and Sons who were leading publishers of such books - together with the obligatory stamped, addressed envelope.

This envelope returned three weeks later with a single sheet of paper which we were certain was a rejection slip. We were wrong. They wanted to see more!

The result was that John Wiley commissioned me to write four such manuals for which they developed a range of self-help books under the titles of "... for the Older and Wiser." The books sold well and, although it is now six years since they published the last one and it is rather outdated, I am still receiving royalties and public lending rights income today. I have had questions and requests from Christchurch, New Zealand, Calgary, Canada and Cleethorpes in Lincolnshire which has kept my mind active in retirement.

The Last Curtain Call

I had been retired for at least ten years when I had to call upon my years of veterinary experience for one last curtain call. Our daughter, Tammy, had bought two male Burmese kittens and asked if I could have them neutered at the surgery when they came down for a weekend. The practice rarely operated on Saturdays but they were kind enough to make an exception in this case and I took the kittens to the surgery after morning surgery had finished. They asked me if I wanted to perform the operation but I felt that since it had been several years since I operated it would be easier - and probably safer - if they did the surgery. I sat in the office outside the kennels while they took the first kitten into the theatre. Five minutes later it was being returned to the cage, and they collected its brother for surgery. Five minutes passed before the nurse came hurrying out of the theatre to collect a drug from the pharmacy. She avoided my eyes. Something was wrong but there was little I could do. Another few minutes passed before she emerged again, looked towards me with a hint of desperation.

"It looks as though we are losing this one, Adrian."

I didn't utter a word but my thoughts were saying "No way. Not on my watch."

I rushed into the theatre where the inert body of the second kitten was lying still on the table and all my years of experience kicked in.

"OK, stand back, let me in. Number one endotracheal tube. Get me the adrenalin."

I slipped the tube down its windpipe and puffed gently into the lungs while my fingers felt for the heartbeat. There was none. I gave a small injection of adrenalin into the heart, pushing and pulling the blood in and out of the ventricles three times before withdrawing the needle and starting external heart massage. The pupils were fully dilated. The tongue was a dull blue, but I was not finished yet. This kitten was not going to die. The silence in the room was absolute with shock. The staff were frozen. This was the old boss's daughter's cat!

Alternating artificial respiration through the tube with the heart massage, I kept going. The kitten was tiny and everything had to be done very, very gently. After more minutes, how long I don't know, there was an involuntary gasp from its tiny chest before a faint heart beat returned at agonisingly irregular intervals. The chest developed a Cheyne Stokes rhythm - coming and going but imperceptibly getting stronger. The blue tongue faded towards a pale pink.

After half an hour the heart was beating on its own and the breathing was almost independent but the brain had been without an oxygenated blood supply for nearly half an hour. What permanent damage would be left?

An hour later I took both kittens home - one, fit as a fiddle, the other clinging to some form of life. The following day the damaged kitten was staggering about - but it was blind. What sort of victory had I won?

It took another week before his sight came back but he was eating, running and playing. He had a tendency to fall off the edge of beds for a few weeks but he seemed to enjoy the experience. He lived to the ripe old age of twelve despite showing many signs of stupidity which endeared it to the family.

What were my thoughts and feelings? "The boss might be old and past his time but he's still got what it takes."

It felt good.

Since that last excitement we have moved to Somerset to be closer to the grandchildren where I am called on from time to time for the odd bit of veterinary advice. I have a few regrets about my veterinary life and, taking everything into account, I have enjoyed my time while feeling rather despondent for those who come after me. It's not the same now but then it never is for succeeding generations and I wish my granddaughter happiness above success in her chosen career.

The Profession Today

I appreciate that, having retired twenty years ago, I am not at the forefront of veterinary financial management. However, since our pension is funded by the rental of the two premises I still own in Colchester, I still keep in regular touch with the practice. There is no doubt in my mind that there is a degree of overcharging in the profession. This is not just a recent development. Many years ago, back in the 80s, I remember some practices trebling their charges for cat flu vaccinations when there was an outbreak of the disease in the area. What concerns me more is the active promotion of questionable investigation or surgical procedures to vulnerable and ill-informed clients.

The profession I was once so proud to represent has changed so much in the 21st century that I am becoming increasingly ashamed to have been a member. Many fees are unnecessarily exorbitant, knowing pet insurance will cover much of the costs. Too many practices are pushing unnecessary laboratory tests and procedures onto ill-informed owners who want nothing but the best for their beloved companions.

Over and above this unnecessary charging, the veterinary schools are not teaching their students how to take a proper 'history' of a case. They no longer rely on their senses of touch, sight, sound, smell and even, sometimes, taste. The resulting graduates have become scientifically lazy and seem happy to leave the process of diagnosis to the laboratory technicians.

A case in point was brought home to me a couple of years ago. Jen and I had moved down to a Somerset village to be closer to grandchildren. Word got about that I was a retired vet and a few local people asked me for occasional advice. On most occasions my recommendations would be to take the patient to the nearest vet. However, one afternoon I got a phone call from a member of the community to say an old age pensioner was in a distressed state about some advice she had received from her vet.

The 80-year-old widow had taken her 14-year-old Labrador, Goldie, to a local vet for her annual booster vaccination. (This in itself is unnecessary as dogs of such an age rarely require boosters.) Goldie suffers arthritis in both elbows, right knee and both hips. Nevertheless, she can potter down the lane with her owner, she eats well, and she is happy. Despite this, the vet strongly recommended to her owner she should spend over £6000 on bilateral hip replacements. This dog is her baby. She would do anything for her and was seriously contemplating taking out a second mortgage to pay for the surgery. The word got around the village and someone asked me to visit Goldie and discuss the proposed surgery with her owner. It took me over an hour to explain that, at Goldie's age, it would probably take at least nine months to recover from the surgery during which time she would be in considerable discomfort if not outright pain. Even if she recovered, she would still have the arthritic elbows and knee.

Then there are the almost superfluous laboratory tests and procedures foisted upon owners when a tentative but strong diagnosis could be made using the God-given implements such as hands and eyes without resorting to a thoughtless barrage of tests in the profit-making practice laboratory.

Too many vets have lost the vocation for their profession and seem to view it as a moneymaking machine. A colleague recently sent me the invoice received by a friend of his from a specialist orthopaedic practice. The patient was a 13-year-old rescue mongrel that had been bowled over by a much heavier dog. The general practice diagnosed a fractured metatarsal - one of the four long bones in the foot. These fractures are easily treated by immobilisation under a Plaster of Paris dressing because the adjacent bones act as splints to hold the fracture in place

Not today, apparently. It had to be referred to the specialist hospital. They took several X-rays both before and after pinning and plating the minor injury. Inexplicably, they took a CAT scan of the dog's pelvis at a cost of £642.97p!! The total bill cost more than £5000. In my opinion this amounts to greed and borders on fraud. Is it any wonder that I am ashamed of my past profession?

Moving away from the "specialist" procedures of these con men before my blood pressure goes through the roof, there are many simple remedies that can achieve perfectly satisfactory outcomes. But you need to use your mind as well as the laboratory. There are also times when the right thing to do is - nothing - to let Nature take its course - but this can be a hard decision to make.

Our neighbours in Somerset were becoming anxious about their own middle aged Springer, Lily, when the vet could not make a diagnosis in spite of a number of laboratory investigations. Suggestions were made of leukaemia, meningitis and cancer before the owners asked me to have a look. Lily presented a number of curious symptoms. She was restless but tired easily, probably because of her anaemia. Her lower jaw hung loose, and she found it difficult to take food. The vets had discovered fluid on her chest on X-ray but neglected to take a sample. They advised the owners to expect the worst despite dispensing various expensive drugs.

When I went round to the house Lily was in a sorry state. The owners were sleeping with her through the night anticipating the end although she was only eight years old. I went right back to the beginning of the problem. Had anything unusual happened prior to the onset of this illness? I learnt that a couple of days before she became ill she had been charged very heavily in the side of her chest by a large dog that the owner had let off the lead.

Extreme impact can create a range of different symptoms. The blood tests had shown that she was anaemic, but she was generating young red blood cells so an internal bleed could be a contributing factor. There was fluid in the chest. Was this blood?

The local vet had prescribed Pregabalin, an anti-epileptic drug. I don't know what the reasoning was behind this decision but since it is known for its side effects among which are lethargy, in-coordination, nausea and vomiting - all of which Lily was already suffering, I advised the owners to stop the medication.

Having examined Lily to the best of my ability, I was as confused as the local vet so I went home, sat in a quiet room and let my mind play around with the symptoms I had found. The X-rays showed fluid in the chest cavity. This was most likely to be blood, serum or chyle which is a milky lymphatic fluid and is an uncommon cause of fluid in the chest. The heavy impact could have ruptured an internal thoracic vein which would account for the fluid. (Unfortunately the vets had not taken a sample of this fluid so it was guesswork.) A sudden haemorrhage would explain many of Lily's symptoms of anaemia, lethargy and the appearance of rejuvenating red blood cells in her system but it would not explain the weakness of the lower jaw and her eye droop.

The last two signs suggested damage, temporary or otherwise, to the fifth (trigeminal) cranial nerve. Whiplash from the impact could have caused such an injury and any recovery could take a long time. Having considered several more uncommon causes of her symptoms I came to the conclusion that the sudden collision with a much heavier dog was the most likely cause. The treatment for which was simple rest - and time. It was difficult to advise the owners to do nothing except nurse the patient but it worked. Lily has made a complete recovery - as the Mack and Mabel song puts it "Time heals everything" - sometimes.

Very often reassurance is what owners are looking for. I had put my feet up one afternoon recently when Jen called up the stairs "Adrian, there's a bleeding horse outside. Can you have a look at it?"

The animal had been spooked by a passing truck, reared and come down on the spiked railings outside the Post Office. The frightened rider asked the postmaster for help who directed them to our house a few hundred yards away.

There was a trail of blood down the road ending in a pool outside our house. The wound looked dramatic but the superficial bleeding was slowing. There was no injury to the underlying tissues so I reassured then that all would be well once they had walked the horse back to the stables and called the vet. It would be a simple matter of suturing the superficial wound under a local anaesthetic.

Chapter 20

Philosophy & Ruminations

After a long career in veterinary general practice what advice, if any, can I pass on my granddaughter or for any of my grandchildren for that matter? First of all, I think she is mad. But we have had that conversation at length and she shows an admirable degree of determination so I will not go down that road again. After all everyone has to make their own way in life and it would be presumptuous of me to suggest that I know many of the answers. So, in hope rather than expectation, let me put down a few thoughts and ruminations which may be helpful later in their lives.

Never stop learning and be prepared to change your mind even if you have always done something the same way for years. There may be a better way of achieving the desired outcome. Conversely, don't make change for change's sake. New techniques, new equipment, new research can all contribute to our better knowledge and treatment but their very novelty does not imply an improvement. Let me give you an example.

A few years after I retired, our wonderful retriever, Buzz, put his foot in a rabbit hole and ruptured his anterior cruciate ligament. He showed the classic anterior drawer movement diagnostic of the condition so I took him down to my old surgery in Colchester where they confirmed the diagnosis.

"We'll have to refer him to the specialist orthopaedic practice in Chelmsford," they said.

"Why? Don't you do cruciate repairs here anymore?"

"Oh, no! There is a new technique used now. They make a wedge resection of the tibia to alter the angle of the joint table and then they attach a T-plate. They no longer replace the ligament."

It all sounded unnecessarily complicated to me. After all, I must have repaired over a hundred cruciate ligaments in my career with no undue problems. But, if that was the best way of doing it, then so be it and I agreed. Buzz needed an overnight stay in the gleaming orthopaedic veterinary hospital to ensure a good recovery. This added to the high cost of the latest operation which easily exceeded our PetPlan allowance for such surgery. (I would like to add that my cases went home happily the same day as the operation.) It took just over four months for Buzz to walk sound on the affected leg. (My patients would walk sound within a week or ten days - but I supposed they knew what they were doing.)

A year later Buzz tore the other leg's anterior cruciate. Taking him back down to the surgery, I told them I wanted the repair done the 'old-fashioned' way, doing a proper ligament replacement. After all I had taught them all how to perform the operation during my years in charge. He came home the same day and walked sound after two weeks. 'New' does not necessarily mean 'improved'.

Never be afraid to change your mind - or advice - in the light of newer knowledge. In my early years, if I had to put down one of a pair of animals I would suggest to the owners that they removed the survivor from the scene until I had done the deed and removed the body. Later research by the Royal College suggested that, if the survivor saw and smelt the body of its late companion, it did not grieve as long while those who had not seen the body spent weeks looking for their friend. In the light of this, I changed my advice to encourage the remaining pet to see the body before it was removed which reduced the grieving process by weeks.

This leads me to more general words of advice which apply equally to the professional life of a vet but also to an enjoyable, personal journey through life.

These are just thoughts that have occurred to me over the past 80 years which may have some resonance today. You don't have to agree with any or all of it and you can ignore it completely if you so wish.

I have always tried to do my best - not always successfully but I have given up trying to be perfect. Not only is perfection difficult to live with, it is just too tiring.

Try to listen more than you talk. (I have repeatedly failed this dictum for many years but I keep trying.)

To the best of my knowledge I have never asked an employee to do something I have never done many times before. I have cleaned up filthy kennels, scrubbed floors, painted walls and captured dangerous animals, although it was always my responsibility to deal with these cases not that of an employee.

In medicine your patient gets better <u>in spite of</u> what you do while, in surgery, they get better <u>because</u> of what you do. It may be cynical but there is an element of truth to it. Having said that, I always enjoyed the challenge of the detective work needed to make a diagnosis whether it was medical or surgical.

Be prepared to learn from anyone. I have learnt important lessons from cowmen, junior nurses, physiotherapists, dentists, chemists and many more unexpected sources - including a plumber.

One of my early non-veterinary lessons came from our family doctor in Hatfield Peverel, Syd Emerick. Jen and I were visiting Mum and Dad for the weekend. Jen had not been feeling too well for a few weeks and, when Dad invited Syd up to the house for drinks one evening, he happened to mention that Jen had not been well. We did not want to bother him professionally on a social occasion but he was happy to help. We were all sitting in the large lounge which had a large bay window.

"Come over here, Jen, and let's talk about it," said Syd, pointing to the window.

I was in the chair closest to them as Syd questioned Jen about her symptoms. While I left them to it, I kept my ears open. His questions were gentle but probing and he listened carefully to the answers and, after about 15 minutes, he was satisfied.

"Right! Come on upstairs. Let's have a feel at you."

Jen later told me he asked her to lie on her back on the bed placed his fingers just below her ribs which made her jump with discomfort.

"There! Got it," he said. "You are suffering from gastric reflux. Normally easily treated but nothing to worry about."

This simple example of imaginative history-taking was a lesson I have never forgotten. He almost had the diagnosis before he touched the patient.

This almost completes the circle of my veterinary life and takes me right back to that Dunstable consulting room. Martin Senior's imposing copperplate certificate which has been a guiding principle in my veterinary life that there is both Art and Science in veterinary medicine.

Simple tips

There are several simple tips I have collected over the years as a practising vet some of which you may find useful. If some of them seem pretty obvious, then forgive me but the 'obvious' is all too often overlooked. For instance, it comes naturally to many people to approach an animal with the back of your hand. It is far less threatening to a suspicious animal than the open fingers and palm. I have seen too many children and quite a few adults still hold out their fingers to a strange animal and suffer injury as a result. Babies do this naturally but their very innocence overrides any threat of the open hand and is normally accepted by most well-adapted animals. By well-adapted, I mean those creatures that have had normal interactions with humans rather than abuse or neglect.

When visiting a house, remember that the front door is the threshold to the pet animal's domain so treat it with respect. Carrying your medical case in front of you provides an unobtrusive shield against a nervous attack. I have already mentioned that an animal in pain, frightened, nursing a litter of young or finding themselves in a strange environment can cause uncharacteristic aggression. Just keep the possibility in your mind but act quietly and as normally as possible.

It takes practice.

Injections, even those given sub-cutaneously (under the skin), can sting but there is a way of creating temporary anaesthesia of the injection site by gripping the fold of skin firmly between thumb and forefinger for a few seconds. The pressure of the thumb numbs the area so gently move the thumb slightly to one side before inserting the needle in the deadened area. Simple but it works. I used a different technique in larger animals where injections are usually given in the muscles of the neck. Grip the needle by the thumb and fingers but use the back of the hand to hit the injection site two or three times before reversing the hand and insert the needle on the last blow. These animals are used to being slapped about the body so the insertion of the needle is barely noticed. The syringe can then be attached, and the injection completed.

Dosing animals by mouth can be difficult and, sometimes impossible, but a couple of tips may help. When giving a cat or dog a tablet, prize open the lower jaw and push the tablet over the back of the tongue while trying to keep it central. Then hold the mouth closed and massage the throat firmly. Don't be fooled into letting go when you feel a swallow. This is a false swallow which is quickly followed by the tablet being spat out. You can be almost certain that they have swallowed the tablet when you feel a <u>double</u> swallow followed by a licking of the lips.

Sometimes a dog will swallow a foreign object such as a piece of Lego or a tasty handkerchief which may create a problem if allowed to pass further down the gut. In the absence of a specific emetic being available, a crystal of washing soda (sodium carbonate), between the size of a small hazel nut and a walnut, pushed firmly down the throat and swallowed will induce vomiting within about five to fifteen minutes. This can be a very effective first aid measure in an emergency but take care. Washing soda is not baking soda, bicarbonate of soda or even worse, caustic soda.

The other reason for care before inducing vomiting is that you may make things worse. Inducing vomiting an hour or two after a foreign object has been swallowed will be too late and sharp objects such as pins, hooks or needles may do more harm on their way back up. Vomiting will only aggravate the effects of swallowing poisons or other caustic substances and the only recourse is to perform a gastric lavage in the safety of the surgery.

Sometimes even the most prompt emergency treatment will fail, which brings me to the subject of euthanasia. This is often the last kindness you can offer an animal, be it a dairy cow or the family cat. Sadly, many owners cling on to their suffering companions for their own selfish, but human, reasons. It may the last association with a late partner or the 'best friend' of a child about to sit an important examination but, if the patient is suffering, the Latin question must be asked "cui bono?" or "good for whom?"

It takes courage to make that final decision and even more courage to 'be' there when the end comes. You will come across quite a few faint hearts in your career but don't judge them too harshly. The brave ones that stay are invariably surprised at how peaceful the end can be.

There will be times when you are off duty without modern therapeutic help when someone asks you if you can help with a veterinary problem. It may be something simple and does not justify an expensive weekend call out fee and they have heard you are a vet. This is when you have to put your 'lateral thinking' cap on. There are many remedies, condemned as old-fashioned, which could be useful in these situations.

Cold tea, with the milk added, will soothe and cleanse an inflamed eye without making the underlying condition any worse. Abscesses can often be 'drawn' using a bread poultice. I don't suppose many people know what a poultice is today, but we often used to use kaolin clay poultices to treat human abscesses - or boils as we called them. To make a bread poultice you warm a small saucepan of milk. Add this to a slice of bread in a heat-proof bowl and mix it to a soft paste. Apply the poultice to the abscess allowing it to dry a little before binding it to the body.

A few drops of olive oil applied to an itchy, dirty ear will help to clean and soothe the ear without aggravating any underlying condition. Once the oil is in the ear canal, massage it firmly for a few minutes and then clean it. Please don't use cotton buds. The best instrument is the tip of your little finger covered by a cap of cotton wool. You will never go deep enough to cause damage and the animal will get relief.

The human remedies of Imodium and Dioralyte will often restore intestinal function to normal without side effects but don't let vomiting or diarrhoea persist for more than 24hrs without calling for professional advice.

When dealing with an animal in pain remember to take extra care. Even the gentlest animals may act aggressively if they are frightened. It is a wise precaution to muzzle an injured dog using a tie, soft belt or bandage. Make a loop in the material to put over the muzzle and pass the two ends under the chin, behind the ears before tying in a tight bow – do not knot it - at the top of the neck. Simple but effective. We can restrain cats to two ways. The first involves the use of a pair of trousers. Feed your arm down one of the legs until it emerges at the top end. Then grab the hind legs of the cat and, while holding one end of the trousers firmly, pull the cat into the leg. When it is enveloped by the tube of the trouser leg, let go of the legs and hold both ends of the "tube" firmly. The second method requires a large towel placed lengthwise on the floor. Holding the cat firmly by the scruff of the neck, hold it at one end of the towel before rolling it into the towel like Ali Baba. It is important to make this roll very tight to prevent the struggling cat from escaping. The tighter, the better, because the more enclosed the space, the safer and calmer the cat will become. You won't suffocate them using either method of restraint. Once in the towel or trousers, the material can be peeled back from one end to reveal the head while the legs - and claws - are safely confined.

Do you need a sterile dressing when there is no autoclaved pack available? Think of newspaper. They have been through presses hot enough to kill off most bacteria and then tightly packed in bundles for delivery so a clean sheet of the Daily Mail would be better than a contaminated dishcloth. I have delivered many a litter onto newsprint. This applies less today with offset printing but it is still cleaner bacteriologically than a soiled blanket.

I remember one occasion when I had to adapt my minor surgery technique for lack of the equipment. My father had a great friend, Keith Palmer, who owned both a gravel company and a large farm in Suffolk to which he would often invite Dad shooting. I went along to one of these shoots and after lunch the 'guns' were sitting chatting in one of the farm barns when Keith called me over to examine his gundog's eye.

Both he and Dad had had their Springer Spaniel dogs trained, very expensively, to the gun. It was on one drive that morning that both men were waiting at their stands for the driven birds to fly out of the wood into their path. Both dogs sat perfectly at their master's side. Just as the first few birds emerged, a hare got up in the field behind them. This was too much of a temptation for the two young dogs which both took off in hot pursuit while their owners turned in fury and rendered the cold air blue with invective in their futile attempts to recall the dogs. Meanwhile the large mass of driven pheasants winged their way over their heads. It was really very funny.

But, back to the veterinary part of the day, it turned out that Keith's dog had a small benign skin growth, or papilloma, hanging from its top eyelid. It was not giving any pain but was causing a distraction to the dog. I advised Keith that it was a simple operation for a vet to take a small length of nylon suture material, make a loop in the material, place the loop over the papilloma to the pedicle base and then tie it off. The small growth would drop off within a week.

He thanked me for my advice and I thought nothing of it as I walked back to chat with Dad. A few minutes later we were joined by Keith who said he thought he could see something small in Dad's rather impressive spade beard. His fingers took a firm hold on one of the longer hairs and he tugged it out, much to the surprise and discomfort of Dad.

"Would this do for the dog's eye, Adrian?" Keith asked as he handed me the thread of hair

"What the hell are you two talking about?" shouted Dad as he nursed his chin.

We explained, and I tied off the eyelid growth using the hair. I had always been fascinated by small things and had tied many trout and salmon flies in my earlier days so using a fine beard hair to remove an unsightly growth from a gundog was a piece of cake.

As you will soon learn, client stupidity comes in all shapes and forms. I was called out one night to a dog that was extremely ill. It was thin, dehydrated and weak. I asked the owner how long it had been ill to which the reply was "Only this evening."

"Has it been sick?" I asked.

"Oh, yes, she's been vomiting for the past three days."

"Any diarrhoea?"

"She's had the runs for the past week."

"So how can you tell me she only became ill this evening?"

"Her nose only went dry this evening."

He had relied on one of the many old wives' tales that said a cold, wet nose meant a healthy dog. As with many of these old adages, there used to be an element of truth in the advice but this dated back to the 1920s when distemper was one of the primary killers of dogs. The common symptoms of distemper included a dry, hard nose and pads of the feet, hence the other name for distemper - "hardpad". A cold, wet nose only means that the dog was unlikely to be suffering from distemper.

Many unfortunate pet dogs have suffered repeated worming treatments because the owner still believed that the cause of a dog dragging its bottom along the ground is the result of worm infestation. In the 1920s this might have been a valid reason but today, following repeated advice, pet owners are now worming their pets much more frequently. This, combined with the fact we are less inclined to feed our pets raw meat from horses, sheep and cattle, has reduced the incidence of both round and tape worms in the pet population. A century ago when tapeworms were common in dogs, the segments of the worm would stick to the area around the anus causing irritation but, today, the commonest cause of such irritation is the blockage of the anal glands which lie under the skin to the sides of the back passage. These are easily expressed by a vet, nurse or groomer but sometimes occur so often that the dog of better off having them removed.

For many years people believed that a year of a dog's life equated to seven human years. It is not as simple as that and current research suggests that a one-year-old dog is equivalent to a fifteen-year-old teenager; a two-year-old relates to a healthy 25yo human and a fifteen-year-old dog is like person close to eighty years old. These ratios vary from breed to breed so there is no "one rule fits all" in the question of equating canine and human ages.

A more recent debunking of a long-held belief is the theory that we should allow a bitch to have one season before she is spayed. We were even taught this at vet school all those years ago. We thought that this was essential for normal physical development. Later research disproved this misconception. Today those bitches spayed before puberty are far less likely to develop mammary tumours later in life.

I hope that most pet owners today no longer maintain the more bizarre beliefs such as garlic curing worms and fleas; raw meat diets making dogs aggressive and pouring used engine oil over a dog cures mange but you never know, there are always idiots abroad in the land.

I will finish this memoir with this synopsis of advice to all my grandchildren -

☐   Try to be the best but don't demand perfection from yourself.

☐   Listen more than talk.

☐   "Please" and "Thank you" are some of the most important and underused words in the English language.

☐   There is a world of difference between the client and the patient and you must be ready to treat them both.

☐   Don't ignore "gut" feelings but don't rely on them.

☐   Few challenges are impossible.

☐   Don't ask someone to do something you wouldn't do yourself.

☐   When you lead, care for those below and behind you.

☐   You will get injured both physically and emotionally - be ready for it.

- Animals tell you things if you really listen and observe.

- Old ways are sometimes the best.

- Broaden your horizons from the blinkers of the veterinary course.

- Just because something can be done does not always justify its action.

- Have a life outside your profession.

- Don't be afraid to admit lack of knowledge - it is not ignorance, it is honesty.

Finally, to paraphrase my favourite poem - "If" by Rudyard Kipling –

If you can walk with kings and not lose the common touch

If all men count with you but none too much

If you can keep your steel within a velvet glove

Then yours is the earth and everything that's in it

And, what's more, I'll be proud of you, my love.